THE
MOUNTAIN MEN

BOOKS BY GEORGE LAYCOCK

The Deer Hunter's Bible
The Shotgunner's Bible
The Bird Watcher's Bible
The Sign of the Flying Goose
The Flying Sea Otters
   (with Ellen L.)
Big Nick
King Gator
Never Pet a Porcupine
Never Trust a Cowbird
The Alien Animals
The Diligent Destroyers
The Pelicans
The Animal Movers
Wild Refuge
Air Pollution
Water Pollution
The World's Endangered Wildlife
America's Endangered Wildlife
Strange Monsters/Great Searches
Mysteries, Monsters, and
   Untold Secrets
Alaska, Embattled Frontier
Autumn of the Eagle
Squirrels
The Camels

Wild Animals, Safe Places
Wild Travelers
Wingspread
People and Other Mammals
Beyond the Arctic Circle
The Complete Beginner's Guide
   to Photography
Does Your Pet Have a
   Sixth Sense?
Death Valley
Caves
Islands and Their Mysteries
Wild Hunters
Exploring the Great Swamp
Tornadoes—Killer Storms
How the Settlers Lived
   (with Ellen L.)
How to Buy And Enjoy
   a Small Farm
Bats in the Night
The Ohio Valley—Your Guide
   to America's Heartland
   (with Ellen L.)
The Kroger Story
North American Wildlife
The Wild Bears

THE
MOUNTAIN MEN

GEORGE LAYCOCK

Introduction by Paul Schullery
Drawings by Tom Beecham

The Lyons Press

Guilford, Connecticut
An imprint of The Globe Pequot Press

Copyright © 1988, 1996 by George Laycock
Introduction copyright © 1996 by Paul Schullery
Illustrations copyright © 1988, 1996 by Tom Beacham
Published by The Globe Pequot Press
Previously published by The Lyons Press

All rights reserved. No part of this book may be reproduced or transmitted in any form
by any means, electronic or mechanical, including photocopying and recording, or by
any information storage and retrieval system, except as may be expressly permitted by
the 1976 Copyright Act or in writing from the publisher. Requests for permission should
be addressed to The Globe Pequot Press, P.O. Box 480, Guilford, Connecticut 06437.

The Lyons Press is an imprint of The Globe Pequot Press.

Design by Catherine Lau Hunt

Library of Congress Cataloging-in-Publication Data

Laycock, George.
   The mountain men / George Laycock.
      p. cm.
   Originally published: Danbury, CT : Outdoor Life Books, c1988.
   Includes bibliographical reference and index.
   ISBN 1-55821-454-2 (paperback)
   1. Fur trade—West (U.S.)—History—19th century. 2. Trapping—West (U.S.)—
History—19th century. 3. Frontier and pioneer life—West (U.S.)—History—19th
century. 4. Fur traders—West (U.S.)—History—19th century. 5. Trappers—West
(U.S.)—History—19th century. I. Title. [F596.L433 1996]
978'.02—dc20   95-47955
                                                                          CIP

Manufactured in the United States of America
First edition/Sixth printing

Contents

Acknowledgments   *vii*

Introduction   *viii*

Preface   *x*

1   Wild Lands and Furbearers   *1*

2   Pursuit of the Beaver   14

     How the Trapper Caught Beaver   23

3   The Buffalo Hunters   27

4   Mountain Man's Wildlife   *35*

5   Eyes West   *46*

6   To the Mountains for Beaver   *57*

     The World of the Mountain Man   *65*

7   For Love of the Wild Places   *67*

8   Birth of the Rendezvous   76

9   King of the Mountain Men   *83*

10   The Legend of Broken Hand   93

     The Mountain Man's Guns   *102*

11   Old Bill, Master Trapper   *112*

12   Trail Blazer   *120*

13   A Grizzly Problem   *132*

14   Some Called Him Thunderbolt   *139*

15   From Apprentice to Pathfinder   *147*

16   The Happy Mountain Man   *155*

     Leatherwork   *164*

17   To the End of the West   *177*

     Fire and Shelter   *185*

18	The Marryin' Kind	190
19	Journal of a Trapper	197
	Trappers Who Fished	206
20	The Bones of Old Black Harris	208
21	Trappers in the Southwest	215
	The Mountain Man's Cache	223
22	The Old Trapper and the Kid	226
	The Mountain Man's Boats	233
23	Long Shadows	236
	Bibliography	241
	Index	244

Acknowledgments

---

*T*o all those individuals and organizations who so generously helped me during preparation of this book I want to express my sincere appreciation. Librarians, archivists, and museum curators guided me to invaluable sources. In particular I want to extend my gratitude to Charles E. Hanson, Jr., Director of the Museum of the Fur Trade at Chadron, Nebraska, and to historians of the National Park Service, especially the staffs of the Jefferson National Expansion Memorial in St. Louis, and The Fort Union Trading Post National Historical Site. Among the librarians and archivists deserving special thanks are staff members of The Old Courthouse Library and the Merchantile Library of St. Louis. The Missouri Historical Society in St. Louis generously made available old documents, correspondence, newspapers, and journals including the Andrew Drips Papers, The Sublette Papers, and the Journals of Jedediah S. Smith, 1826–1827. I am also grateful to the modern buckskinners who shared with me their interpretations of the mountain man's ways. My wife Ellen's skilled assistance was a major contribution at all times.

—G. L.

Introduction

*F*ew North American adventurers inspire the same mixture of awe and envy today as the mountain men described so well by George Laycock in this book. As the vanguard of European exploration of the American West, as independent souls in a strange, wild land, or just as a bunch of guys out having amazing adventures, they engage the interest of generation after generation of Americans. And no wonder. Their accomplishments seem fairly simple, but their legacy is complex and ironic.

Consider the complexity. We see these men as exemplifying a wild, free life, unfettered by social constraints; yet it was commerce and industry that paid their way, and that drove most of them to the wilderness in the first place. In stereotype, we see them as simple, hardy men, all more or less alike; but they were a multinational crowd, with intense and even violent allegiances to their various employers or home countries. And they were interacting with a remarkably complex set of native cultures, whose own political relationships were as subtle, involved, and convoluted as any in the Old World.

Then consider the irony of the mountain men's legacy. The very wildness they represented—both in themselves and in the western landscape—was doomed in good part by their own activities. As they "explored" the country (the natives of the region had explored it quite thoroughly during the previous 10,000 years, so the term seems a little odd), they were preparing the way for hordes of people whose primary goal was to civilize it beyond recognition. As they adopted the ways of the native people, they were among the first to affect those native cultures, putting them on the long and painful path of subjugation to the ways of the white society.

On the other hand, as they traveled the vast western ranges and valleys, a number of them were literate enough to leave us with our only descriptions of what this country was like prior to the destruction of the great wildlife herds, or accounts of the massive alteration of the prairie-vegetation communities under agriculture and livestock. Besides, as wild as the country was in the early 1800s, it had already been affected in many ways by Europeans, even though those Europeans had never seen it. European diseases (of both human and livestock), European horses, and European firearms and other technology had all reached the High Plains and the Rockies well before Europeans themselves spent any significant time there. The mountain men would have had to arrive two or three centuries earlier than they did if they wanted to see a western landscape truly unaffected by European ways.

But while environmental historians, anthropologists, and a variety of other scholars spend more and more of their time wondering about such things, most people are still interested in the mountain men primarily because of their adventures. Those adventures are what Laycock provides in abundance in this new edition of his book, introducing us to some of the most important and quirky personalities of the time and sharing with us some of their most outrageous exploits. Perhaps as important, he opens a window onto the fascinating details of their lives by showing us how they managed their trade, developed their tools, and made the most of their resources. I consider this book an excellent starting point for anyone newly attracted to the mountain-man era, and a handy reference for those already familiar with it. For anyone wanting to learn more, it's a good start; you could do a lot worse than spend a few years of your recreational reading time following the trails of the men George Laycock introduces you to in this book.

—Paul Schullery
Yellowstone

Preface

*T*he mountain man, weathered and wind-bitten, searched out the beaver, sent his packs of furs back to market, and in the process proved himself to be the ultimate outdoorsman. He was a survival specialist in the face of bitterly cold winters, antagonistic Indians, and unbelievably powerful bears. He was unsurpassed as a marksman and skilled as horseman and naturalist.

Typically the free trapper was young when he went to the mountains. He was single, poor, farm reared, and he had long hair, but kept his face shaved, except perhaps for a moustache. He was sinewy, powerful, and possessed of lightning reactions. He was perhaps the finest woodsman the country has ever seen, surpassing even the Indian in mastery of the outdoors.

These beaver trappers pushed back the wilderness frontier. They were explorers who led America into new regions deep in the Rocky Mountains and beyond. Our curiousity about the nature of the mountain men, and how they lived, is as sharp today as ever.

—GEORGE LAYCOCK

· 1 ·

Wild Lands and Furbearers

From the day he first led his little party out of New Orleans and up the Mississippi River in 1763, Pierre Lacléde Liguest was thinking of furs, and the best ways to get possession of them. He blazed marks on a few forest trees in what seemed to him to be the most desirable place for a riverside settlement.

The following spring he sent Auguste Chouteau, with a crew of thirty men, who found the marked trees on the west side of the river, and began constructing a large shed which was followed by dingy little buildings where people could live. "Little huts," one historian characterized them later, "unsuitable for the purposes of a stable. . . ," but there were few complaints about the lack of facilities. These were hunters and trappers and, as one writer said, "They could pillow on the earth and sleep unsheltered under the canopy of heaven without thinking it a hardship."

As the settlement took shape that spring of 1764, its founder named it in honor of his king, Louis XV of France. He had picked a choice location in view of what he hoped to accomplish. There were furs to be collected through trade with the Indians, and a trading post here was within reach of tribes in the Mississippi and Missouri river valleys.

Six years later, in 1770, St. Louis numbered one hundred and fifteen families with five hundred people. Livestock had the run of the streets whose surface varied from mud to dust depending on the season.

When early mountain men began trickling in, on their way to the beaver streams of the Rockies, the town had come through its first half century and its buildings were becoming larger and finer. The busy town by the shore of the Mississippi became the hub of the budding fur business. It also became the last memory of civilization that the lonely trapper carried with him through the western mountains.

NATURE OF THE MOUNTAIN MAN

Born into every generation are restless men with feet that will not stand still, eyes that search for distant mountains, hearts that long to go where the scene is new and the promise of adventure alive. The possibility of danger only whets the appetite. Opportunity to satisfy this longing for adventure changes with time and place, but few men ever found a greater challenge than these buckskin-clad woodsmen who traveled westward to trap beaver in the early eighteen hundreds.

In many ways this mountain man was like other young men of his time. His nineteenth birthday was past and there he was—stuck on the farm. If he wanted to know what his life was going to be, he could look at his father or his uncles, plodding along behind their oxen, or see them milking cows and tending crops until, at last, their aging bodies weakened and their dreams died. Not a bad life perhaps, but didn't travelers in the village speak of trappers back from the Rocky Mountains, telling how they had bested Indians and grizzly bears while reaping fortunes in beaver furs?

So, at the end of a long winter of dreaming of the distant mountains, the gangling lad who had never been more than fifty miles from home hitched up his suspenders, buttoned his homespun coat, pulled his old felt hat down over his shock of brown hair, and set off carrying his long gun, powder horn, bullet pouch, blanket, and little more.

Ahead of him stretched the trail to St. Louis. Beyond that, he would just wait and see. If he could get to the mountains, he had choices. In the fur industry there were various levels of employment and once in St. Louis he listened to the stories and began to sort out the possibilities. The safest plan was to sign on as an *engagé*, a hired hand, with one of the fur companies. This was the beginning for a lot of young fur trappers with little or no money or equipment. The company outfitted them as day laborers, paid them maybe two hundred dollars a year, and everything they caught belonged to the company. So did their souls.

There were also contract trappers who were set up in business by one of the fur companies. Instead of becoming camp tenders, common laborers, or boatmen, they worked as trappers, but were obligated to bring all their furs to the company and buy their goods from it at whatever exorbitant prices it charged.

At the top of the structure was the genuine free trapper who ". . . never had to say 'yes, captain' to no man." He owned his outfit and made his own decisions. He might go to the mountains, as part of a group for safety, and help with the chores on the way, but once there he traveled and trapped where he liked, then sold his furs where he chose.

This legendary free trapper in the early Rocky Mountain beaver industry became as unfettered by social constraints as any American who ever lived. He was the world's most skilled outdoorsman, unequaled in marksmanship, expert in hunting and trapping, a superb woodsman alert to the ever-changing scene around him. He knew the signs of danger and his specialty was survival in a world filled with hazards. Given his skills and his love for wandering the lonely valleys, he could accomplish what he set out to do—if he lived long enough.

As the young English adventurer George F. Ruxton wrote after living and traveling with the beaver trappers in the Rocky Mountains:

> It was the roving trader and the solitary trapper who first sought out these inhospitable wilds, traced the streams to their sources, scaled the mountain passes, and explored the boundless expanse of territory where the foot of white man had never trodden before . . . For the free hunter of the Far West was, in his rough way, a good deal of a knight errant . . . every footstep was beset with enemies and every moment pregnant with peril. The great proportion of these intrepid spirits who laid down their lives in that far country is impressive proof of the jeopardy of their existence . . . They were the pathfinders of the West.

The clothing and equipment that the mountain man brought to his profession were not new to the American outdoors. The trapper adapted the methods and equipment of frontiersmen before him in the Appalachians, and those of the Plains tribes to whose land he had come.

For clothing, he required protection from the elements, freedom of movement, and an outfit that he could mend with the materials at hand and replace when it wore out. His outfit had to be practical and it had to be
trimmed down to minimum weight for easy transport. The loose-fitting
cloth garments with which he started west, and which he often preferred,
were replaced eventually with practical clothing fashioned from soft,
smoked buckskin.

If he chose to let his clothes get slick with buffalo grease, the op-
tion was his. Old pictures drawn by artists on the scene make it plain that
there was individual variation in clothing, hat styles, and the amount of
decoration worn on buckskins. The decoration often depended on
whether or not the trapper traveled with an Indian wife.

Early traveler Rufus B. Sage was only one of several to leave behind a description of the typical mountain man's appearance. After three
years among the trappers, Sage wrote of the mountain man:

> His skin, from constant exposure, assumes a hue almost as
> dark as that of the Aborigine, and his features and physical
> structure attain a rough and hardy cast. His hair, through inat-
> tention, becomes long, coarse, and bushy, and loosely dangles
> upon his shoulders. His head is surmounted by a low crowned
> wool-hat, or a rude substitute of his own manufacture. His
> clothes are of buckskin, gaily fringed at the seams with strings
> of the same material, cut and made in a fashion peculiar to
> himself and associates . . . His waist is encircled with a belt of
> leather, holding encased his butcher knife and pistols—while
> from his neck is suspended a bullet pouch securely fastened to
> the belt in front, and beneath the right arm hangs a powder-
> horn traversely from his shoulder, behind which, upon the
> strap attached to it, are affixed his bullet-mould, ballscrew,
> wiper, awl, &c. With a gun-stick made of some hard wood,
> and a good rifle placed in his hands, carrying from thirty to
> thirty-five balls to the pound, the reader will have before him
> a correct likeness of a genuine mountaineer, when fully
> equipped . . . The mountaineer is his own manufacturer, tailor,
> shoemaker, and butcher, and can always feed and cloth him-
> self, and enjoy all the comforts his situation affords.

His outfit customarily included his horse on which he rode, and his mule on which he carried all his worldly goods, including his packs of furs as they accumulated. He carried buckskin for repairing and replacing moccasins and clothing, robe and blanket for bedding, lead, tobacco, and, if he had them, pemmican and jerky. The items he used daily—fire-starting equipment, spare flints, usually a straight razor for, contrary to common belief, most mountain men shaved, an awl for making repairs—were toted along in buckskin bags of various sizes and designs.

Following the rivers and creeks, he learned the nature of the streams and their tributaries—and tributaries of the tributaries—reaching into every valley large and small where beaver lived. He followed the mighty Missouri across the prairie and into the Rockies, turning up the Niobrara, Grand, Little Missouri, and Musselshell.

He carried his traps along the Yellowstone and up the rivers that feed it, the Powder, Tongue, Bighorn, and Clark's Fork, taking beaver all the way. He found the three beautiful mountain streams that form the Missouri, the Jefferson, Madison, and Gallatin, and followed each of these snow-fed rivers high into the mountains until water and beaver gave out. He tramped the broad valley of the ribbonlike Platte, discovered a route over the Continental Divide, and came down into headwaters of the river the Indians called the "Seedskeedee"—the Green—and this led to the Colorado and the beaver waters of the Southwest.

To the north, he explored the waters of the Salmon, Snake, and Columbia. He came upon river after river until he had mapped, in his mind, the surface of the western half of the continent, for he was far more than a beaver trapper, he was also an explorer. He opened the West. At the risk of his life, he counted coup on the grizzly and defied the native tribes that tried to halt him. He moved the borders of the country westward on his shoulders.

RISE OF THE COMPANIES

Long before the journey of Lewis and Clark, and the heyday of the mountain man, the fur industry was a major New World enterprise. Early European arrivals bought furs from the Indians and trapped the beaver of streams, lakes, and ponds themselves from Canada south to Virginia. Before the time of the mountain men, Hudson's Bay Company traders were dealing with the Indians while the French voyageurs paddled giant canoes through turbulent northern waters carrying packs of beaver down the St. Lawrence.

Reports brought back by Lewis and Clark of the wealth of furs for the taking in the Rocky Mountains were welcome news in the fur industry. One who was especially interested was a New Yorker in his early forties who had risen rapidly to become head of the American fur industry.

John Jacob Astor happened to be in the right place at the right time, but any fair-minded person would admit that he had other things going for him. Astor was born in Waldorf, Germany, in 1763, but left for London as a teenager. There he joined his brother in the manufacturer of musical instruments.

Young Astor, ambitious, energetic, and self-confident, was still a teenager when he decided to sail for America to make his fortune. He took along a shipment of flutes which constituted his entire capital. The ship on which he sailed was destined for Baltimore, but in the winter of 1784, enough ice formed in the mouth of the Chesapeake to hold the ship up until March. There was little to do except visit with other passengers and one of these turned out to be a New York fur dealer. Said the fur dealer to John Jacob Astor, "Young man, what you should do is take your flutes to New York and sell them and put your money in the fur market."

That was the beginning of a business enterprise that was to make the young immigrant one of the wealthiest men in America. He came to understand the fur business on a global scale as well as any man alive. His moves were bold ones, and there was not a beaver trapper in the mountains who did not in some way feel the impact of John Jacob Astor's dealings.

In 1808, he founded the American Fur Company, which was so powerful that it became known across the West simply as "The Company," while every other fur company, large or small, was lumped together and known as the "Opposition."

Government trading posts had been set up to lure the Indian trade away from the British. Astor's manipulations helped get these outposts closed by act of Congress. This abolition of the government factory system cleared the way for private industry which, to Astor, meant his own American Fur Company and its western department headquarters in St. Louis. Furthermore, to deal with the fur production, and compete with the British in the Pacific Northwest, Astor formed the Pacific Fur Company, which became a victim of the War of 1812. Astor then concentrated on establishing a string of fur trading forts throughout the Missouri River drainage.

To the north, the fur industry was dominated by the Hudson's Bay Company, which the British had established in 1670, and its competition the North West Company, operating in western Canada. Their trading posts spread through the rich fur country dealing with the Indian tribes. Among the free trappers and the smaller fur outfits, neither the Hudson's Bay Company nor the American Fur Company was loved. One trapper said he would as soon be a slave in Missouri as an *engagé* for the Hudson's Bay Company.

Competition between the fur companies was cutthroat in nature. The American Fur Company ruthlessly used every tactic it could devise to break the backs of smaller outfits. One of its milder tactics was to jack up prices and buy furs at prices higher than their real market value, taking a loss rather than allow smaller companies to acquire furs and bring them to market.

Opposition companies came and went, and among their leaders were the more famous mountain men of all times. Jedediah Smith, David E. Jackson, and William Sublette bought out the pioneering William Ashley and Andrew Henry outfit in 1826, and ran their new company under their own names. But four years later they sold out to Jim Bridger, Tom Fitzpatrick, Milton Sublette, Jean Gervais, and Henry Fraeb, who set up the Rocky Mountain Fur Company. The Rocky Mountain Fur Company later changed hands. Leading trappers and traders continued to go with The American Fur Company as Astor's lock on the fur industry tightened. Numerous companies rose and fell.

The leading companies had constant competition as the smaller companies and free trappers spread out over the central Rockies. There were few restraints on business methods. Companies connived with Indian leaders to send their warriors against rival fur companies. They hired away each other's trappers, and had no compunction about taking over trapping grounds others had found.

At one point Astor's agents dispatched a trapping party to dog the footsteps of the Rocky Mountain Fur Company until the frustrated trappers seemed unable to elude them. Astor's men, William H. Vanderburgh and the noted Andrew Drips, showed up wherever Tom Fitzpatrick and Jim Bridger led their Rocky Mountain Fur Company trappers, until Bridger and Fitzpatrick decided to lead Astor's people right into a trap.

They kept moving, and each move took them deeper into Blackfoot country. All of them must have known the seriousness of the game they were playing. The outcome was as predictable as punching a hornets' nest. The Indians finally attacked and Vanderburgh was killed in the battle. About the same time, Bridger and his men stumbled into a band of Pigeons, one of the Blackfoot tribes, and Bridger escaped with a couple of arrows stuck in the back of his shoulders. He pulled one out but had to leave the other where it was, at least for the present.

Another weapon used in the mounting competition was the trade whiskey brought into the forts and rendezvous. Even when it was illegal, it was used. Wrote Rufus Sage, "Trading companies, however, find ways and means to smuggle it through, by the wagon load, under the very noses of the government officers . . ." When the United States government did try to cork off the flow of whiskey to the Indians, the Hudson's Bay Company began trading whiskey for furs to entice the Indians across the border. This promptly brought whiskey back to the trading posts in the United States, law or no law, and in at least one case, a still was established inside a fort. The big losers, as usual, were the Indians, who were cheated, robbed, and ruined physically and mentally by the heavily watered but free-flowing alcohol.

Pressure applied by Astor's people was eventually too much for the smaller outfits to withstand, and the predatory American Fur Company swallowed the competition. Astor, however, always had his eye on the bottom line. In 1834, when there were early signs that the fur industry was slipping, he sold out.

BEAVER MEETS THE TRAP

Long before white people came to North America, native men were taking the beaver both for their meat and their dense furs. These ancient beaver trappers had their own methods. Some of them made beaver traps of long poles, fashioned into conical baskets that came to a point on one end. The Indian trapper would kick a hole in a beaver dam and set his trap in it with the small end downstream, well beneath the surface.

The beaver, leaving its lodge in the evening and arriving to inspect the dam, soon discovered the break where the water rushed through. It sensed danger to its orderly world, and inspecting the hole, moved deeper into the basket until its head became stuck in the small end of the trap and it drowned.

The Indian trappers also built pens with drop doors that were triggered either by a waiting trapper pulling on a line or by the beaver itself.

In winter, they used another system. Ahead of time, they made nets of vines. On the day of the hunt, the band of beaver takers arrived at the pond with their nets and spears, took soundings on the ice with the shafts of their spears and could check by the hollow tones where the beaver had burrows. Then they chopped holes in the ice and pushed their nets through to the bottom.

Finally, everything was ready. Nets waited across every entrance to burrows and lodges. On top of every frozen beaver lodge stood a man with his spear posed. Above each hole stood the beaver trapper, holding in his hands a drawstring to jerk the net the instant a beaver bumped into it.

The leader gave the signal. Men pounded on the ice and punched their spears into the lodges. They stomped on the ice and the lodges. Frantic beavers, rushing for safety, bumped into strange nets and were hauled up onto the surface and clubbed before they could escape. This plan put beaver furs on the back of many an Indian and set beaver tails to roasting beside the campfires.

Beaver catchers were still using these old systems when white trappers imported the first of their metal traps. The real inventor of the steel trap will never be known, but historians tell us that sweating iron-mongers were pounding them out of hot iron at their glowing forges perhaps five hundred years ago. Settlers from European countries brought leg hold traps to North America as early as the 1650s and used them to take two million or so beaver, which were exported during the 1600s and 1700s by French, English, and Dutch colonists.

The steel trap was certain to undergo changes in design as more trap makers came to the business, but the basic design remained the same. The typical beaver trap had to weigh enough to hold a beaver underwater while it drowned. This trap evolved to weigh three and a half pounds without chain. It had two strong springs powerful enough to keep a struggling beaver from pulling free. Attached to it was a chain, perhaps six feet long, with a ring in the end. There was no standardization in these days prior to mass production. Furthermore, the blacksmith turning out traps might never have tested them. For this reason, the leader of a beaver trapping brigade, or the free trapper setting out alone, usually remembered to set each of his new traps and trip it a few times to see that it worked smoothly. Then, each new trap was folded and wrapped in its chain before being packed into a wooden box or barrel for transport. The mountain trapper at work normally carried half a dozen traps, folded, wrapped, and carried in a sturdy rawhide trap sack.

Traps, individually made, usually costing the trapper from two to five dollars each, were irreplaceable in the wilderness. They were valuable enough that trappers watched over them as faithfully as they would their powder horn and bullet pouch. One mountain man discovered that three Indians had lifted four of his traps. He trailed them through the snow all day, walked into their camp that night, and reclaimed his traps at gunpoint. He threatened the thieves' lives if they followed him, and scanning his back trail repeatedly, hurried back to his own camp, completing a twenty-four hour, forty-mile, round-trip march.

The best remembered name in the manufacture of steel traps is Sewell Newhouse, who is sometimes credited with inventing the steel trap. The leg hold trap, however, was already in use hundreds of years before Newhouse was born. But Newhouse improved the old designs and put such quality into his traps that he founded a famous trap-making industry, bringing the manufacture of traps from the iron monger's forge to factory production.

The successful trapper in good beaver country often took a beaver in every trap, probably half a dozen skins in a day. The beaver was skinned out on the scene to lighten the trapper's load for his return to camp. Along with the fur, he usually took the castoreum for making additional "medicine," to use, sell, or trade. He also skinned out the broad, flat tail and carried this delicacy back to roast beside his evening fire, or took the whole carcass if he needed meat. Then, he scraped and fleshed out each skin until it was free of fat and muscle, and finally stretched it tight and laced it to a circular frame that he made by bending a willow sapling until its ends could be tied together. He cured the beaver pelts by hanging them around his camp to dry.

When he moved from valley to valley, his mule carried his accumulated furs, dried and pressed into bales weighing a hundred pounds or so. If he planned a long trip, he cached his valuable furs to be reclaimed later from this primitive storage chamber—if he returned, and if the Indians had not discovered the hiding place.

Eventually, he packed off his dried furs, each carrying his personal mark, to the summer rendezvous for sale or trade. Most of the time he expected each plew, or beaver skin, to weigh a pound and a half and bring him four dollars a pound or six dollars for a quality beaver. An able trapper, working in good beaver country, might normally take a hundred and twenty-five to a hundred and fifty beaver in a good year, and know his friends at summer rendezvous would exclaim, "Wagh! That shines some. He made the beaver come, he did, or I wouldn't say so."

After selling his furs and replenishing his supplies at rendezvous, the trapper turned back to the mountains, probably broke. His aim was always the same—to find a new supply of beaver and make it back with their hides to the next rendezvous. His was a perilous and risky business, but it was a special life, and he would stay with it as long as he had his hair and the beaver lasted—if that's the way his pole floated.

But before the fur business would really get underway there was business to settle with the British. The British-inspired Indian pressure on the Americans forced temporary closure of Fort Osage, which the United States government had set up near today's Kansas City. The North West Company sent its agents into the headwaters of the Missouri. Intense international competition for furs helped spawn the War of 1812, and the North American fur trade ground to a halt until after the 1814 treaty.

The fur trade in the Rocky Mountains was blossoming by the early 1820s and in the following fifteen years, between 1820 and 1835, the western beaver trapping industry flourished, peaked, and started downhill. New trappers still went to the mountains, and some of the old-timers could not bring themselves to leave. But they had methodically removed the beaver, breeding stock and all, from valley after valley, and the furbearers had to rebuild their numbers before they could again be profitably trapped.

There was another disaster visited on the fur industry. For hundreds of years hatters had turned beaver fur into fine felt hats. Both in this country and Europe, any properly attired gentleman wore his beaver hat proudly. Because Europe had long since used up its beavers, there had been a strong demand for furs from North America. Even prior to 1800 there were years when the Hudson's Bay Company sent enough beaver pelts to Europe to manufacture more than half a million hats. Then, suddenly thousands of skins of the South American nutria, a large aquatic mammal, began flooding into New York and London providing a cheap substitute for beaver, and the demand for the mountain man's major product plummeted. On top of this came a change in style. The once fashionable beaver hats fell from favor as silk hats replaced them and this further depressed the beaver market. Meanwhile, the beaver supply had dwindled as trappers cleaned out the beaver valleys across the West.

In time, both the market and the beaver made modest revivals, and a few hard-core trappers continued to take some beaver, along with other furs and buffalo hides, profitably through the 1840s and 1850s. But never would there be a new land for the fur takers to explore. The mountain man of the American West had come and gone, and in his brief tenure, he became a legend that would not die. His story properly begins with a very special animal.

Pursuit of the Beaver

*W*hen the earliest settlers came to North America's eastern seaboard, the beaver lived from Alaska to northern Florida. It flourished where every mainland state is today, and throughout Canada north to the tree line.

In this country alone there may have been four hundred million beaver. This was the estimate made by the naturalist Ernest Thompson Seton. Enos Mills, another naturalist, and an authority on the beaver, placed the estimate closer to a hundred million. Nobody knows. But beaver were so abundant that early trappers finding their way into untouched wilderness valleys were astounded by the wealth of fur waiting for the harvest.

The beaver of the East were the first to go, disappearing as civilization pushed westward. Western beaver, wintering in the frigid, high mountain country, wore the finest of all beaver fur. Captain Meriwether Lewis had his first opportunity to inspect these furs in April 1805, when his party encountered French Canadian trappers on the Missouri River, and he declared the quality to be ". . . by far the best I have ever seen."

Before many years passed, the westering trappers were drying thousands of beaver skins around their camps. Warren Angus Ferris, an American Fur Company clerk, left us a vivid description of the scene as he found it in the early 1800s, in present day Idaho.

> In a narrow bottom beneath the walls of Grays Creek we found a party of trappers, headed by Bridger . . . Their encampment was decked with hundreds of beaver skins, now drying in the sun. These valuable skins are always stretched on willow hoops, varying from eighteen inches to three feet in diameter, according to the size of the skins, and have a reddish

appearance on the flesh side, which is exposed to the sun. Our camps are always dotted with these red circles in the trapping season when the weather is fair. There were several hundred skins folded and tied up in packs laying about their encampment.

The history of the beaver goes back millions of years before the arrival of the earliest humans on the continent and not all beaver have always been the same as those we know today. In 1889, scientists discovered in eastern Indiana the nearly complete skeleton of an ancient Ice Age beaver larger than a modern black bear. This extinct beast once waddled around the marshy country from Nebraska to the east coast, reaching its greatest numbers in modern Indiana and Illinois. There is evidence that this massive animal lived as far north as Alaska. Scientists know it today as *Castoroides ohioensis*, and believe that both it and the modern beaver, *Castor canadensis*, were here until some ten thousand years ago.

The giant beaver probably fed on sedges, grass, and other plants harvested in the marshes around the edges of lakes, and may never have chewed down trees for food, or possessed the highly developed engineering skills practiced by the modern beaver.

The beaver we know today is, on first glance, a dull-witted, dumpy looking animal with beady little eyes set in a small head of no great beauty. On land, it stands higher in the rear quarters than it does at the shoulders. But the beaver belongs in the water where it is beautifully adapted to its element. From its pug nose to its powerful hips, the tear-shaped animal's sleek body lines allow it to glide smoothly through the lakes and streams.

There is more. Not only is the beaver thoroughly matched to its environment, but it is also that rare wild animal capable of altering its habitat to meet its own needs. The beaver literally converted large parts of North America to wetlands and provided better living conditions, not only for itself, but also for a host of other wildlife.

Deer and moose came to the beaver pond to eat and drink. Waterfowl stopped to feed and rest and sometimes stayed to nest and raise their young. Rails, herons, kingfishers, prothonotary warblers, and a host of other birds, along with turtles, salamanders, and insects, found food and refuge in the beaver ponds. One modern biologist, keeping track of the wildlife using a beaver pond, counted, in one year, one hundred and twenty-four species of birds and thirty-seven kinds of mammals.

Largest of North American rodents, the adult beaver may be four and a half feet in length and reach a weight of sixty or seventy pounds. There are stories of beaver that weighed more than a hundred pounds. Its size depends largely on its age and the foods available to it.

The beaver's specialized equipment includes a broad, flat tail, furred at the base, but otherwise covered only with dark, leathery scales and a few coarse hairs. The tail of a large adult beaver may be six inches wide and twice that long, and it serves several purposes. As the animal swims, the tail becomes its combination sculling paddle and rudder. If you have ever surprised a beaver when you were canoeing or fishing, you know that the tail is also the beaver's early warning system, serving as a device to alert other beavers by slapping it against the water surface with a riflelike crack. Then it, and most other beaver within hearing, dives for deep water.

In addition, the tail serves as a thermoregulatory mechanism, helping the animal lose body heat when it is on land in hot weather. Furthermore, the beaver sitting on its hind legs and cutting on a tree will use its tail as a convenient prop to help support its body, then as a balance, if it must make a dash for safety. The tail is also a place for the beaver to store fat ahead of winter.

The teeth of the beaver are vital to its way of life. The long, curved, orange-colored incisors with which it fells trees, then cuts them into manageable sections never stop growing. Lowers and uppers overgrow each other so their edges rub together, and because they are soft on the inner surfaces and hard on the outside, their cutting edges are self-sharpening as they work. A beaver can drop a five-inch aspen in less than five minutes.

The beaver is especially equipped for underwater work. A transparent nictitating membrane covers and protects each eye. The ears and nose are equipped with valves that close automatically as the animal submerges, then open again when it surfaces. Underwater, the lips shut tightly behind the incisors so the beaver does not have to worry about swallowing water as it works.

In addition, before it dives, the beaver takes in extra oxygen, inflating the lungs. It has an especially large liver that stores highly oxygenated blood. When submerged, its blood pressure drops and the flow of blood to the muscles slows, although added blood flows to the brain. With these provisions, the beaver can stay submerged for five, ten, or even fifteen minutes without surfacing for air.

In the water, where it swims with grace and confidence, its broad, webbed hind feet paddle alternately, while it tucks the smaller front feet up neatly out of the way beneath its neck. Each hind foot has a split nail on the second digit that the beaver uses as a comb to groom its fur and spread protective oil on it.

This is essential to the animal's health because its fur must keep it dry and protect it against severe temperatures. The fur is of two layers. The outer layer of long, shiny guard hairs gives the beaver its glossy brown color. Beneath the guard hairs is a dense layer of shorter, brownish-gray hair that insulates the body.

Male or female, the beaver carries a pair of scent glands that provide it with a substance carrying the strong odor it uses for marking territorial boundaries. To a beaver, the odor becomes a personal identification tag, telling the curious whether the calling card was left by family member or stranger, and probably whether the visitor was male or female. During the breeding season, the beaver marks its home territory by building mud patties a foot wide and two or three inches high, then individualizing each with a mixture of urine and the liquid from its castor glands. Trappers collected these glands and used the castoreum to bait beavers to their traps. This substance is also used in the making of perfume.

In the wilderness, the beaver's natural enemies included wolves, coyotes, bears, bobcats, foxes, otters, and great horned owls, with the smaller predators probably limiting themselves to taking the kits. The Indians took beaver for both food and fur, but the human population was low enough, and the hunting methods primitive enough, that the beaver, especially in the mountains, could replace its losses and maintain its numbers.

But with the arrival of people from Europe the pressure on the beaver increased as trappers pursued the animals relentlessly. The beaver, whose watery refuge often saved it from natural predators, lacked defensive tactics against this new enemy. Nor were there laws to curb the trapper's fur harvest or control his methods and seasons, so he quickly eliminated the animals from whole valleys, and entire states. Pennsylvania, for example, still had elk, wolves, and mountain lions in the mid-1800s—but its beaver were gone. The white man had encouraged Indian trappers to take the beaver and trade them for beads, lead, powder, guns, and kettles. Then settlers moved in to finish the job.

To the west, through Ohio, Indiana, and Illinois, the great beaver harvest continued. People multiplied. In 1819, a Wisconsin hunter killed a large beaver on Sugar Creek in Walworth County, Wisconsin, the last known wild beaver in southern Wisconsin. According to Hartley H.T. Jackson's *Mammals of Wisconsin*, by 1900 the beaver of that northern state were down to perhaps five hundred living in a few scattered locations.

But the following year Wisconsin made its first efforts to protect the animal. The populations recovered. Wisconsin stock was even shipped to Pennsylvania to start new populations there and today the beaver prospers in both states as it does throughout much of its original range. In some areas it thrives in pest proportions, flooding farm fields and highways with its dams. It can, however, never again be as abundant as it was when the mountain men began their historic sweep through the beaver's Rocky Mountain stronghold.

One mountain man wrote of a river his group trapped for beaver, saying, ". . . we found the richest place for beaver we had yet come across, and it took us forty days to clean that section." That was the attitude that eliminated the beaver from valley after valley—find the beaver and clean them out. The trapper might not pass this way again, and why leave fur for the competition?

The beaver has been billed as a super engineer, and that reputation is well earned. Water is the beaver's refuge, and where the animal can find food it sets about building dams and creating ponds for its protection. The beaver tows sticks to the dam site, and places them in the water parallel to the current. The butt ends are upstream and the sticks are held in place by rocks, mud, and vegetation. On the upstream side the dam builders pack mud and rocks into every crevice until the mass of materials begins to hold back the water. Then autumn's falling leaves float down on the current and help seal the dam.

Scientists have determined that moving water triggers the beaver's urge to construct dams. Maintenance of the dam is a constant chore. As the beaver emerges from his lodge into the soft evening light, it normally goes directly to inspect the dam, then sets to work plugging any newly discovered leaks. Long dams may be the work of more than one family. The longest beaver dam on record is one that Mills found on the Jefferson River near Three Forks, Montana. It measured twenty-one hundred and forty feet in length.

Ahead of winter the beaver begin storing food to see them through the months when the pond will be frozen over. They cut small trees if they can find them, and larger ones if they must. There is a Canadian record of beavers cutting down a tree that measured a hundred and ten feet high and five feet seven inches in diameter at breast height. The animals cut the larger trees into lengths they can handle and move them to the water's edge. Once afloat, the branches are towed to a place near the lodge where they are weighted down and held in place with rocks or soil until they form an underwater mound of interlocking branches. During the winter these sticks are towed through an underwater tunnel into the lodge as needed, and there the bark is stripped off and eaten. Beaver also eat oak mast and aquatic vegetation. Modern beaver have learned to eat corn.

The pond-dwelling beaver must also build a lodge and the materials are the same as those used in constructing the dam. The lodge continues to grow as the water rises. There must always be an above-water chamber where the beaver family can rest and eat, and the young can be snug and dry. Entrances are underwater, allowing the animals to emerge beneath the ice to get to their stores of winter food while taking their air from bubbles beneath the ice. When there is no ice, the beaver can dive at the first sign of danger and swim underwater a considerable distance to its lodge without ever surfacing.

As the colony depletes its supply of aspen and willows, the beaver must work back farther and farther from the water's edge. Dragging branches overland is difficult and hazardous work that keeps the beaver out where the coyote and bobcat hunt. Sometimes a beaver colony brings water closer to the food source by raising the dam, but the beaver also knows how to construct and use canal systems for floating lengths of wood from the aspen grove to the beaver pond.

Early in this century, Enos Mills, on the slope of Long's Peak in Colorado, studied perhaps the most remarkable beaver canal system ever discovered. Mills, who had studied beaver for twenty-seven years in every state where beaver lived, as well as across Canada and into Alaska, watched the autumn activity of these Colorado beavers every day for two months. By notching standing trees in the grove the beaver were cutting, he could follow the course of individual logs as they moved through the beaver community.

"This was an old beaver settlement," Mills wrote in his book *Beaver World*, "and the numerous harvests gathered by its inhabitants had long since exhausted the nearby growths of aspen . . ." Studying the colony, Mills realized that the beaver would have to move their winter food supplies a quarter of a mile from a hillside aspen grove. Furthermore, they had to move the wood one hundred and twenty feet downhill to the level of the lodge.

These beaver had not dammed a stream to make their home pond but instead had built a semicircular dike around a system of hillside springs. Then they built other ponds below it until the slope was terraced with five ponds. The lower pond had a circumference of six hundred feet and was formed by a dam four hundred feet long and six feet high that almost encircled it.

"At its upper edge," wrote Mills, "stood the main house, which was eight feet high and forty feet in circumference. There was also another house on one of the terraces." Mills was able to follow the beavers' progress as they cut trees in their aspen grove and moved the sections down through or past the series of ponds to the big lodge.

One tree, six inches in diameter, had been cut into sections and the logs moved out of the grove. "From the spot where they were cut," said Mills, "they had evidently been rolled down a steep, grassy slope . . . dragged an equal distance over a level stretch among some lodgepole pines, and then pushed or dragged along a narrow runway that had been cut through a rank growth of willows. Once through the willows, they were pushed into the uppermost pond. They were taken across this, forced over the dam on the opposite side, and shot down a slide into the pond which contained the smaller house."

This would have been an amazing feat in itself, but Mills still did not find his marked logs. "On the opposite side of the pond I found where the logs had been dragged across the broad dam and then heaved into a long, wet slide which landed them in a small, shallow harbor in the grass. From this point a canal about eighty feet long ran around the brow of the terrace and ended at the top of a long slide."

The canal looked to Mills to be recently dug. It was thirty inches wide and fourteen inches deep. The earth removed to make it had been neatly banked along the lower side.

Water from the pond above was moving through it slowly. By now Mills knew that the logs cut on the slope, a quarter of a mile above, had all been moved by the beavers down into the big pond to supply the main lodge with winter food. He waded out into the water, and near the lodge where the winter food was being stored he found sections of the aspen trees he had notched where they stood, a quarter of a mile uphill.

For sixty-four days in succession, Mills visited the colony and studied the work of the occupants. "When I took my last tour through the colony," he wrote, "everything was ready for the long and cold winter."

Stream-dwelling beaver generally avoid much of this labor and live in burrows they dig in the banks.

The beaver is quiet by nature. If you are nearby on a quiet night, you may hear it gnawing at a tree. Then the tree crashes and all is silence, for as the tree begins to crack and tilt, the beaver hurries off to dive into the water. There it waits, and if the noise of the falling tree attracts no predator, it returns. But if there is a hint of danger, the beaver lifts its broad flat tail and smacks it down upon the water with a crack like a rifle firing, and the alarm sends all the beaver in the pond diving for deep water.

Beavers normally live in colonies and the male and female are monogamous. They mate in winter, usually in the water, under the ice. About a hundred days later, the female gives birth to perhaps three or four kits, and then days after that, the young ones begin to eat bits of vegetation. They stay with the family until their second year when they disperse to find new homes.

The mountain men knew some months were better than others for taking beaver pelts. The best season is autumn, beginning around mid-October, when the prime furs reach maximum length and reflect a sheen that pleases the buyers.

This fur was the prize luring the mountain men over the plains and into the mountains. The promise of the beaver sent him up a thousand streams, exploring the wildest country. To him the beaver was the most important wild animal in the world. Next came the grand beast on which he relied for his favorite food.

HOW THE TRAPPER CAUGHT BEAVER

The mountain man's major occupation was finding and catching beaver, and he became exceptionally skilled at it.

His first step when coming to new waters was to search for fresh signs of active beaver colonies. He looked for well-maintained lodges and dams as well as fresh cuttings where the beaver had felled trees to provide the bark on which they live. He studied the river shorelines looking for beaver burrows in the banks.

Typical beaver trap used by the mountain men of the early 1800s.

He normally worked with half a dozen traps. Preferably, he set his trap in water shallow enough for him to wade but with holes deep enough to drown a beaver quickly. The water was generally ice cold, and his footwear was not waterproof, but by wading he could put the trap right where the beaver lived and at the same time depend on the water to mask human odor that the beaver's sensitive nose could detect. Once caught, the beaver normally rushes for deeper water, and the long chain on the trap enabled it to reach deep water where it would drown before it could chew off its leg.

Once he selected the spot for one of his traps, the trapper drove a stout pole into the water. He set the trap, either by putting his foot on the springs and lifting his weight onto them, or by using squeezers to clamp the springs down. He depressed the springs long enough to set one jaw beneath the dog that fits

If the trapper had trouble depressing the springs of his trap with his feet, he often used a trap squeezer. The squeezer was made of stout, dried sticks, about eighteen inches long, held together at one end by a metal ring or rawhide binding. The open end was bound shut to hold the trap spring in place until the trap was set. The trapper could either carry two squeezers or save weight and space by substituting a U-shaped metal trap holder so he could use only a single squeezer for both springs.

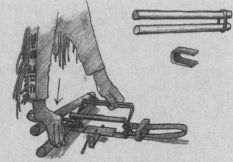

into a notch on the back of the pan. This holds the trap ready and waiting in its set position until the foot of the beaver puts pressure on the pan.

Next, he secured the trap by fitting the ring over the end of the pole and placed the trap in the shallow water. If the struggling beaver tore the anchor pole loose, the trapper searched downstream until he spotted the float pole, then retrieved trap and beaver.

Once the trap was in place, he baited the set. He stuck a fresh cut willow branch into the bottom of the lake or stream so that it was exposed to the air directly above the trap. He then carefully daubed the stick with a little of the "medicine" carried in his bait box.

The first beaver to arrive sniffed the evening air and knew there was the odor of a strange beaver in the territory. It followed the odor to the trap, stretched to check the bait, and in the process, lowered one foot to the bottom for support. The foot settled on the trap's pan.

Half a dozen well-set traps could keep the mountain man busy, making his sets and caring for the furs.

Beaver Bait

Three parts of the beaver were valuable to the mountain man, the fur, the tail for food, and the castor glands.

Both sexes carry the twin castor glands at the base of the tail. The glands are twin sacs about three inches long. Their weight is about six pairs to the pound. The substance stored in these sacs mixes with urine to form castoreum, a thin yellow liquid which

The trapper's bait box could be made from a six-inch length of cherry limb. This drawing is based on a "medicine" bottle displayed in the Museum of the Fur Trade at Chadron, Nebraska. The trapper hollowed out the limb and inserted a plug in the bottom and a plug and stopper in the top. He carried it suspended from a rawhide thong, probably hung from his powder horn or belt.

the beaver deposits on scent posts around its home range. The mountain man collected the castor sacs to make the bait used in his sets and for sale.

To set his trap, the mountain man drove a stout pole into the water, depressed the springs of the trap, and slipped the ring at the end of the chain over the end of the pole. Then he baited the set.

The bait he carried, and which he called "medicine," was kept in a small horn or wooden bottle with a tight stopper and a thong from which it swung in a handy location. Depending on the whims and experiences of the trapper, the bait might contain other ingredients in addition to the essential castoreum. "The Journals of Lewis and Clark" include the recipe followed by one of the group's most skilled woodsmen for making beaver scent. "This bait," wrote Clark, "will entice the beaver to the trap from

When a beaver caught the odor of the scent, it approached the trap, and in checking the bait lowered one foot to the bottom for support. The foot often touched the trap's pan, and the jaws sprang shut.

as far as he can smell it, which may be fairly stated to be at the distance of a mile, as their sense of smelling is very acute."

This two-century-old recipe requires half a dozen castor glands. Added to the container were a nutmeg, twelve or fifteen cloves, and thirty grams of cinnamon, all

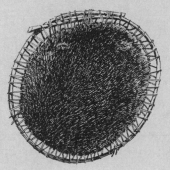

finely pulverized. The mixture was stirred

Sometimes the trapped beaver headed for deeper water, tearing the anchor pole loose. But the trapper only had to spot the floating pole to retrieve trap and beaver.

well, ". . . with as much ardent spirits added to the composition as will reduce the whole to the consistency of mustard."

A few drops of this bait were enough to attract the attention of the beaver as it checked out its range. Tightly stoppered, the "medicine" retained its strength for weeks.

After removing the tail, which he often roasted over the fire for his evening meal, the trapper scraped and fleshed out each skin, then laced it to a frame made of a willow sapling. The pelts were hung in camp to dry.

· 3 ·

The Buffalo Hunters

The mighty buffalo played its role in the beaver's downfall. The fur trappers hungered for the fat cow whose flavorful meat provided energy to tramp the cold mountain trails and wade the icy streams. Given plenty of buffalo meat, the living was good, and the mountain man needed no beans or bread to maintain his health and sense of well-being.

Strips of the freshly butchered beast, still warm and oozing blood, were impaled on sticks or ramrods and suspended close beside a campfire of dried buffalo chips to sear and roast. When the rich, dark meat was cooked, or at least warmed through, the hungry trapper, squatting beside his fire, held the meat close to his face, and carved slice after slice directly into his mouth, unconcerned that the dark, warm juices ran down the handle of his butcher knife, along his arm, and dripped onto the blackened front of his greasy buckskin jacket. He could joyfully eat pound after pound of such meat. Then, wiping his hands and knife upon his clothes, and running the back of his hand across his face, he settled down beside the fire to fill his pipe before he slept.

Meat that could not be consumed at once was cut into strips and dried to make jerky for the days ahead when there might be no buffalo in sight.

The fur trapper was only the latest in a long list of people to depend on the bison. Thousands of years earlier, men wrapped in animal skins and carrying stone-tipped weapons followed these giant herbivores across the Bering Sea land bridge from Asia, and man and bison together spread out across the continent.

Then bison, or buffalo, changed its form over the centuries. Once there were giant bison with horns three or four times as long as those of modern bison. These ancient monsters gave way to the modern species which spread over the continent and reached its peak numbers in those broad grasslands stretching from the Mississippi River into the Rocky Mountains. There may once have been, as some have estimated, sixty or seventy million buffalo across North America. No other part of the world, Africa included, had a single species of wild big-game animal in such abundance.

Hunting Methods

Indian hunters took what they could from the sprawling herds and scarcely made a dent. Then, the Spanish introduced horses, and the Indians learned to race alongside the stampeding buffalo, guiding their ponies with the pressure of their knees, while bringing the beast down with well-placed arrows. This enabled the Indian hunter to feed more people, and the tribes grew. Modern firearms brought the buffalo down faster yet. But when the fur trappers began invading the West, the herds of buffalo still roamed the grasslands in unbelievable numbers.

To the Indian hunter and mountain man alike, the most exciting way to take a buffalo was to ride it down on horseback and, clinging to the side of the sweating pony, shoot the buffalo on the dead run. As the "buffer" stampedes, the hunter readies his rifle, puts his heels to the ribs of his horse, lets out a bellow, and feels the cold air rush past his face. He takes his point blank aim in a cloud of brown dust, knowing that if his lathered horse senses a shift in the buffalo's course, or a swing of its horns, it will change direction with the speed of thought.

"The horse that is well trained for this purpose," wrote mountain man Osborne Russell in his famous *Journal of a Trapper*, "not only watches the ground over which he is running and avoids the holes, ditches and rocks by shortening or extending his leaps but also the animal which he is pursuing in order to prevent being 'horned' . . . if the horse in close pursuit wheels on the same side with the Buffaloe he comes directly in contact with its horns and with one stroke the horses entrails are often torn out and his rider thrown headlong to the ground."

The experienced hunter knew the need for a well-placed shot. As George Frederick Ruxton wrote, "The first attempts of a greenhorn to kill a buffalo are invariably unsuccessful. He sees before him a mass of flesh, nearly five feet in depth from the top of the hump to the brisket, and consequently imagines that by planting his ball midway between these points, it must surely reach the vitals. Nothing, however, is more erroneous . . . he must be struck but a few inches above the brisket, behind the shoulder . . ." Ruxton adds that he once shot a bull through the center of the heart and watched it run half a mile before it fell. Another time, he saw a bull shot nineteen times at six paces before it fell.

As the animal goes down, horse and hunter are already speeding off in pursuit of the next buffalo. Guiding his horse with his knees, the hunter reloads on the run and closes on his next target.

There were other effective ways to take the buffalo and the mountain man knew them. One was to stalk the animals on foot from upwind and work your way into range before the buffalo knew you were there. Avoid standing erect in plain view. Crawl along the gullies, hide behind the rocks, or hold a bush out in front of your face for camouflage.

The Indians had favorite killing places where they could, if conditions were right, take a hundred or more buffalo in a single drive. They sometimes drove a herd into box canyons from which there was no escape.

Or if there was no natural place for trapping buffalo, the Plains Indians made their own traps. They built a corral and inside it imbedded sharpened poles set at an angle to keep the buffalo from knocking them down. Then, they built a V-shaped approach by setting two lines of rock piles out across the grasslands for a mile or two. When all was ready, the animals were herded toward the broad open mouth of this trap. As the buffalo moved along, women and children jumped from behind the rock piles yelling and waving skins. The buffalo ran straight into the trap where they were killed with arrows and spears. The Indians, collecting meat for the coming winter, took amazing numbers of buffalo in this manner. Near the head of the Missouri River a band of four hundred Flathead Indians was observed killing five hundred buffalo in a three-hour hunt.

Easier yet was driving a herd of buffalo over a cliff. In the *Journals of Lewis and Clark*, we find Captain Clark's description of this method. The Indian chose one of the swiftest runners among their young men and draped a buffalo robe over his body with the head and horns worn as a helmet. Then, they sent him out between the cliff and the grazing herd. The rest of the party surrounded the herd and began moving in on them. The decoy out front ran toward the cliff, leading the alarmed buffalo to their doom.

At the last moment, the decoy dropped down among the rocks and took refuge in a crevice as the thundering animals came to the cliff and were pushed to their deaths by the multitude behind them. One May day in 1805, along the Missouri River, upstream from the Musselshell, Captain clark wrote: "Today we passed on the Stard. side the remains of a vast many mangled carcasses of Buffalow which had been driven over a precipice of 120 feet by the Indians and perished . . . they created a most horrid stench."

The Plains Indians also worshiped the buffalo. The animal possessed a mystic appeal for these people whose lives depended so heavily upon it. Shamans prayed to the spirit of the great beast. Mandan dancers wore buffalo head masks and chanted sacred songs to bring the buffalo back. At the conclusion of a feast they offered a bowl of food to the preserved head of a buffalo hanging in the lodge so the buffalo would think well of them. Similar ceremonies were part of the culture of Pawnees, Assiniboines, Hiditsa, and Sioux.

But these people were also practical enough to carry out North America's earliest efforts at game management. Each spring they burned the prairies, encouraging the tender new growth that tempted the wandering buffalo back to the tribal lands and spared the hunters the need to risk their lives venturing onto the hunting grounds of neighboring tribes.

DECLINE OF THE BUFFALO

The trappers blazed new trails for the settlers who followed and growing numbers of people claimed the land of the buffalo. At first, buffalo had been so numerous that few people saw any need to worry about their future. A fat cow might be slaughtered for the tongue alone, or to supply supper for a couple of trappers, and the remainder left in the grass for the wolves.

So heavily did the trappers draw on the buffalo supply that the more observant among them could see the great herds dwindling. Osborne Russell wrote, ". . . this noble race of animals . . . will at no far distant period become extinct . . ."

The waste continued beyond the day of the beaver trappers until Russell's prediction very nearly became truth. The official policy of the United States Army was to destroy the food source of the Plains Indians, and thereby the Indians themselves. Men whittled away at the once vast herds until only small bands of buffalo remained.

While the animals remained, noblemen from Europe and wealthy hunters from the East invaded the West to shoot buffalo they did not need. In 1872, Buffalo Bill Cody, General Phil Sheridan, and Lt. Colonel George Armstrong Custer played host to Grand Duke Alexis of Russia and his party. The Duke eventually managed to ride in beside a racing buffalo, place the muzzle of his gun close to the side of the beast, and bring it down. He was so elated that he leaped from his horse, cut off the trophy's tail and, whooping and hollering with delight, called for champagne to be served that all might toast the magnificent beast and the Russian who, with the aid of horse, gun, and a platoon of helpers, had conquered it.

E. Douglas Branch, in *The Hunting of the Buffalo*, writes of the $10 round-trip ticket for which, in 1866, a man and his gun could board a train in Leavenworth, Kansas, for a four-day buffalo-shooting trip. Railroad companies advertised that "Buffaloes are so numerous along the road that they are shot from the cars."

For the buffalo, the worst was yet to come. First, there was a demand for the meat in military posts. In winter, meat could be shipped to the cities without spoiling. Thousands of buffalo were shot to supply the demand for tongues that were dried in the sun and shipped east. In one year, twenty-five thousand tongues were shipped to St. Louis alone. Then, demand increased for the hides and this brought thousands of professional buffalo hunters to begin the final process of clearing the plains of the great beasts.

The professional buffalo hunter never made much money but if he liked to shoot big animals he had found the best of all lives. He worked with a crew of skinners and sometimes he could have fifty or so buffalo on the ground in an hour, giving the skinners as much work as they could handle for the day.

Riding out in early morning he dropped a feather to test the wind, moved downwind of the herd, stalked to within two hundred and fifty to three hundred yards and set himself up to kill as many buffalo as he needed without moving his shooting station.

As long as the buffalo did not suspect that a man was close, they might not run. They seemed to stay within range even after members of the herd began to drop dead around them. The buffalo hunter commonly used a gun support made of two crossed sticks. His Sharps, effective at three hundred yards, was usually sighted in at distances great enough to keep from spooking the animals.

The aim was to shoot the leader of the herd first, and always in the lungs instead of the heart. The buffalo shot in the lungs usually stayed with the herd and soon died. A heart-shot buffalo might run and spook the entire herd.

Several buffalo hunters, or "buffalo runners" as they called themselves, established records of more than a hundred animals taken from a single stand. Tom Nixon once killed a hundred and twenty in forty minutes. One hunter, shooting at three hundred yards, killed seventy-nine buffalo from a single herd with ninety-one shots. Another hunter killed fifty-four with fifty-four shots.

Always the object was to make a clean kill with a single shot. Shells were costly, and the herd might spook at any moment. Besides there was the matter of professional pride. Let a man set a record and word spread.

Among the favorite guns used by these hunters were the Remington 40/90, the "Buffalo" Sharps 40/120/550, which loaded with 120 grains of powder gave the 550-grain projectile a muzzle energy of around twenty-three hundred pounds, and the 50 caliber Sharps made especially for killing buffalo.

As beaver trapping died out, the occasional trapper turned to selling buffalo robes. By the hundreds of thousands, the shaggy, black hides were baled to wait beside the railroads. In the 1880s, the herds were so nearly gone that the hide business was history. Bleaching bones remained the only physical evidence that these plains once held buffalo numbering in the millions. Then, a market opened up for the bones as well and destitute homesteaders, along with their wives and children, scoured the grasslands, collecting cartloads of buffalo bones. Box cars moved the bones to eastern factories where they were converted to fertilizer, glue, and charcoal, or the boneblack used them in refining sugar.

By the arrival of this century, the remaining evidence of the once abundant buffalo that had fed the early trappers consisted of here and there a deeply rutted trail, a grown-over wallow, or a huge prairie boulder rubbed smooth and glossy by generations of rough-coated beasts.

With the disappearing buffalo went the culture of the Plains Indians. Plains Indian historian Thomas E. Mails, in his book *The Mystic Warriors of the Plains*, lists nearly a hundred products and uses to which the Indians converted the various parts of the buffalo's body, ranging from glue to rawhide buckets. The scrotum was used in making rattles or as a vessel. The stomach contents were saved to become medicine for treating frostbit.

The mountain man also found uses for buffalo parts. The hides became beds and great coats. Horns were turned into powder horns, spoons, cups, and ladles. Strips of hide were woven into ropes, and rawhide became the standard material for making moccasin soles.

At the last moment, the nearly extinct plains buffalo was given protection in Yellowstone National Park, then elsewhere and, gradually, their numbers increased. But never again would these great beasts that had nourished Indians, trappers, and settlers for centuries be truly wild animals. Today, they live mostly in captive herds. There is no longer space for the free-roaming buffalo on the broad, sweeping plains. The saga of the buffalo that once "blackened the prairies" is a depressing bit of American history.

What many modern tourists never realize is that the buffalo was never fully domesticated. In parks and pastures, it still carries in that woolly head the ancient instincts of the wild beast and anyone carelessly invading the animals' safety zone may be tramped and gored. This is a constant concern of rangers in Yellowstone National Park, Wind Cave National Park, and South Dakota's Custer State Park where remnant herds of buffalo wander the grasslands. The animals are especially cantankerous during the rutting season and in April and early May when the new rust-colored calves arrive. The mountain man and the Indian knew how to gauge the moods of a buffalo. If it elevates the tail or arches it and moves toward the person instead of away, the time has come for the person to depart and protect himself. When the tail points up in the air, the agitated buffalo is ready to charge.

Even though the mountain man measured all other meats against "fat cow," there were frequently times when "buffer" could not be found. Then, he turned to the lesser choices, and these hunters in buckskins knew them all.

4

Mountain Man's Wildlife

Typically, the mountain man grew up following the trails of wild animals. Back in Tennessee, Kentucky, and Virginia he was born into a hunting community. While still a tad, he joined his daddy following the rangy coon hounds through the night, and stalking elusive deer and alert turkey gobblers. He learned how to trap muskrats, mink, and wolves. He could read the tracks of the wild creatures and understand the seasonal ways of the animals. Often he could shoot well enough to bark a squirrel and bring it undamaged from the limbs of a shagbark hickory.

He took these woodsman's skills with him to the western grasslands, and on into the mountains, but there he met a remarkable variety of animals new to him. How well he came to appreciate and understand them determined how well he succeeded as a trapper, and often how well—or how long—he lived. Trapper Osborne Russell said of the mountain men, "They have not the misfortune to get any of the luxuries from the civilized world but once a year and then in such small quantities that they last but a few days." He added that, "Sheep, elk, deer, buffalo and bear skins mostly supply the mountaineers with clothing, bedding, and lodges while the meat of the same animals supplies them with food."

THE GREAT BEAR

Russell also wrote of the beast the trappers feared most, the grizzly bear. "In going to visit my traps a distance of three or four miles early in the morning," he wrote, "I have frequently seen seven or eight standing about the clumps of cherry bushes on their hind legs gathering cherries with surprising dexterity not even deigning to turn their grizzly heads to gaze at the passing trapper but merely casting a sidelong glance at him without altering their position."

If this was all the grizzly did, the trapper was fortunate. More often than not, when mountain man met grizzly, one or the other, usually the trapper, picked a fight. The trapper, especially if traveling with a companion or two, customarily tackled the grizzly bear for the hell of it, more than from any need for the meat or fur. Hunting the great bear was exciting business.

When trapper Thomas James brought his memories together in a book he called *Three Years Among the Indians and Mexicans*, his recollections of Marie, a French Canadian trapper, remained vivid in his mind. He could not forget Marie's appearance after the Frenchman tangled with a grizzly.

After setting his traps one morning, Marie ". . . strolled out into the prairie for game, and soon perceived a large white bear rolling on the ground in the shade of a tree." Marie did what any redblooded mountain trapper was expected to do, he leveled off a shot at the grizz. He missed. The bear paid only scant attention to the noise, so Marie, with more persistence than common sense, reloaded and tried again.

This time he succeeded—after a fashion—by wounding the bear. "His majesty," wrote James, "instantly, with ears set back, flew toward his enemy like an arrow . . ." Marie ran like the wind, but there was no good place to run, so he dashed out onto a beaver dam, then dived into the shallow water. The grizzly did a belly-smacker right beside him, and there began a game of tag which continued for some minutes. Every time Marie came up for air, the grizzly was waiting until the trapper finally, in a judgmental error even worse than shooting at the bear in the first place, surfaced directly beneath the animal's chin.

The bear clamped his open mouth over the trapper's head and sank its teeth in deep enough to prevent any hope of escape. One tooth punched through beneath Marie's right jaw, another through his right eye. As the bear swam for shore, towing his catch by the head, Marie's partner came running and shot the beast through its head while missing Marie. "I saw him six days afterward," said James, "with a swelling on his head an inch thick, and his food and drink gushed through the opening under his jaw made by the teeth of his terrible enemy."

Grizzlies were also pursued by Lewis and Clark's men. On a July day in 1805, the Lewis and Clark party decided to get even with the grizzlies that had been wandering around their camp at night, frightening the horses. The bears were believed to be hanging out in the willow thickets on a nearly island.

The hunters divided into parties of three and began pushing their way through the willows. They found a single bear in the thicket. This bear had the misfortune to choose for its target George Drouillard, called Drewyer in the explorers' journals, the best hunter in the expedition. As the great bear rushed down on the hunter, Drouillard calmly sighted and put a bullet through the animal's heart. The bear was twenty paces from Drouillard when it stumbled and gave the hunter his opportunity to escape. "We then followed him 100 yards," says the journal, "and found that the wound had been mortal."

This still did not satisfy the hunters. They continued to tramp around through the thicket, like rabbit hunters, trying to flush another bear. "Not being able to discover any more of these animals we returned to camp."

Sometimes it was the bear that made the first move. Zenas Leonard told in *Adventures of a Mountain Man* about the two trappers who came into his camp after a close encounter with a giant grizzly. These trappers had set their traps and were busy arranging their camp for the night when the bear rushed down upon them, chuffing and snarling, teeth flashing in its open mouth.

This sent the trappers diving for the guns they had leaned against a nearby tree. Their problem was compounded by the fact that one gun was double-triggered while the other was single-triggered, and in the excitement of the moment, they both grabbed the wrong muzzleloader.

The bear's first target was the man holding the double-triggered gun. Because the trigger was not set, it would not fire, so he could do little but beat the furious bear over its broad head with the butt of his friend's rifle.

The grizzly soon had enough of this treatment and turned on the other trapper, but this man too was immediately in trouble. Thinking that he held the double-triggered gun, he tried to set it and as he did so, the gun went off, after which he took his turn pounding the angry bear on the head.

These trappers were fortunate. The bear finally withdrew without doing much damage other than tearing a sleeve off one man's coat and biting him through the hand.

"The grizzly bear is the most ferocious animal that inhabits these prairies, and are very numerous," wrote Leonard. "They no sooner see you than they will make at you with open mouth. If you stand still they will come within two or three yards of you, and stand upon their hind feet and look you in the face, if you have fortitude enough to face them, they will turn and run off; but if you turn they will most assuredly tear you to pieces . . ."

Today the grizzly bear is exceedingly rare in the Lower Forty-Eight, but when the mountain men roamed the plains and valleys, thousands of these great bears still occupied the western country all the way east into Kansas and Nebraska. Wherever the mountain man wandered, he was suddenly in the land of the great bear, and the grizzly was king.

The grizzly is an awesome animal. The adult male may weigh six hundred pounds, or more, and stand almost four feet high at the shoulders. He is recognizable by his broad head with the dish-shaped face, and the hump over the shoulders. Although the color varies, a common color is yellowish brown. The front feet are equipped with long, sharp claws capable of opening the belly of an elk or man, or lifting a three-hundred-pound rock to see what small creature lurks beneath it. Its remarkable sense of smell may lead it unerringly upwind two or three miles to food sources, including the odor of food from the camper's fire.

The great bear is a loner, except during the mating season or in the case of females with cubs. Newly weaned cubs, already in their second year, now large and powerful, may travel together for some months.

A grizzly anywhere is a threat if surprised, especially if the bear is injured, guarding food, caring for cubs, or otherwise feels that its space has been invaded. Threat or not, the giant bear added spice to the mountain man's life. Next to the roving Indians, whose lands the trappers invaded, the grizzly was their most persistent enemy.

WOLVES AND PRAIRIE WOLVES

In the evening, and into the night, the mountain man listened to the song of the coyote. This plaintive wild music became a familiar serenade. The little song-dogs were everywhere. They sat on the slopes, lifted their faces to the skies and practiced a wilderness harmony. The trapper's night would have been empty without them.

These prairie wolves lived mostly on small animals and seldom caused problems for the trappers except when they became pests around camp. One trapper blamed the coyotes that had been pestering the trapping party for taking the fur cap off his head while he was sleeping. The hat was not found.

The coyote's big cousins, the gray wolves or timber wolves, were never trusted. In the early years of the 1800s, wolves were a prominent part of the wildlife community which surrounded the mountain men. The low, mournful howl of the hunting pack was enough to set a man's nerves on edge and start him to studying the shadows around his campfire. Trapper Tom Fitzpatrick told of his encounter with a pack of wolves he claimed that he met when already down on his luck. He had come close to death in an attack by a band of Indians. To escape, he had left his horse behind. Then, while crossing a stream, he lost all his belongings including his gun, powder, extra clothing, and food, leaving him nothing to eat but plants and roots.

"I followed the banks of this river for two days," he wrote, "subsisting on buds, roots, weeds, &c." On the second evening, Fitzpatrick was digging the sweet roots of a swamp plant when he became aware of a pack of growling wolves coursing down the slope and closing rapidly on his position.

Fitzpatrick leaped for the nearest tree and scrambled into its branches. While the wolves howled around the base of the tree, the trapper perched uncomfortably above them with only his butcher knife for protection. "The wolves [were] tearing up the ground and gnawing at the tree so that I sometimes feared they would cut it through," said Fitzpatrick.

Before morning, the wolves gave up and moved on. Fitzpatrick descended from his perch and departed "with great speed." Another time, wolves did him a favor—they killed a buffalo and left him enough meat for a meal.

In time, the wolves, like the beaver and the grizzly bear, would be eliminated from most of their range.

The wolf is German-shepherd size, or larger. A big one may stand three feet high at the shoulders and weigh a hundred pounds. They are social animals, living and hunting in packs in which the members are often related. This cooperative lifestyle enables them to kill the large animals on which they customarily feed. The male and female mate for life. Once a year, usually in mid-May, the female gives birth to a litter of five to seven pups.

The wolves that met the early trappers and explorers were not always fierce beasts, threatening to kill and devour. Perhaps more often than not they slipped away unnoticed at the first sign of human presence. Meriwether Lewis wrote in his journal on May 29, 1805, as the expedition moved up the Missouri, "We saw a great many wolves in the neighbourhood of these mangled carcasses; they were fat and extremely gentle."

He adds that Captain Clark killed one with his "espontoon," and leaves the reader asking if Fitzpatrick was really as threatened by the wolves that treed him as his story implies. Perhaps the nature of wolves has changed with time as the adaptable wolf became acquainted with the white man's threat and wolf numbers dwindled. There are various accounts of wolf packs attacking early settlers in the eastern forests, as well as the western mountains. We may no longer be able to separate wolf fiction from wolf fact, but wolves, rare and scattered, pose little threat to people today, and perhaps never did.

BIG CATS

Although the "yarners" surely included mountain lion tales in their campfire repertoir, old records rarely mention these big cats. Mountain man James Ohio Pattie did write of awakening in the middle of night to stare into the eyes of a giant panther, crouched on a log six feet away. Said Pattie, "I raised my gun gently to my face, and shot it in the head."

But Pattie's reverence for facts is open to question. Perhaps Osborne Russell left a more reliable picture when he described the cougar as ". . . very destructive on Sheep and other animals that live on high mountains but will run at the sight of a man and has great antipathy to fire."

We can forgive the yarning mountain man who made the giant cat into a man-killer. Successful storytelling around the campfire was often built of imagination more than fact, and the cougar remained a most impressive cat, lending itself well to the storyteller's art. The adult mountain lion, measuring perhaps seven feet from tip of tail to nose, may weigh one hundred and fifty pounds or so, and larger ones have been recorded. The golden brown mountain lion with its short, smooth hair, quietly stalks its unsuspecting prey—usually a deer or elk—on padded feet. It moves with the shadowy stealth and grace of cats everywhere.

The adults are loners except in the season of mating which, for the female, comes every second or third year. She commonly has a litter of three helpless kittens which she hides among the rocks or downfall timber. For two years the kittens stay with their mother, learning the art of survival, and are finally cast out to find their own territories. Once they gained their full size and strength they were a greater threat to the mountain man's grazing horse than they ever were to the trapper himself.

THE ELK

As September brought cool autumn nights to the mountains, the shrill whistle of the bugling elk echoed down the slopes. Let the call come from close at hand and the trapper picked up his gun and slipped silently out of camp. Killing an elk meant a large supply of choice meat—second only to fat cow. Furthermore, elk were found in the high country where the buffalo were often scarce.

The trapper hunted elk free of our modern legal restraints or concerns about what is sporting. Instead of the careful stalk, these earlier hunters sometimes ran the elk down on horseback. Osborne Russell wrote that the elk, although swift and elusive when found alone, were highly vulnerable when running in herds. ". . . if they are closely pursued by the hunter on horseback they soon commence dropping down flat on the ground to elude their pursuers and will suffer themselves to be killed with a knife in this position." Hunters coming upon a band of elk ran them and hazed them, yelling and shooting over them, until the weaker ones began to drop.

The reward for taking an elk was an animal that might weigh up to a thousand pounds and carry a hide that was choice for making moccasins and other items of clothing.

THE DEER

Deer, both mule deer and whitetail, were always welcome in the fur trapper's camp. Not only was the meat considered excellent, but the hides were needed for making clothing.

The mule deer, already given its name by the earliest explorers because of the size of its ears, was a welcome sight, feeding on the grassy slopes. The smaller whitetail that the trappers had known in their eastern homes, lived among the cottonwoods and willows along the riverbottoms.

THE PRONGHORN

If there was one western animal that astounded the mountain men, it was the pronghorn, which they sometimes called "goat." Any man who saw it run had to marvel at its all-out speed. Trappers admired its vision for it could spot them across miles of open grasslands, and they were astounded by the distances over which the animal could maintain its top speed.

From the Indians they learned that the pronghorn had a serious weakness that worked to the hunter's advantage—it was highly curious about anything it did not recognize or understand. So, the hunter would lie on his back and kick his feet in the air, and the pronghorn moved in closer to investigate. One mountain man wrote that, by getting down low and waving his hat in the air slowly, he could bring them within thirty paces and easily shoot them.

To the trapper in search of meat, the pronghorn ranked far down the list. One mountain man called it a "species of meat we would not look at when in the vicinity of deer and buffalo," but added that, in times of hunger, they considered themselves fortunate to take antelope.

In his book *Ruxton of the Rockies*, George Frederick Ruxton described the scene he witnessed in the beautiful San Louis Valley of south-central Colorado. On the plains they watched bands of antelope cruise past them, but the bone-chilling cold kept them plodding along on their horses unwilling to shoot. Finally Ruxton could stand it no longer. He didn't even pick out a target but made a covey shot instead.

"I jumped off *Panchito*," he wrote, "and, kneeling down, sent a ball from my rifle into the thick of the band. At the report two antelopes sprang into the air, their forms being distinct against the horizon above the backs of the rest; and when the herd had passed, they were lying kicking in the dust, one shot in the neck, through which the ball had passed into the body of another."

Eventually uncontrolled hunting, and later the building of fences across the ranchlands, cut heavily into the number of pronghorns. One estimate places the population of these animals on their native western grasslands, at the time of the mountain men, at thirty-five million. By the beginning of this century they were down to dangerously low levels. But sound management has brought them back. There are hunting seasons again and travelers can see antelope from the highways. If coyote, dog, or man approaches, the whole herd, white rumps flashing, dashes off at forty miles an hour. This is the speediest of all North American land mammals.

BIGHORN SHEEP

Another favorite food of the mountain man was the flesh of the bighorn sheep. As one trapper said, when comparing bighorn sheep to mutton, "its flavor is more agreeable and the meat more juicy." In addition, the mountain man who had an Indian wife hunted the bighorn because leather from its hide was softer and superior to that of deer for making clothing. But taking the wild sheep was seldom easy. It is at home in the highest country, commanding a view of the slopes and valley below.

The bighorn were hunted anyhow, even in winter when the hunter had to scramble over treacherous snowfields and icy ledges. ". . . but the excitement created by hunting them," wrote Russell, "often enables the hunger to surmount obstacles which at other times would seem impossible." He tells of the winter hunt when, crawling over rocky ledges, he spotted a dozen ewes below him. He shot one through the head and she ". . . fell dead on the cliff where she stood."

The hunter was ready for this. He carried a rope which he promptly tied to some bushes and let himself down the face of the cliff to the dead sheep. He rolled the sheep off the cliff and watched her fall a hundred feet to another ledge. "I then pulled myself up by the cord," he adds, "and went around the rock down to where she fell . . ." There he butchered her, shouldered some of the meat, and climbed back to his starting place. He started a fire, set the ribs to roasting, and obtained water by dropping hot stones into a skin filled with snow. After a night of sound sleep, he climbed back down to claim the remainder of the sheep, but a wolverine, which was still on the scene, had eaten the remains.

OTHER WILD ANIMALS

Given the opportunity, the trapper also took prairie chickens, sage grouse, and other game birds, and sometimes non-game birds, as well. Wrote Rufus B. Sage, "Upon the opposite side of the river was a bald eagle's nest with two half-grown fledglings. One of our party, ascending the tree, captured the young ones, and we had a fine meal from their carcasses." He added they robbed a wood duck nest of a dozen eggs, then did the same to the nest of a goose, and even added to their feast the eggs from a raven's nest.

Wild turkeys were always welcome in the trapper's camp fare, and Sage tells how he took the big birds from the roost at night. "My experiments in turkey-hunting made me a proficient shot by moonlight, a feat which adds materially to the sport. This is done by maneuvering so as to have the turkey in a direct line between the marksman and the moon, causing its shadow to fall upon his face—then raising his rifle to a level from the ground upwards, the instant the sight becomes darkened, he fires, and, if his piece be true, seldom fails to make a centre shot."

The mountain man met other wild animals—the fox, prairie dog, skunk, mink, bobcat, porcupine, packrat, magpie, and raven. At night, he heard the owls add bass notes to the coyote's song. Jedediah Smith once wrote in his journal, in California, "I saw wild geese, white and gray brant, blue and white heron, buzzards, and hawks of all colors." In season, the trapper was alert for the rattlers in his path and, if he owned a hair rope, he sometimes stretched it around his bed on the questionable theory that a reptile would not cross such a barrier. He became a practical naturalist. His welfare, and often his life, depended on how well he understood the habits of the wild animals around him.

We can hope that sometimes the mountain man, drawing on his pipe in the late evening, or moving along the beaver stream at his work, took time to smell the flowers. He must have heard the liquid notes of the western meadowlark, and watched the antics of the chattering pine squirrels. Perhaps he spoke to the playful otter even as he set his trap where it lived, and paused to watch the soaring eagle. He lifted his leathery face to the mountains at the bugling of the elk, heard the throaty calls of the trumpeter swan, and saw the bighorn sheep on the rocky crags—for he was a part of the wilderness. The world of the Rocky Mountain wildlife was his world too.

5

Eyes West

---

*I*n the early years of the 1800s, as the United States expanded its borders westward, monumental events happened swiftly. Through treaties in 1800 and 1801, the vast lands of the Louisiana Territory, including much of the western half of the Mississippi Valley as far north as Montana, passed from the government of Spain back to the French, although the Spanish continued to administer the region. In 1801, President Thomas Jefferson dispatched his minister, Robert Livingston, to Paris, hoping to buy New Orleans and parts of Florida.

Napoleon meanwhile, worried that the British might move in and take the Louisiana Territory by force, decided that perhaps the best answer was to sell the whole area to the United States. This grand offer caught Livingston by surprise, but in due time they agreed on a price of $15 million, and the agreement was signed in treaty form on April 30, 1803, about doubling the size of the United States.

In addition, the purchase brought the United States into possession of a vast wilderness territory about which little was known. Jefferson conceived the idea that a small party of rugged outdoorsmen, using St. Louis as a starting place, could follow the Missouri River north and west through what would someday become the Dakotas and Montana. They could cross the Rocky Mountains through unknown territory, and explore for a west-flowing stream that would lead them all the way to the Pacific Ocean.

The leader of such a group would have to be young and tough—a man with determination and drive, but one whose men would respect and follow him and President Jefferson had his man in Captain Meriwether Lewis, who worked in the White House as his personal secretary. The president knew the young officer well.

Lewis was eager to go. He worked hard at preparing himself for the trip, studying under professors in Philadelphia, learning botany, zoology, celestial navigation, and even medicine. Meanwhile he drew up a list of equipment and supplies, and considered the skills he must find in the men who would accompany him.

As a guideline, he had the president's instructions on what the trip should accomplish. "To Meriwether Lewis, Esquire, Captain of the 1st regiment of infantry of the United States of America: Your situation as Secretary of the President of the United States has made you acquainted with the objects of my confidential message of Jan. 18, 1803, to the legislature. You have seen the act they passed, which, tho' expressed in general terms, was meant to sanction those objects, and you are appointed to carry them into execution."

Here was an order that would catapult the young captain into lasting fame. The journey would fire the imaginations of dreamers, while turning the thoughts of practical men to the valuable beaver furs waiting in western waters.

The president's memo explained that Lewis was to explore the Missouri River and its major tributaries, searching out the most direct route to the Pacific. The explorers were directed to study the wildlife, especially the animals that might be new to science, and describe the plants and animals in their journals. They were also to study the Indian tribes and learn how these people lived, practiced their religion, settled their conflicts, and to consider how they might be brought into a system of fur trading with the white man.

Jefferson told Lewis to select a co-leader to share responsibility for the journey, and Lewis knew the man he wanted. While serving under General Mad Anthony Wayne in Pennsylvania, he had soldiered with William Clark, the tall, red-headed, personable younger brother of the famous General George Rogers Clark. Lewis enjoyed Clark's company and respected his remarkable abilities as a frontiersman. Clark was at his home near Louisville, Kentucky, when he received the invitation from Lewis. He quickly dispatched a message to Lewis expressing his eagerness to be a part of this historic wilderness journey.

These two soldiers proved to be a good team. Lewis outranked Clark, even though Clark was four years older. But command of the expedition was shared from the beginning and, although equal command of a military unit is an unusual arrangement, these two young officers made it work—and smoothly. Lewis, the better educated, was responsible for much of the scientific study while Clark, a skilled woodsman and boatman, became the geographer and shared the daily business of running the operation. Both men kept journals which, combined with the writings of a few others in their party, left us the records we have today of the travels of these pioneering mountain men. Among all American adventure stories, the journey of Lewis and Clark stands unequaled for its daring, as well as its success, and the skill with which it was conducted.

Lewis traveled overland to Pittsburgh where he arranged for construction of a fifty-five-foot-long keelboat, complete with mast. Here he also chose some of his soldiers, and they were with him when he set off down the Ohio River.

Captain Lewis and Captain Clark, putting their little military unit together, were searching for a special breed. The crew they assembled was a small select band of twenty-seven young, unmarried soldiers. In addition, there were a number of French river boatmen who, with a corporal and five privates, would accompany the group upstream and return before the first winter, bringing back the keelboat and the notes and scientific specimens the captains had collected to that time. Captain Clark also brought along York, a powerful black slave whose color astounded the Indians along the way.

There was another person in the permanent party who deserves special mention because, except for the captains, he became the most important reason for the success of the venture. After Captain Lewis picked up Captain Clark, as well as some of the other new members in Louisville, they drifted on down the broad waters of the Ohio to Fort Massac, the location today of Metropolis, Illinois, some thirty miles from the Mississippi. Here the captains met George Drouillard, called Drewyer in their journals, for the first time. This was the big, tough outdoorsman of whom Captain Lewis would later write in his journal, "I scarcely know how we should subsist were it not for the exertions of this excellent hunter."

Drouillard, the finest marksman in a crew of excellent marksmen, became the Lewis and Clark expedition's official hunter. The journals tell of a day when rations were low and several hunters were dispatched on both sides of the river. They returned with a total of seven deer. Drouillard had killed six of them.

Another of his duties was to serve as interpreter in dealings with the Indians, since Drouillard was familiar with the sign language universal among the Plains tribes.

The little party came out of the Ohio onto the Mississippi and turned up that stream toward the mouth of the Missouri. Final details of the transfer of the Louisiana Purchase lands had not all been worked out. Across the Mississippi, even though the land now belonged to the United States, it was still administered by foreigners, so Lewis and Clark anchored for the winter on the east side of the Mississippi just opposite the mouth of the Missouri. There, at Camp Wood River, they spent five months in thorough preparation, putting the finishing touches on their outfit. They trained. They took on supplies. Meanwhile, they talked with any travelers who could give them bits of information about conditions on the Missouri.

UP THE MISSOURI

On May 14, 1804, the keelboat and the two pirogues in which the Lewis and Clark party traveled shoved out into the waters of the Mississippi and were soon headed up the Missouri. Their trip had begun in earnest. Through Herculean effort with poles, oars, lines, and sail, they pushed upstream against the current, fifteen miles or so a day until autumn, when they reached the Mandan villages near the mouth of the Knife River in North Dakota. Here they cut logs and built Fort Mandan where they sat out the bitterly cold winter until the following April.

At their first winter fort, they added an interpreter, a French Canadian, Toussaint Charbonneau, and his wife, Sacajawea, a young Shoshone Indian woman, captured from her people and later purchased by Charbonneau. After Charbonneau and Sacajawea joined the party, Sacajawea gave birth to a son, the male child that Captain Clark always fondly called Pompey.

At Fort Mandan, Lewis and Clark first heard from the Indians of bears, larger and more ferocious than any they had known in the eastern forests. They could not easily believe that the grizzly bears would offer any serious hazard to their well-armed hunters. In due time, however, they would gain a deeper respect for the strength, speed, and temper of the animal.

When spring came, they moved upstream in a little flotilla consisting of two large pirogues and half a dozen canoes. In addition to their boats the party had two horses. These were largely for the use of Drouillard, and the hunter who accompanied him, as he went after deer, buffalo, or other game. When he shot an animal, he field-dressed it and packed it to camp by horseback.

Lewis spent considerable time on shore, studying the native plants and animals, making notes and collecting specimens to send back to President Jefferson. Clark, the better boatman, usually stayed with the boats.

By June 21, they had crossed much of Montana and arrived at the Great Falls, an impassable barrier for the boats. Lewis described the river as ". . . raging among the rocks and losing itself in foam." It dashed and roared through a series of whitewater rapids and falls, and the boats had to be dragged ashore and portaged more than eighteen miles around the rough water. This demanded more than two weeks of superhuman effort, the most difficult labor the explorers had encountered on the trip.

They tried to simplify the task by building primitive wagons, using sections of cottonwood logs for wheels and tongues. These cumbersome vehicles broke down frequently as they were being pushed over the rough land. When there was a strong wind, the crew sometimes hoisted sail and let the elements help move them.

The heavy work around the falls was made more difficult by terrible weather. Cold rain pelted the travelers and made their buckskin clothing cling to them. Huge hailstones sometimes bounced off their hatless heads. Wherever they walked, carrying their burdens, the path was laced with the needle-sharp thorns of prickly pear cactus, until everyone limped on sore feet. Even the double-thick rawhide soles the Indians taught them to sew onto their moccasins did not keep the thorns from penetrating.

Furthermore, there were now plenty of grizzly bears—white bears, as they were called by Lewis and Clark—and they threatened the travelers daily. The great bars were so abundant, and by this time so highly respected, that Lewis wrote, ". . . I do not think it prudent to send one man alone on an errand of any kind." Lewis's dog, a black New-foundland that traveled with him to the West Coast and back, kept him awake at night barking at the bears. Lewis wrote that one grizzly came within thirty yards of camp to snack on thirty pounds of buffalo fat left hanging from a pole.

Lewis and Clark and their men shot grizzlies whenever possible, partly for meat, but mostly for the thrill. Drouillard shot one grizzly through the heart and was promptly chased by it, at high speed, for a hundred yards before it fell. Another grizzly rushed a hunter and chased him into the river where he escaped by hiding beneath an overhanging bank.

One grizzly that qualified for mention in the journals was a bear the men spotted resting in the open, as their canoes moved upstream. Men in the last two canoes pulled to shore and half a dozen men went after the bear.

The squad of hunters moved to within forty yards of the grizzly and took cover behind a bank. Four of them fired at once while the other two, by prior arrangement, held their fire in reserve. All four shots scored; two went through the lungs. But the huge bear was up at once charging toward the puffs of smoke.

The last two hunters now fired. Both hit the bear. One broke the grizzly's shoulder, which slowed the bear down but did not stop him.

The hunters had little time to reload so most of them chose to make a speedy exit. Two of them leaped into a canoe and shoved off into the current while two others, hiding in the willows, were able to reload and fire again. The shots told the bear where the hunters were and allowed him to correct his course in pursuit of them. Two hunters, with the bear gaining on them, dropped their guns and dove from a twenty-foot-high bank into the river. The bear, not even slowing down, followed them over the edge and crash landed beside them. The chase ended only when one of the men still on shore managed to reload his gun in time to shoot the animal through the head. As they butchered the bear, they found that ". . . eight balls had passed through him in different directions."

One afternoon Drouillard and Joseph Fields, while out hunting for camp meat, killed nine elk and three grizzlies, one of which was the largest bear the party had yet seen. The hunters discovered the bear's tracks on the edge of a thicket but wisely decided not to go into the thicket. Instead they climbed twenty feet into a large tree where they found a secure limb.

Once comfortable, they began shouting insults at old Caleb until their whooping brought the desired results. ". . . this large bear instantly rushed forward to the place from whence he had heard the human voice issue . . ." That was all for the grizz; Drouillard shot him through the head, dropping him on the spot. The animal's hind feet measured seven inches across and nearly twelve inches in length ". . . exclusive of the tallons."

In addition to bears, there was an abundance of other wildlife, and while working at the Great Falls the party ate as well as it had anywhere. Herds of fat buffalo wandered into range. Drouillard and other hunters could easily add elk, deer, and antelope to the meat supply. The men not only ate well, but also dried meat for the coming weeks, because Indians had warned them that they would find no buffalo on the western side of the mountains.

On July 25, 1805, they reached the point where the Jefferson, Gallatin, and Madison rivers, named by Lewis and Clark in honor of the president and the secretaries of treasury and state, come together to form the Missouri. This Three Forks area would soon become famous among the mountain men for both its wealth of furs and the high risk of dying here at the hands of the Blackfoot Indians.

Among the remarkable accomplishments of Lewis and Clark was

the skill with which they dealt with the Indians along their trail. They carried a good supply of trade goods and offered gifts to Indians they met. They seemed to possess an uncanny knowledge of precisely how to mix firmness with kindness to keep the native people from threatening the expedition.

The streams grew smaller and increasingly difficult for the boats to negotiate until, in August, they had to leave their boats behind. Sacajawea was now back at home in the Three Forks country where the Minnetatrees took her captive five years earlier. The party met the Shoshones, and the chief was Sacajawea's brother. With her help, they traded with her people for a number of horses to transport their equipment over the passes of the Continental Divide.

Sacajawea recognized features of the landscape and pointed out for the explorers the pass over the Bitterroots in western Montana. They negotiated the pass and crossed over to find the waters flowing toward the Pacific.

They left their horses, and in five newly made canoes, they rode down the Clearwater into the snake, then the Columbia. "Here I first tasted the water of the great Columbia river," wrote Lewis. Now for the first time they were going with the current instead of against it, and new experiences in river running lay ahead. The rapids were often overwhelming and frightening. They walked the shores and lined their canoes through with the help of ropes made of elkskin. Their canoes were sometimes swamped, or upset, but no lives were lost.

They wanted to spend the coming winter near the coast where the climate would be mild. Here in the land of the Clatsop Indians, they built their shelter, named it Fort Clatsop, and settled in for the winter. Some of the crew went to work evaporating seawater to collect the salt. Others hunted, or worked on the equipment, or made clothing of skins. They sewed a supply of moccasins for the return trip.

THE RETURN TRIP

Food shortages made the winter disagreeable and so did the persistent rains. The local Indians, perhaps corrupted by earlier dealings with the crews of ships coming to the coast, were constantly attempting to steal goods from the explorers. By late March, Lewis and Clark were headed back up the Columbia on the long return trip to St. Louis,

Even Drouillard had bad days when he could find no game. But on one day he killed a total of seven elk. Clark mentioned in his journal that some others also hunt but do not understand the fine points of elk hunting and are, ". . .unsuckssful in their exertions." In the Pacific Northwest, Lewis and Clark frequently traded with the Indians for dogs which they had become accustomed to eating. Writing about a supper consisting of a piece of elk, plus bone marrow, Lewis said, "This for Fort Clatsop is living in high stile."

Their long winter at Fort Clatsop had given Lewis and Clark time to review their notes and draw maps. Perhaps there was a better route than the one they had followed up over the Bitterroots. To find out, they decided that on the return trip they would split the party into two groups. In July 1806, Lewis, leading a party of ten, set off cross-country for the falls of the Missouri.

Near the end of his trip, when Lewis was expecting any day to rejoin Clark, he fell victim to a strange hunting accident. Lewis decided one day to go ashore to shoot an elk or two for camp meat. Peter Cruzatte seemed not to be especially busy so Lewis said, "Cruzatte, you come along."

Lewis was apparently unconcerned that Cruzatte had only one eye and that his impaired vision in that one rendered him seriously nearsighted. They went ashore, stalked and killed one elk, and wounded another. They began stalking the downed animal from different directions. Lewis came within range, carefully brought his rifle to his shoulder, sighted down the long barrel, and was about to squeeze the trigger when he was nearly knocked down by a terrific impact in the buttocks. At the same instant he heard the report of Cruzatte's gun from the underbrush nearby. Lewis was furious. "Damn you," he yelled, "you've shot me."

Although Lewis granted Cruzatte's the benefit of the doubt, saying that he didn't think the man had done it on purpose, it is doubtful that he ever again felt warmly toward the one-eyed hunter.

Meanwhile Clark's group had headed for the Three Forks, then crossed the Continental Divide to the headwaters of the Yellowstone, which they followed until they met Lewis on the Missouri near the mouth of the Yellowstone.

Back in St. Louis and Washington, D.C., Lewis and Clark and their party had long since been given up for lost. One person, however, who still expected them to return was the President of the United States. Thomas Jefferson had faith in these men, and perhaps a sounder understanding than most of the time-consuming hazards and delays they could face on a wilderness trip all the way to the Pacific.

About midday on September 23, 1806, after traveling for more than two years, Lewis and Clark's boats came back down the river and into sight of St. Louis. They fired their guns in salute and the whole town turned out to welcome them.

This little group of determined people had set in motion the exploration of the American West. Incredibly, they had lost only one man. His symptoms indicate to modern doctors that he might have suffered a ruptured appendix which, in his day, he could not have survived, even with the best medical care of the times.

The Lewis and Clark adventure stands today as the most important and successful piece of exploration in the history of the United States. Men of vision extended the boundaries of the nation's explored lands toward the western sea, discovered mountains, found passes, and traveled rivers never known to white men before. They had opened the wild and lonesome lands beyond the Mississippi to the beaver trappers and the settlers who followed.

A grateful president, seeking a suitable reward for his favorite mountain men, appointed Clark, who had respect and understanding for the Indians, to become Superintendent of Indian Affairs at St. Louis. He was also promoted to brigadier general of the territorial militia. In 1813, William Clark became governor of the Missouri Territory. He died in 1838 at the age of sixty-eight.

For Meriwether Lewis there was the post of Governor of the Louisiana Territory, in 1807, but this appointment was unfortunate.

Lewis, always serious and introspective, never adapted to the political life of compromise and public relations.

He had been in office about a year when he set out along the Natchez Trace for Washington to consult with his superiors. He stopped to sleep at a roadside hostel near Collinwood, Tennessee. He died that October night, in 1809, almost surely by his own hand. Some believed that he was murdered and robbed. Whatever the real story, the thirty-five-year-old hero's life ended in a shoddy little tavern beside the Natchez Trace.

His big work was done. He and his friend Clark, and their crew of pioneering spirits, had opened the gate to the West. Next would come the fur trappers, and these skilled woodsmen would become not only takers of beaver but explorers as well, learning about the American West as it had never been known before.

· 6 ·

To the Mountains for Beaver

---

*W*hen Lewis and Clark first arrived at the Mississippi to spend the winter of 1803–04, preparing for their wilderness travels, the merchants of St. Louis were already on hand to serve them. Prominent among these frontier businessmen was Manuel Lisa, a swarthy, New Orleans-born Spaniard with an excellent business sense. When Lewis and Clark established their camp on the Illinois shore across from the mouth of the Missouri River, Manuel Lisa was among their early callers.

As he visited with the explorers in their camp, Lisa observed the soldiers and their leaders, noting the competence of the two officers, and the skills and energy of their crew, at labor and in their training. Without doubt, his busy mind was already linking the plans of this little band of explorers to the promise of valuable furs. There would be riches for the right people willing to risk following Lewis and Clark up the Missouri and into the mountains.

Lisa was blessed with abundant energy. His work as merchant and trader had taken him to an assortment of jobs along the Ohio and Mississippi rivers. Before arriving in St. Louis, he had been an itinerant merchant piloting his own boat on these inland waters. Those who dealt with Lisa knew him for his cold, calculating, sometimes ruthless, pursuit of his competition. He could go for the jugular, and he was a bulldog in a business deal. His combination of shrewdness and tenacity lifted him to the top in the early fur industry and left enemies in his wake. Lisa wanted into the fur industry, and he was not one to sit back in St. Louis playing the gentleman and pulling strings. Instead he became a skilled wilderness traveler and an acknowledged expert in dealing with the Indians, who were always the major problem facing the beaver trappers. These skills were due, in part, to his experience as a trader with the Osage tribe, in a lucrative and monopolistic trading post that the Spanish governor granted Lisa even before the Louisiana Territory was passed back from the Spanish to the French.

Lisa's temperament became well known to government authorities. He disliked the high-handed dealings of the Spanish, and the manner in which they sold their favors, or handed them out to friends. Some believed the Spanish had given Lisa the coveted Osage trading post just to keep him quiet. What he wanted most was an open market and the chance to beat his competition, free of meddling officials and shady government deals, and his opportunity came with the Louisiana Purchase in 1803. Now, Manuel Lisa was free to claw his way to the top.

In the next few years, while Lewis and Clark were in the West, and out of touch with their St. Louis base, Manuel Lisa was consolidating his resources. Lisa began calling in his chips from those who owed him even if it meant going to court to collect the debts.

Lewis and Clark returned with good news of abundant furs in the mountains. The mountain streams were said to harbor beaver with the finest fur in the world, and in numbers beyond counting. This report came when beaver was good as gold on the market.

Lisa met with partners, raised funds, and assembled boats, men, and supplies. He stocked trade goods to supply forts he would build among the Indians of the Missouri River country. In the spring of 1807, he launched two keelboats on the Missouri.

Lisa was adding a fresh approach by taking along his own trappers instead of depending on Indians to bring in all the beaver. He would outfit his trappers from established posts.

That spring his company had perhaps fifty traders and trappers when his boats pushed away from the shore at St. Louis. Manuel Lisa himself was in charge. In his new crew were a number of men who had already traveled the route with Lewis and Clark, and following their discharge had drifted about searching for new opportunities until signing on with Lisa. Among these veterans who knew the mountains and their moods was George Drouillard, representing Lisa's partners, who chose to stay back in St. Louis.

There was competition from the beginning, and the fur companies employed rough tactics. When one of Lisa's crew members repeatedly found ways to delay the expedition, Lisa suspected that the problem causer was a professional obstructionist employed by the competition. About one hundred and twenty miles out of St. Louis, another one of the group, Antoine Bissonette, defected. Manuel Lisa talked with the best hunter in his crew. "George," he is believed to have said to Drouillard, "I want you to track that bastard down and fetch him in." Then he added three fateful words that were to get them both into trouble. "Dead or alive."

Bissonette might have escaped from a lesser man. But with Drouillard on his trail, his chances of getting away were slender. Furthermore, whatever Drouillard shot at fell down. He was not a bully or braggart; he was friendly and well-liked by the men who traveled the mountains with him. He was, however, a good soldier who understood that if a group was to survive in Indian country, and get its work done, there had to be discipline.

Predictably, Drouillard caught up with Bissonette. But the deserter made the mistake of trying to escape. Acting on Lisa's orders, Drouillard winged Bissonette, then helped him back to camp. Lisa had Bissonette loaded into a canoe and sent him downriver for medical help. The trip was too long. On the way Bissonette died, a fact for which Lisa and Drouillard would eventually have to answer.

Lisa had opportunities to display his skill at dealing with the Indians. Usually a show of strength was enough to help avoid confrontations. The always warlike Arikara threatened them as the keelboats moved upstream past their villages, but the chiefs hesitated to attack a group as strong as Lisa's band of trappers.

One day Lisa's keelboaters met a solitary dugout canoe being paddled downstream by another Lewis and Clark veteran, John Colter. The Lewis and Clark men who were already with Lisa probably figured Old Colter had long since gone under and given up his hair to a pack of howling natives. But the buckskin-clad trapper was in excellent health, and had a joyous reunion with his old friends that evening as they ate fat cow around the campfire.

Lisa, meanwhile, was thinking. His job was to maximize the company's take of beaver, and he needed this man, Colter. The mountaineer knew the country, was an expert in traveling alone, and had traveled among the Indians. Lisa began talking with Colter. "Put off going back to St. Louis for a while. Come work for me and be our guide." When Lisa's party pulled out and headed upstream again, Colter went along.

Lisa turned his boats away from the Missouri and up the Yellowstone, perhaps at the urging of Colter, who knew the country and its beaver, as yet undisturbed by trappers. Late that year the party came to the mouth of the Bighorn, which seemed an excellent place to settle down for the winter. There was wood and water in abundance, and the wildlife came down from the surrounding Wind River Mountains and the Bighorns to winter in the more protected region. The appeal of the place was known to the Indians and Lisa could expect the Crows, once they knew of his presence, to come in to trade furs for his cloth, beads, lead, powder, awls, and other goods.

The party set to chopping trees and building a fort which Lisa named Fort Raymond in honor of his son. Prospects looked good for the success of this fort and, although the snows of winter already blanketed the mountains, Lisa dispatched Colter into the land of the Crows to inform them of a new trading post established where the Bighorn empties into the Yellowstone. The Crows, unlike the Blackfeet, had learned to trap and cure furs as the white man wanted them.

That season was a successful one for Lisa. His trappers harvested the beaver in good numbers. By spring, Lisa was preparing to return to St. Louis with his haul while leaving most of his trappers behind to be ready for the trapping season in the fall of 1808.

When Lisa and Drouillard finally arrived back in St. Louis that spring, Drouillard was promptly seized and held for trial for the murder of Bissonette. He was found not guilty, and this verdict seemed fair enough to the fur company organizers who led trapping and trading expeditions. "If you let a man get away with desertion, how can you ever figure to maintain discipline in the mountains? And if you got no discipline, and nobody pays heed to the bourgeois, everybody's in danger when the pesky redskins hit you."

With Lisa back in St. Louis showing a profit from his first successful mountain trip, other fur traders knew beyond any further doubt that the abrasive Spaniard was serious competition. Even before the water stopped dripping off his canoe paddles, Lisa was planning his next trip up the Missouri to collect the packs of beaver his fur trappers had brought to the fort.

His next trip was on a much grander scale. The first expedition had been made with a crew of about fifty men. This second trip, beginning in the spring of 1809, included more than a hundred trappers and traders, as well as a military detachment escorting the Mandan chief Shahaka back to his village on behalf of the government. Lewis and Clark had invited Shahaka to accompany them on their return trip out of the mountains to visit the Great White Father in Washington, D.C. Part of the deal was that they would escort him home, guaranteeing safe passage through the lands of his ancient tribal enemies. The time had come to make good on the promise. For this purpose, a hundred and forty soldiers had joined the party.

Much of what historians know of this second Lisa trip into the Missouri River headwaters comes to us in the journal of Thomas James, a member of that expedition. The twenty-seven-year-old James, tall, powerfully built, quick-witted, intelligent, and sometimes pugnacious, never had much love for Lisa, and one may assume that the feeling was mutual. But, like many another young man, Tom James wanted to see what the wild country was like up there where the Indian, buffalo, and grizzly bear lived. Some years after his adventures he recorded his first-hand accounts of his years in the mountains.

There were thirteen barges and keelboats in the flotilla, and James was captain of one of the unwieldy boats with about two dozen men aboard, including Reuben Lewis, brother of Meriwether. "We started from St. Louis in the month of June, A.D. 1809," wrote James, "and ascended the Missouri by rowing, pushing with poles, cordelling, or pulling with ropes, warping, and sailing.

"My crew were light hearted, jovial men, with no care or anxiety for the future, and little fear of any danger . . . Six weeks of hard labor on our part had been spent when our provisions gave out and we were compelled to live on boiled corn with no salt."

James claimed that, meanwhile, those on the other boats continued to eat well, and that Lisa forbade James's crew from opening any of the thirty barrels of salt pork they were transporting on their barge. Finally, the crew threatened mutiny and forced the issue at gunpoint. After this, James, who was more than ever ready to give Lisa a bad report, wrote, "Rascality sat on every feature of his dark complexioned Mexican face—gleamed from his black, Spanish eyes, and seemed enthroned on a forehead villainous low."

Eventually the military, having safely delivered Shahaka back to his joyous people, departed. Meanwhile, so many of Lisa's men deserted that the party was down to thirty-two. Part of the time during the following months these men trapped in little bands of three or four. James and three others trapped together. But the following May the men wanted to go farther afield, so the party planned a venture up the Jefferson River with their traps. This time, twenty-one of them traveled together because the Blackfeet were more troublesome than ever.

The famous Lewis and Clark woodsman George Drouillard left camp one day and went upstream a mile or so to set his traps. The next morning every one of his traps held a fine beaver. James warned the more experienced Drouillard that if he kept on roaming so far from help it might be he and not the beaver that got caught. Drouillard had a quick answer. "I'm too much of an Indian to get caught by Indians."

The next day he came back, again carrying a full load of beaver skins, and claiming that this was the way to catch them.

The third day Drouillard set out to repeat his solo act, but failed to return when he should have. Meanwhile, two other trappers, ignoring warnings, went off by themselves to hunt meat. They also failed to return. Soon the whole company set out searching for the missing ones. They came first to the bodies of the two meat hunters, "pierced with lances, arrows, and bullets and lying near each other."

A hundred and fifty yards farther, they discovered what remained of Drouillard and his horse. Tracks told the story. The noted mountain man had put up a good fight and probably killed some of his attackers, ". . . being a brave man and well armed with a rifle, pistol, knife, and tomahawk." According to James, Drouillard had been "mangled in a horrible manner; his head cut off, his entrails torn out, and his body hacked to pieces." The famous hunter who had traveled all the way to the West Coast and back, had fought his last battle.

James, however, admired the Indians. "I have seen some of the finest specimens of men among our North American Indians. I have seen chiefs with the dignity of real princes and the eloquence of real orators, and braves with the valor of the ancient Spartans."

By the time the decimated party reached St. Louis again, James, and most of the others were, according to his account, deeply in debt to the company. They had been underpaid for their beaver skins and overcharged for their supplies. The company had sold the trappers powder at six dollars a pound and lead at three dollars a pound, while tent cloth brought a dollar and a half a yard, and a shirt went for six dollars. Whiskey was twelve dollars a gallon. Against these charges, the company allowed the trappers a dollar and a half for each beaver skin turned in. Back in St. Louis, the beaver pelts would bring six dollars each.

After a year of trapping the headwaters of the Missouri, James returned, owing three hundred dollars. To him, Lisa and his partners in the Missouri Fur Company would always remain swindlers. Manuel Lisa almost surely viewed such transactions as justifiable, and the profits as fair, considering the long and hazardous routes over which supplies and furs were transported.

Lisa, and various partners, disbanded and reorganized the Missouri Fur Company several times. Lisa was always ready to travel back into the Rockies in pursuit of profitable beaver skins. More than any of his partners, he was convinced that the fur trade held the promise of riches.

While he continued to trade and organize trapping parties, he also served the government among the Indians of the Missouri River country. The Indian agent was now Captain William Clark, and Lisa became his sub-agent. He married the daughter of a chief of the Omahas and, whatever the other benefits, this alliance was good for trade; and as historian and Lisa biographer Richard E. Oglesby suggests, Lisa's relationships with the Plains Indian tribes were vital in keeping these Indians loyal to us during the War of 1812.

Lisa, who apparently relished traveling in the wild country of the Rocky Mountains, made his final trip into the headwaters in the fall of 1819. When the pioneering trader and trapper came back downriver the following spring, he was a sick man. Later that year he died and was buried in St. Louis.

Pipe Carrier
The trapper's pipe and twist of tobacco were usually close at hand. The common pipe was the long-stemmed clay pipe used as trade goods with the Indians. These pipes were easily broken but inexpensive enough to be replaced readily. Some trappers carved their pipes from cherry or other wood.

One common method of carrying the pipe was to suspend a carrier for it from the neck. The system varied with the ideas of the trapper. Some pipe carriers had a compartment for tobacco and, if the trapper had an Indian wife, were decorated with fancy beading. This style of pipe bag was cut from a single piece of leather to fit the pipe and allow room for tobacco. It was stitched and, if desired, equipped with a flap that fastened down with a button, then decorated with fringe. Calico was also a popular pipe-bag material when available.

Another plan was to carry the pipe secured by tight leather thongs that held it to a small rawhide heart-shaped disk suspended from the neck.

THE WORLD OF THE
MOUNTAIN MAN

For the fur trapper, the land beyond the Mississippi was filled with mystery. Stories of the hazards and the rewards of traveling there filtered back, but the only way a man could know the secrets of the plains and the mountains beyond was to go and see. The West sang a siren's song. Once the trapper tasted the wine of freedom, he could never erase the memories of wilderness from his mind.

His trails had led him to the world's grandest scenery. He would recall the spectacular landscapes, the broad plains, towering mountains, rushing streams, and blue alpine lakes. The enchanted mountains and valleys he discovered would one day be the places people would set aside as national parks to keep for their pure beauty. They would call them Yellowstone, Grand Teton, Rocky Mountain, Yosemite. These glimpses of the wilderness, as it appeared to the first mountain men to come for the beaver, are our links with history. If, in these remaining wild places, we turn our backs on the paved roads and close our ears to the modern sounds, we may still sense the wildness that the mountain man knew.

But to really see his world as he knew it we must view it through his eyes. Typically he came from farm or settlement where civilization was becoming entrenched, and turned westward to face the unexplored.

Over the plains and into the mountains he walked with a degree of freedom he had never known before. He could go where he pleased. There were no property lines. He could take the animals as he wanted. If he chose not to work, he was free to rest. If he worked hard there was the promise of wealth. The world was his as far as the eye could see, and there was no family or high sheriff to tell him otherwise.

The free trapper knew also that every day was the ultimate test; he could stay alive and prosper if he was man enough and shot straight. Out here he was master of his own destiny. He was some, he was! Maybe for the first time in his life, far from the crowds, he felt comfortable.

This attitude led him deeper and deeper into the unexplored valleys, over the ridges, and along the age-old game trails. For days, months, and years he camped in the shadow of the mountains. There was only one way to know what lay around the next bend in the trail or stream, or beyond the looming mountain pass. Awaiting him might be Blackfoot or grizz. Or maybe just the yellow evening sun, soft against the distant snowy peaks.

He had to go and see.

The Yellowstone River was of vital importance in the fur industry. From its headwaters south of Yellowstone National Park, to its confluence with the Missouri near the North Dakota border, this scenic stream remains the country's longest free-flowing river south of Alaska.

Yellowstone's Mammoth Hot Springs, geysers, and Firehole River, which draw millions of tourists today, were magic places to the Indians, and unbelievable to mountain men who first heard descriptions of them from exploring trappers.

At the confluence of the Missouri and the Yellowstone stood Fort Union, perhaps the most famous of all the fur trading posts, and for many, the last taste of civilization.

In Jackson Hole, in northwestern Wyoming, the early trappers discovered the Grand Tetons, as spectacular as any mountains in North America, rising abruptly from the valley floor. The Snake River, flowing through Grand Teton National Park, was a favorite stream with the mountain men, as it is with modern fishermen and rafters.

· 7 ·

For Love of the Wild Places

Through the soft days of early October, the easterner moved swiftly along the woodland trails, always headed west, up and over the mountains. His trip turned out to be an adventure as wild as any North American outdoorsman has ever known.

The mountainsides around him and the forest giants forming their canopy over his trail were splashed with fiery autumn colors. He must have watched the gray squirrels gathering nuts for the winter, the wild turkeys walking in the forest, the deer and the black bear hurrying out of sight. But he was in a hurry too. Word was out that Captain Meriwether Lewis was signing on hunters and boatmen for a grand journey into the distant Rocky Mountains, to places new to the white man.

The traveler's immediate destination was Limestone, Kentucky, a settlement on the south bank of the Ohio River, fifty miles or so upstream from Cincinnati. The little riverside village was already famous as a landing for flatboats and keelboats bringing people down the Ohio to the western frontier.

In Limestone, which we now call Maysville, the woodsman soon spotted a big keelboat tied to the bank. He introduced himself to the captain and outlined his qualifications. He had been a hunter, trapper, and horseman since he was a boy on the farm in Virginia. Captain Lewis sized him up. The applicant stood five feet ten inches tall, looked strong, and seemed to be quiet and reserved but quick-witted and decisive in his manner. The captain noticed that this stranger was not the loudmouthed braggart often found along the rivers. He was instead somewhat inclined to weigh his words. When the keelboat eased into the current to head on down the Ohio toward Louisville, a new member was aboard. Captain Lewis had signed on John Colter, and apparently neither of them ever regretted the decision.

The deeper Lewis and Clark traveled into the wilderness with their little band of explorers, the more they came to rely on the skills of Private John Colter. They frequently relieved him of his other duties and sent him with Drouillard to roam the countryside on foot or horseback and supply the company with meat. Colter was a specialist in traveling alone in the wilderness, sometimes for days or weeks at a time, always finding his way back.

As Lewis and Clark were returning to St. Louis near the end of their two-year-long journey, Colter seemed in no rush to return to civilization. The Lewis and Clark party was within six weeks of reaching St. Louis when it tied up beside a little two-man camp on the banks of the Missouri.

The two strangers explained that they had come into the mountains from their homes in Illinois in 1804, to trap beaver. They found beaver aplenty in the mountains, but Indians had robbed them so often that they had little to show for the time and work. They still nurtured their dreams of growing rich trapping furs in the western mountains.

Colter was especially interested when the two trappers, Forrest Hancock and Joe Dixon, said they were headed back toward the wilderness, up the Yellowstone River, where the beaver lived. Furthermore, they needed a partner who knew the Yellowstone country. There was then probably no white person anywhere who knew it better than John Colter did.

Colter took the idea to Captain Lewis and Captain Clark. Would they perhaps discharge him here on the Missouri instead of back in St. Louis? Lewis and Clark considered the long months of faithful service Colter had rendered. Why not? They took the matter up with the rest of their crew. They would release Colter, providing no others in the party would make similar requests before reaching St. Louis. The chances are good that no other man in the group gave serious thought anyhow to turning back into the mountains with St. Louis so close at hand.

The Lewis and Clark party moved off downstream and was soon out of sight. The three trappers, Hancock, Dixon, and Colter, turned upstream toward the distant peaks and ridges. They spent that winter of 1806–1807 in the upper Yellowstone where, it is believed, they built a shelter and waited out the worst of the weather.

None of these three pioneering mountain men was strong on writing. Little can be known for sure of what they saw. But their association was not especially profitable and did not last long. By the following spring, Colter had carved himself a dugout canoe from a cottonwood log and was soon headed downstream alone, once more St. Louis bound.

By this time, however, Manuel Lisa, the crusty fur trader who guided the fortunes of his Missouri Fur Company, was moving toward the Rocky Mountains in pursuit of beaver plews. In due time Lisa's party had wrestled his keelboats up the Missouri River as far as the mouth of the Platte, and were tied up there when John Colter's little canoe slid into view around the bend.

Colter, the mountain man, once more turned his back on St. Louis and headed for the mountains, this time working for Manuel Lisa.

Lisa moved his party up the Missouri as far as the Yellowstone, then turned up that tributary and followed it to where the Bighorn River fed into it sixty miles or so downstream from where Billings, Montana, stands today. Here Lisa's men began felling timbers and constructing an unimpressive shelter that became the first fur trading post in the upper Missouri country. It was probably close to where Colter, Dixon, and Hancock had wintered the year before.

Although Lisa intended to send his own trappers out on the beaver waters, he also expected to barter for furs with the Indians of surrounding tribes. He had, with Colter's guidance, selected a good location. People of the Crow nation wintered in this region, and so did large numbers of wild game animals that would provide food for the trappers.

But unless someone went out among the Indians to spread the word about Lisa's arrival, and his new commercial enterprise, there would be few furs. This may have been the hazardous assignment Lisa had in mind for Colter from the first. Nowhere could he have found a better qualified person.

Colter said he would travel alone. He liked being alone in the mountains, depending on his own survival skills, making his own decisions, going where he pleased. He would seek out the Indians in their wintering camps, and he would spread the word—there was now a trading post at the mouth of the Bighorn. He put together the essentials—powder, lead, flint and steel, sharpening stone, jerky, some lightweight trade goods, a blanket or robe, in a pack weighing thirty pounds—picked up his rifle, and set out on a five-hundred-mile winter hike through the mountain stronghold of the Crows.

About where Cody, Wyoming, stands today he came upon an Indian village of perhaps a thousand people. They talked with the lightly equipped trapper and allowed him to go on. This camp was on the Shoshone River, which was then called the "Stinking Water." It was near here that Colter witnessed springs bubbling from the ground and filling the air with their sulfurous odor. When he later described the scene to his fellow trappers, they laughed and slapped their buckskin leggins, declaring, "That's some, that is! This child's heard it all now. Old Colter's found his hell, sure enough 'er I wouldn't say so." In due time, the springs of Colter's Hell subsided.

Colter crossed the mountains over Shoshone Pass and down into the Wind River Range, then turned northwest toward Yellowstone. Among the mysteries surrounding Colter's life are the details of the route he followed on the remainder of this journey. But there is agreement that he crossed the area that later became Yellowstone National Park. He skirted Yellowstone Lake. Then traveling north, he went down the Yellowstone River and finally turned east again to cross the mountains and come down into the headwaters of Clark's Fork of the Yellowstone. He was now making his way back toward Cody.

There are no records telling us how long Colter needed for this winter hike of more than five hundred miles. He may not have considered the time important and surely did not anticipate that researchers would one day scour old records, hoping to uncover bits and pieces of information revealing the details of his life and travels. To the mountain man, his trip on foot, while living off the land, was a job, and he did it.

Spring was probably at hand by the time Colter returned to Lisa's fort. But soon, he was sent off again on another journey as ambassador to the Indians. He was going about his business visiting with the Crows, when the Crows' traditional enemies, the Blackfeet, attacked. An attack by the Blackfeet was always a serious matter. On that spring day in 1808, Colter had little choice: he joined his hosts in their efforts to repel the Blackfeet.

Some historians believe that the Blackfeet held a grudge from that moment on against not only Colter but all white men. At any rate, this marked the beginning for John Colter of a series of almost unbelievable close encounters.

Coming from Joe Meek, Jim Beckwourth, or some other trapper famed for his storytelling skills, the account of Colter's amazing escape might have been questioned. But the quiet Colter was known for his honesty. He later told the story to Thomas James, and James wrote it down. He also vouched for Colter. "His veracity was never questioned among us," wrote James, "and his character was that of a true American back woodsman . . . of the Daniel Boone stamp. Nature had formed him, like Boone, for hardy endurance of fatigue, privations, and perils. He had gone with a companion named Potts to the Jefferson river which is the most western of the three forks, and runs near the base of the mountains."

Colter and Potts, each in his own canoe, were working their way slowly upstream, running their beaver sets, and Colter was edgy because they were deep into Blackfoot territory. He had good reason for his uneasiness. Suddenly several hundred Indians materialized on the east shore of the river and there was little hope that the white trappers could escape.

When the chiefs ordered the trappers to come ashore, Colter obeyed, figuring that he would thereby add, at least briefly, to his life span. Killing him where he sat in his canoe would be easy enough for this many warriors. He no sooner touched shore than the squaws began ripping the clothes off his body and soon he stood before the yelling warlike Indians, stripped of all clothing and weapons.

The chiefs again demanded that Colter tell Potts to come on in. Colter relayed the message. He also advised Potts to do as he was told. Potts said something akin to, "Wagh. Them red devils will kill this child, sure enough, same's they're fixin' to do you and from here I can leastways take one of 'em with me." With this, one of the Indians put a ball in Pott's shoulder.

Potts did what he said he would do; he recovered enough to lift his gun and kill the Indian who shot him. In the next minute Potts was, in Colter's words, "made a riddle of."

The screaming Indians now dragged Potts's body from the river while others turned their fury on Colter. He fully expected to black out, permanently, from the quick blow of one of the tomahawks being lifted against him, but the chiefs managed to push back the young warriors. Meanwhile, some of the Indians were hacking off chunks of Potts. One of the squaws walked up close to Colter and threw Potts's penis and testicles in his face. They continued pelting him with various bloody parts of his partner's body, using for the purpose, as Tom James wrote, "the entrails, heart, lungs, etc."

Then came a squabble about what to do with their white captive. Colter figured maybe Potts had taken the best way out after all. But his wits were still with him, and given the slightest opportunity, he was keyed up for escape.

One of the chiefs walked up to Colter. Was he a good runner? Not very, Colter lied. The satisfied chief, surrounded by powerful young men eager to prove how fast they could run, gave Colter his instructions. He led the naked trapper out behind the main group of warriors onto the open plain, and told Colter to start running.

Colter noticed, in a glance, that the warriors were stripping themselves of all clothing and extra weight and now he fully understood the odds against him. He dashed off across the flatlands toward the river six miles away.

Perhaps no runner ever had greater motivation than John Colter did in that hour. Ignoring the thorns of the prickly pear cactus through which his bare feet raced, Colter, toughened by his years in the mountains, ran at his fastest speed. Glancing over his shoulder, he saw the band of runners racing along silently, each intent on being first to come within spear-throwing range of the white man.

Colter got his second wind. He did not slow his pace. Blood began flowing from his nose. It spattered against his sweating chest, dropping onto his bare legs. He raced on beneath the brilliant sun, oblivious to everything but maintaining his grueling pace.

One by one, the exhausted Indians fell far behind. One of them, however, was an exceptionally strong runner and Colter knew that the warrior was closing the distance between them.

When it became obvious that he could not outrun the Indian, Colter took a bold chance. He jerked to a halt, and wheeled to meet the Indian, calling to him to stop and talk the matter over. The Indian kept coming and, as he drew near, he raised his spear over his head and lunged at the trapper. Colter side-stepped, grabbed the spear, and put enough pressure on it to throw the off-balance Indian to the ground. The tumbling Indian was no sooner rolling on the ground than Colter ran him through with the spear point, pinning him to mother earth.

He grabbed the Indian's blanket and, once more, began running. He was now well ahead of the nearest warrior. At last he came to the river and, for the first time, began to think that he might have a good chance of escaping. He swam to the end of a small island where he dove under a pile of tangled driftwood that had washed up against the land.

Within minutes, dozens of Indians were running up and down the riverbank. They probed each hiding place with their spears, and searched around the roots of the cottonwoods. They even swam out to search the island. They climbed onto the pile of logs beneath which Colter clung in the darkness with his head barely above water. He waited for them to drive their spears through the brush pile, or set it afire.

The search continued throughout much of the day. Darkness settled over the river. At last the Indians withdrew, and Colter slipped from beneath his shelter and swam the river. Instead of crossing the mountain pass, which was the easiest way out of the valley, but probably guarded by the frustrated Indians, he climbed the nearly vertical slope to the distant ridge. For the next eleven days he stopped only to sleep or to gather the roots and plants that sustained him. When he reached Lisa's Fort, the other trappers scarcely recognized him.

Colter told the story of his escape in detail to Tom James and others on a later trip as they traveled through the area where he had made his unforgettable run for freedom. He pointed out the mountain he had scaled. As Colter quietly related the details of that day, his companions grew silent. One of the trappers listening to the story, fully aware that they were in hostile country said, "I never felt fear before, but now I feel it." His fear should have been a warning. A few days later this trapper was caught by the Blackfeet and killed.

Those traps Colter had quietly dropped overboard when the large band of Blackfeet discovered him and Potts were very much on his mind. Traps were hard to come by in the mountains and there was no substitute for them if a man was to take plews. The possibility of recovering the traps lured Colter back to the scene. He had stopped to cook supper and rest, and as he settled down he heard the sound of rustling leaves in the darkness.

The mountain man, like the hunted animal, lived with all senses alert. Every sign was weighed for what it might mean in terms of survival. Now, he heard a noise the meaning of which was known to him instantly; beyond his campfire guns were being cocked.

He leaped over the fire and raced off through the brush as shots rattled around him. Once more he scaled the mountain to avoid the pass, and once more John Colter escaped. But he was beginning to get the message. He came back to the fort this time saying that he had made a promise to his Maker; providing he could survive, he would leave the country.

He still had one test ahead of him. He was finally on his way downriver with a companion headed for the distant sights and sounds of St. Louis when the Blackfeet attacked. This time Colter and his companion hid in the bushes, and the Indians, who had high respect for the trappers' rifles, did not come after them.

John Colter never counted coup. He was no braggart and no

bully. Perhaps in all his years in the mountains he killed only one Indian, and that time to save his own life. For all this, he had little to show. He came down from the mountains without much more than memories. He moved to a farm near where Dundee, Missouri, is today. He married, and all we know of his wife is that he called her Sally.

Colter, the pioneering trapper and explorer, who specialized in traveling alone, had spent six years in the mountains. He had played his role in the historic adventures of Lewis and Clark, traveled where no white man had gone before, discovered on his own the wonders of Yellowstone, and set an example for hundreds of fur trappers who would soon follow him to the mountains. John Colter, the soft-spoken mountain man, became a legend in his own day. He died in bed in November 1813, of jaundice.

· 8 ·

Birth of the Rendezvous

O f all the fur gatherers going to the mountains, no individual had a more profound effect on the life and methods of the beaver trappers than William H. Ashley. He was not the colorful and carefree mountain man wandering unfettered over the hills with horse and trap bag. Instead, he was a tough and daring organizer, a businessman, and sometimes a politician, who saw in furs the opportunity to get rich. He had the rare ability to stand back from the fur business, see why it was not working as it should, then substitute his own new methods. All this would prove valuable in the risky beaver-trapping business.

Ashley, who was of medium height and weighed perhaps one hundred and forty pounds, arrived in Missouri from his birthplace in Virginia about 1803. He was serious about the fur business—or anything else he tackled. His earliest Missouri venture was the operation of lead mines and the mining of saltpeter. His partner in this business was Andrew Henry, already a seasoned old-timer who had trapped beaver deep in the Rocky Mountains. The two men served together during the War of 1812 when Ashley was a brigadier in the militia, and Henry served with him as a major.

After Missouri became a state in 1821, Ashley was elected lieutenant governor. His political duties, however, left him time to continue his business career and by 1822, when the fortunes to be made in the fur business were much on the minds of men in and around St. Louis, Ashley and Henry turned their eyes toward the mountains. At the time of the war the fur business had slacked off, but it was again picking up momentum, and it was logical enough that Henry would go to Ashley with his plan for a continuation of their partnership. "General, I been there, I have, and I tell you there's a heap of beaver up in those mountains if we can just bring 'em out."

The longer these partners discussed their plans for the fur business, the more they believed that they were a good working combination. Ashley was the businessman and Henry was a veteran field leader. A dozen years earlier, Henry had been Manuel Lisa's partner in the Missouri Fur Company. He had led the first trapping party to venture west of the Rockies. He had pioneered trapping on the Three Forks of the Missouri, and also on Henry's Fork, and wherever he led trappers he earned their respect for his courage and skill as an outdoorsman. Said one mountain man of Henry in those early days, "I have a lot of confidence in . . . Mr. Henry." He spoke of Henry's "humor as well as his honesty and frank manner and without beating about the bush." It was natural that Henry would lead the first party of trappers Ashley and Henry fielded.

The partners developed a plan that was a new wrinkle for the Rocky Mountain fur industry. Instead of relying so heavily on barter with the Indians, Ashley and Henry decided to depend mainly on their own trappers. They intended not to simply take them along as hired hands, but to outfit them, then give them half of the furs they brought in. Ashley wanted to line up the best men he could for Henry to take into the mountains, so early in 1822 he inserted an unusual advertisement in the *Missouri Gazette and Public Advertiser*.

To Enterprising Young Men

The subscriber wishes to engage ONE HUNDRED MEN, to ascend the river Missouri to its source, there to be employed for one, two or three years—For particulars, enquire of Major Andrew Henry, near the Lead Mines, in the county of Washington (who will ascend with and command the party) or to the subscriber at St. Louis.

—Wm. H. Ashley

Word spread rapidly around St. Louis, and the men Ashley recruited included names that would become famous throughout the mountains.

The trappers could break up into little crews of two or three men instead of the large party, so easily spotted by the Indians. The smaller groups could slip unnoticed from one watershed to the next, quietly taking the beaver as they came to them. In April 1822, Henry and his trappers set off up the Missouri. Six months later, when October winds were already bringing the first storms of winter, they reached the mouth of the Yellowstone.

They built a small fort near the border of Montana and North Dakota where the Yellowstone River flows out in a broad, shallow delta to join the Missouri. It was called Fort Henry. Later the American Fur Company built a large fort in this strategic location and called it Fort Union. Today the National Park Service maintains it as the Fort Union Trading Post National Historic Site.

Ashley arrived later in October with supplies, then turned around and went back to St. Louis. Henry's men moved into the headwaters of the Missouri and tried to trap the beaver-rich country in Blackfoot territory around the Three Forks. Henry finally had to lead his men over into the Snake River country to escape the relentless pressures put on them by the Blackfeet.

Meanwhile, Ashley, back in St. Louis, was accumulating goods with which to supply Henry during their second year. The biggest barrier to travel up the Missouri in those years, and everyone in the fur business was well aware of the hazard, was the warlike Arikara Indians whose territory the white trappers were invading. Their fortified villages, standing near the water's edge, were in a strategic position to block boat traffic. All who had ascended the Missouri, including Lewis and Clark and Manuel Lisa, had to use various combinations of bribery and bluff to get their parties past this human barrier.

The Arikaras, or "Rees," as the trappers called them, were situated upstream a few miles from the mouth of the Grand River near the border between North and South Dakota. Whenever they chose to, the Indians, several hundred strong, could shoot down on the exposed boatmen. The warriors, as well as their families, could go about their activities quite safely behind the log fortification. It was a strategic bottleneck to make the bravest mountain man wonder what he was doing there.

This was where Ashley ran into serious trouble in 1823. He was taking two keelboats of men and supplies upstream to Henry. Meanwhile, Henry had dispatched Jed Smith downstream, to meet Ashley and tell him to bargain for horses which he needed badly to replace stock stolen by the Blackfeet. Smith was with Ashley when the keelboats came abreast of the Arikara village.

Ashley dropped anchor in midstream to talk peace with the Indians and deal for horses. At first, the negotiations went smoothly enough, and the Indians traded horses for powder, guns, and other goods. Nobody on either side, however, was truly at ease. Ashley decided to lift anchor at first light the following morning and get out of there before the Arikara began turning their newly acquired guns and ammunition on his trapping party. Unfortunately, the new day dawned so stormy that the boats could not move against the gale.

That night the Arikaras did not seem to bed down the way peaceful people should. Ashley increased his guard. After midnight the noise from the villages increased, and Ashley was determined to get away as soon as there was light enough.

The day had scarcely dawned when the Indians began shooting. Half of Ashley's men had been put ashore to guard the horses on the sandbar in front of the Indian villages. They had no barricade of any kind except the falling bodies of their horses and comrades.

By the time the skiffs could carry out a rescue mission, twelve of Ashley's men lay dead. Another eleven were wounded and three of these would soon die. It became the most serious defeat yet for the trappers at the hands of Indians, and the whole thing had lasted about fifteen minutes. The general tried to rally his troops and run the gauntlet but his boatmen, who included a number of French Canadians unaccustomed to Plains Indian tactics, refused to rally.

Ashley had to face the fact that the Arikaras had stopped him cold and turned him back. But he was a determined man and he turned this disaster into a triumph of sorts by completely changing his method of supplying the brigades of trappers. If the river route was closed, he would go overland. From this time on, the mountain men traveled by horseback and supplied their brigades by pack animals. This was a better plan. The trappers could now travel faster and range farther afield.

Next, Ashley and Henry decided to send two parties out. Henry led the first one to Fort Henry by crossing Nebraska and the Dakotas. The other group followed young Jedediah Smith into the Wind River country and on to find the South Pass over which thousands of people would move to California and Oregon.

In the summer of 1825, Ashley was about to create another legendary element of the mountain man's story. Setting out from St. Louis he led his pack train of supplies overland toward a meeting with his trappers. The preceding spring, in the Green River country, Ashley had split his group into small parties and sent them off trapping and exploring with instructions to meet later that summer on Henry's Fork for what would become the first summer rendezvous of the mountain men.

This was also Ashley's opportunity to explore the mysterious Green River. The Green rising in the Wind River Range of the Rocky Mountains of Wyoming and flowing south to join the Colorado in southeastern Utah, was one of North America's truly wild rivers. This turbulent whitewater stream, thundering down between towering canyon walls, gave Ashley, a nonswimmer, the wildest ride he ever had. Bobbing along like corks in the mist, he and his seven men slid down the spectacular rapids, rode the tossing rooster tails through Flaming Gorge, into the Canyon of Ladore, and over Disaster Falls, filling their boats with water and, minute by minute, flirting with disaster.

They left no description of this ride that does justice to their wild adventure. But this was the river which, forty-four years later, Civil War veteran John Wesley Powell ran on his famous whitewater ride down the Canyon of the Colorado, and we can find what it was like by turning to Major Powell's account. Powell was on a scientific expedition for the U.S. Geographical and Geological Survey and his boats were the best of the times. He had them especially built of oak, double-ribbed, and strengthened with bulkheads and double posts.

This was the canyon that Ashley and his little crew negotiated in two boats made of sticks and buffalo hides. They were lifted to the peaks of the waves time and again, then slid into the troughs and continued bouncing along in their flimsy craft until they eventually floated out of the canyons. Years later, Major Powell found where Ashley had written the date and his name on the weathered rock walls deep within the canyon.

From his Green River adventure, Ashley moved on to join the first of the summer rendezvous.

The following year Ashley returned for the second rendezvous, which was held in Willow Valley near today's Hyrum, Utah. The event attracted perhaps a hundred mountain men, their Indian wives, and assorted visiting tribesmen. This time his pack animals carried the kegs of whiskey which Ashley failed to pack in for the first rendezvous. The system of summer rendezvous created by Ashley became a permanent and colorful part of the mountain man's life, and would continue until 1840 when the fur business was winding down.

The rendezvous was unlike anything before or since, a gathering of uninhibited men down from the mountains. Camped nearby were perhaps ten times as many Indians, who brought their families, lodges, dogs, and horses. Amusement ranged from horse racing to dalliance with Indian maidens. Wrestling matches, shooting contests, tomahawk throwing, and storytelling continued day and night, all the time stimulated by heavy drinking.

A favorite gambling game, with Indian and white man alike, was hands. The rules were simple. The contestant tried to guess which hand held the pebble. It is an old game, but perhaps it was never played as seriously, and for such high stakes, as it was in those beautiful mountain-rimmed valleys in the days of the rendezvous. A warrior or a trapper, playing hands, could lose his horse, gun, and even his wife.

George Frederick Ruxton, after talking with trappers who attended, wrote, "The rendezvous is one continued scene of drunkenness, gambling, and brawling and fighting, as long as the money and credit of the trappers lasts." He tells of the gambling—one trapper even bet his scalp—and how a man might lose his year's work in a couple of hours. "These annual gatherings," adds Ruxton, "are often the scene of bloody duels, for over their cups and cards no men are more quarrelsome than your mountaineers. Rifles at twenty paces, settle all differences . . ."

The rendezvous ended when the trapper had once more spent his year's earnings on diluted, overpriced whiskey, and a few items of clothing and equipment to serve him in the mountains through the coming year. His woman, if he had one, was outfitted with new clothing and trinkets.

The trader and outfitter, with his newly acquired wealth, packed his stock of furs on his animals, waved to those staying behind, and rode off down the valley. If he made it safely back to St. Louis, and the price of beaver had not plummeted, he might be several thousand dollars richer. Ashley, returning from the second rendezvous, brought some nine thousand dollars worth of furs back with him.

Jedediah Smith had taken over Henry's place as a partner in the business. Henry, discouraged by the constant pressure from the Indians and the failure to move enough furs to market to make the enterprise the success he and Ashley had hoped, had given up.

Before leaving the rendezvous, Ashley struck a bargain to sell his business to Jedediah Smith and two other noted trappers, Bill Sublette and David E. Jackson. General Ashley was leaving the mountains too. Politics were still on his mind and now he had money to campaign on. In his short time in the mountains he had introduced the concept of the free trapper, created the mountain-man rendezvous, and dispatched the men who discovered the South Pass. General Ashley went on to serve three terms in the United States Congress. He died of pneumonia in 1838.

King of the Mountain Men

*I*f you roamed the Rocky Mountains in the golden days of the free trappers, you would recognize the names of the real leaders among the mountain men—Fitzpatrick, Meek, Smith, Sublette, Walker, Clyman, Harris, and others, each with his own remarkable story. You would surely hear of Old Jim Bridger, the tall, muscular mountaineer once described as having a thick neck, high cheek bones, long brown hair, blue-gray eyes, and a hooked nose. To many, he represented the near-perfect physical specimen. Carl Russell, authority on the beaver trappers and their tools, wrote of Bridger as being "mostly rawhide."

Bridger was always friendly, but always serious. Jed Smith once said of Bridger that when it came to leading men, Old Jim possessed the skills of the angel Gabriel. Thereafter, Jim Bridger, who was not very old and did not look angelic, became "Old Gabe" to a generation of trappers, and he was the mountain man whom younger trappers tried to emulate.

Old Gabe never learned to read and write, but if this was a handicap it was shared by many trappers. Nor was it handicap enough to keep Bridger from becoming a gifted trapper, guide, businessman, Indian fighter, and, most of all, explorer. He possessed the photographic memory for streams, ridges, passes, and trails that made him a walking encyclopedia of western geography.

When he was still a boy on his father's land, Bridger began acquiring the woodsman's skills that would prepare him for the solitary mountain man's hazardous lifestyle. He grew up loving to hunt. He began riding while still young and, when he started west, could sit on a horse as if he were part of it.

In 1812, when little Jim was eight years old, his family turned its livestock and wagons toward Missouri. His father, a farmer and surveyor, settled on land along the Mississippi River near St. Louis. Within the next five years death reduced the family of five to two, young James and a sister. His sister went to live with an aunt, while a kindly blacksmith named Phil Creamer took the shy boy into his home as an apprentice.

During the next four years Jim pumped the forge bellows and breathed the heated sulfurous fumes as he struggled to master the blacksmith's skills. He still found time to explore the rivers by canoe and run a trapline. In these years too he bought his first gun and quickly mastered it. With the sharp eye and steady hand of youth, he became a crack shot.

Visiting with travelers in the blacksmith shop, young Bridger heard tantalizing stories of distant mountains where a young man could make his mark even without an education.

The door to his career as a Rocky Mountain trapper opened for Bridger in the spring of 1822. He was finishing his apprenticeship with Creamer and looking around for employment when someone told him of General Ashley's advertisement in the St. Louis newspapers. Aboard Ashley's first keelboat, as it edged out into the river that spring, was Jim Bridger, one of a crew of twenty-two men.

The keelboat, with Major Henry in charge, labored slowly up the Missouri River to the mouth of the Yellowstone where the crew set to building a fort ahead of winter.

That winter was excellent schooling for Bridger. Along with others in his party, Bridger was soon to learn the harsh lessons of dealing with the warlike Blackfeet who were fighting the white man's takeover of the Upper Missouri country. The following spring, near Great Falls, Montana, a war party of Blackfeet, in a hit-and-run operation, struck a group of Henry's trappers, including Bridger, killing four and injuring others.

The following winter the trapping party wintered on the Bear River on the west side of the Continental Divide in southern Idaho. As they sat around their campfires speculating on where the Bear River went, some thought it might lead all the way across the southwest to the Pacific Ocean. Bets were made. But unless somebody followed the river to the end of its course, the question would never be settled. Young Bridger, eager to prove himself, volunteered to go downstream and find the answer.

Years later, Robert Campbell, one of General Ashley's trappers, wrote for a government geographer what he remembered hearing Bridger tell about his solo voyage down the Bear River. The river led Bridger eventually to the edge of a great lake, so broad that it seemed to be an arm of the ocean. Bridger dipped his hand into the clear water and tasted it from the tips of his fingers. "She war some salty, Hoss. Dogged if she warn't!" Bridger had apparently become the first white man to find Great Salt Lake.

It was also about this time that Jim Bridger became famous as a whitewater boatman. General Ashley had to get his shipments of furs out of the mountains, and he was short on horses. Perhaps they could float part of the furs through the canyon of the Bighorn, but this section of the river was a complete mystery. Nobody had ever run the twenty miles or more of treacherous water through the Bighorn Canyon—the place the Indians called "Bad Pass."

Bridger allowed that the best way to find out about the navigability of the river was to scout the canyon by boat, so he began building a log raft. He made his craft as sturdy as he could, hoping it would withstand the canyon's rocks and the force of the churning waters.

The sheer, vertical walls of the Bighorn Canyon, which has since been flooded by Bighorn Lake behind Yellowtail Dam, rose as much as six hundred feet above the river, blocking the sunlight from the floor of the canyon and keeping the rapids in perpetual twilight. Some short stretches of the river were relatively quiet. But where the Bighorn had carved its course through solid rock, the river was squeezed into narrow, constricted passages, and the noise of the rapids was thunder to the ears. There were sharp, unexpected turns, forcing the water around towering boulders, while tumbling mountains of water crashed against sheer rock walls and filled the canyon with a soft, ghostly mist. For miles, the river bounced Bridger's little, unresponsive raft off boulders and into roostertails while the trapper hung on and fought for control. Bridger swept down the chute between the brilliantly colored rock walls, and in due time his little log raft came bouncing out of the Big Horn Canyon carrying a lone trapper in soggy buckskins.

Bridger had seen enough. Furs could not be risked in the wild canyon of the Bighorn. Ashley packed his plews on the weary horses and transported them the long way around. This wild river rafting added to young Bridger's growing reputation. The trip was much talked of among the trappers and was also a revelation to the Indians who had insisted that Bad Pass could never be run.

In 1830, Bridger and four partners bought out the Rocky Mountain Fur Company from Ashley for about sixteen thousand dollars.

Within a few years competition in the fur business became intense. The best waters were trapped and retrapped. Bridger met the pressure by moving his trapping operation into the headwaters of the Missouri, fully aware that they were in the heart of Blackfoot country. Wherever the trappers and the Indians crossed paths, the Indians were more likely than not to greet the invaders with bullets and arrows.

One day in 1832, Bridger's group encountered a party of a hundred or so Blood Indians and Bridger sensed trouble immediately. The trappers fired a single shot, perhaps to show the Indians that the white men were not afraid to fight. This might normally have set the battle in motion, but the Bloods did a surprising thing: they hoisted a white flag.

Bridger sent two representatives out halfway to talk, and two sub-chiefs came to meet them. The remaining parties on both sides hung back in nervous readiness. The curious Bridger, unable to withstand the pressure, then rode forward cautiously to where the leaders were smoking the peace pipe.

According to the description written by Washington Irving in *Captain Bonneville*, the chief, seeing Bridger, also rode forward. The chief, a powerful-looking man, offered greetings but Bridger did not buy his peace talk. In his view, the Bloods, a branch of the Blackfeet, were treacherous and never to be trusted. Bridger was fully alert—perhaps too alert. As the chief approached, Bridger, almost by instinct, cocked his rifle.

The chief was as edgy as Bridger was, and the metallic click spoke a universal language. The chief, who had at that moment been extending his hand in friendship, suddenly grabbed the barrel of Bridger's gun and twisted it downward so the bullet thudded into the ground between them. The chief then followed through by twisting the Hawken from Bridger's hands and using it to swat Old Gabe out of his saddle. Almost at the same instant, Bridger felt two arrows thump into his back.

Other hits scored during the skirmish that followed. Both sides withdrew to cover and continued, throughout the day, to take pot shots at each other. The losses totaled nine Indians and three trappers. Bridger's men pulled one of the arrows from his back, but the second point was embedded in the bone and had to stay there.

Three years later, in 1835, during the Green River rendezvous, Bridger went to Dr. Marcus Whitman and asked if he could remove the arrowhead from his back. The operation was complicated by the fact that a calcareous growth had formed around the embedded arrow point. As the doctor, wielding his butcher knife, struggled with the three-inch-long iron point, a ring of spectators, including visiting Flatheads, Utaws, Nez Percés, and Bridger's friends, the Shoshones, stood around the sweating trapper marveling at the surgeon's skill and the trapper's stoicism. Apparently the operation was a success because Bridger soon resumed his duties.

This was also the year of Bridger's first marriage. He was friendly with the Flatheads, and his new wife, Cora, was the daughter of a Flathead chief. They were married for eleven years and had three children before Cora died in 1846.

Among Bridger's more memorable fights with various tribes was an encounter with a band of Crows brought on by Bridger's friend, the ebullient Joe Meek. Meek's story was recorded by Frances Fuller Victor, who wrote that Joe was returning to Bridger's brigade in the Yellowstone country from a trapping session along the headwaters of the Snake. Meek knew that, in the Yellowstone country, there was always the possibility of falling into the hands of the Crow warriors, and one day that is exactly what happened.

Meek had been out trapping on his own for five days when the

Crows spotted him. The Indians quickly blocked his only escape route, forcing him to take to the muck and willows along the creek. His horses soon bogged down, and as he floundered in the mud and water, struggling to escape, the band of Indians descended on him, screaming and shooting.

"When they war within about two rods of me, I brought Old Sally to my face ready to fire, and then die," Meek said. But the chief liked the looks of Old Sally and, perhaps to keep her out of the mud, yelled at Meek to give up his gun and he would live. Meek said, "Well, I liked to live." Bidding Old Sally farewell, he sadly surrendered his flintlock.

In due time the chiefs finished their deliberations over what to do with the white trapper. The head chief asked Meek what group he belonged to. He said his captain's name was Bridger, known to the Crows as the Blanket Chief. The Indians wanted to know how many men the Blanket Chief had and Meek, who knew the number was two hundred and forty, calmly allowed as maybe there were forty. The chief greeted this as a splendid omen. His two hundred men could easily overwhelm forty whites. He told Meek, "You shall live, but they shall die."

Meek says, "I thought to myself, 'hardly'."

The entire band of Indians, along with their prisoner, who was now traveling on foot with the squaws, carrying burdens, walked for four days before coming into the vicinity of Bridger's camp.

The farther they walked, the more somber Meek became about the prospects for his future health. He knew what his penalty would be for lying. He would need extraordinary luck to get him out of this one— luck plus Old Gabe's cool thinking.

The Crows' first contact was with Bridger's horse guard, bringing in the mounts and pack animals. The chief ordered Meek to call the horse guard over to parlay. Instead, Meek yelled for the white man to stay away and to send Bridger to rescue him.

"In a few minutes," as Mrs. Victor wrote it, "Bridger appeared on his large white horse." Bridger told Meek to inform the chief that he wanted to confer with one of the sub-chiefs. The chief sent his second in command, Little Gun, off to smoke with Captain Bridger. Little Gun had no way of knowing that Bridger had already sent out a party of his finest marksmen who were creeping within range, hidden by a deep ravine. As Little Gun drew near, the trappers' deadly long guns came up over the lip of the ravine and pointed directly at the second chief. Meek stood waiting quietly for the fall of the tomahawk that he had been promised if he betrayed the chief.

Bridger next instructed Meek to explain to the chief that he was proposing a prisoner exchange. By now a hundred or so trappers, deadly shots with itchy fingers, were on hand, and the chief decided that maybe he had better trade prisoners after all. Not only did they send Meek back to his party, but they also returned his mule, gun, and furs. The chief paid Meek a high compliment; even the Crows, he said glumly, couldn't lie as skillfully as Joe Meek could. That evening, telling Jim Bridger about his experience, Meek relaxed for the first time in four days.

As the fur industry became less and less fruitful, and the first wagon trains of settlers, bound for California and Oregon, wound through the Indian country, Bridger took as his partner Louis Vasquez. They had a plan. In 1843, on a tributary of the Green River in southwestern Wyoming, they began building a wilderness store they called Fort Bridger. Their fort was strategically located right in the path of the travelers.

The fort's log buildings were surrounded by a wall formed of sharpened logs set upright in the ground. There were two parallel rows of these logs and the space between them was filled with earth and rocks. The fort included a blacksmith shop where travelers' wagons could be repaired. Both Bridger and Vasquez worked at hauling supplies from St. Louis, then transporting furs out to market.

In the following ten years, Fort Bridger became a famous landmark for westbound travelers, as well as a way station for the Pony Express. Then the Mormons, uneasy about Bridger's influence with the Indians, sent an armed party of forty or so men to capture him. Bridger learned about the vigilantes' approach in time to escape, but he had to leave his property behind. The *Missouri Republican*, reporting a traveler's account of this action in its November 5, 1853 issue said, "Being apprised of their approach, he took to the mountains . . . where he could watch all the movements of his pursuers . . . Bridger, when he thought it was safe, was joined by his wife and children and they are now on their way in, and will probably reach Westport next week." Fort Bridger became an army post in 1858.

In 1848, Bridger had married again, this time a woman of the Ute tribe. His new wife died a year later in childbirth. The old trapper bought a farm back in Missouri and eventually took his third wife, a Shoshone chief's daughter, there to live.

By this time, Bridger had made numerous trips, leading groups to many different western destinations and he still did not give up his travels. Since he was the authority on rivers, valleys, mountains, seasons, and supplies of wild game, travelers had confidence in his ability to get them through the difficult times. Scientists, explorers, and sportsmen sought out the famous old mountain man to lead them into the mountains and beyond.

Perhaps the strangest hunting party Bridger ever guided was that of an English sportsman, Sir George Gore, who launched a big-game hunt like none the American West had ever seen before. Gore arrived in Wyoming territory with a full complement of servants, including some forty specialists, cooks, valets, horsemen, and dog handlers. He had more than a hundred horses and a dozen yoke of oxen. After outfitting in St. Louis, the party made its way to Fort Larramie, Wyoming, for the winter of 1854, and here Gore met Bridger and listened to his mountain stories. The result was that Old Gabe came aboard as a guide.

For the next year and a half, Bridger stayed with Gore as he journeyed through the hills, seeking large animals to kill. Gore's daily routine called for sleeping until mid-morning, then, after a leisurely bath and a fine breakfast, riding off, often alone, sometimes staying out far into the evening. He often asked Bridger to join him at dinner. Then they relaxed while Gore read Shakespeare and Bridger added his homespun commentary. According to Randolph B. Marcy's book *Thirty Years of Army Life on the Border*, Gore one evening read Sir Walter Scott's account of the Battle of Waterloo, then asked Bridger what he thought of that one.

Bridger allowed that the Battle of Waterloo must have been a "considerable skrimmage," then added comments to the effect that . . . "them Britishers must a fit better thar than they did to New Orleans where Old Hickory give 'em the forkedest sort of chainlightnin' you ever did see—and you can just go yer pile on it, Mr. Gore."

According to Marcy, Gore, guided by Bridger, shot forty grizzly bears, twenty-five hundred buffalo, and uncounted hundreds of deer, elk, antelope, and other creatures. Furthermore he had the trophies to prove it. Eventually, Gore had his fill of this sport in the American West. The Indians, and perhaps the whites as well, had seen quite enough of this Englishman and his excess killing of American game.

The world, and surely its storytellers, has sometimes been unkind to Jim Bridger's memory. He was not the braggart that some painted him, nor was he a drunkard or polygamist. Most of the stories he told of strange and remarkable scenes, including the marvels of Yellowstone, were found, in time, to be true. For years, he served the government as an expert scout. One cavalryman, serving on an expedition Bridger guided, called the old scout ". . . a prince among men, the uncrowned king of all the Rocky Mountain scouts." This cavalryman noticed that all the other scouts, hunters, and army officers treated Bridger with respect. It was proper that they should for few, if any, outdoorsmen anywhere matched his skill or equaled his accomplishments.

Bridger's advancing age itself was a testimonial to his mountain skills. He had fought the Indians and bears, suffered the icy streams and bitter winters. Old Jim was a survivor. As he grew older he looked back on his rich life of remarkable adventures with a sweet sadness. His old mountain friends were gone. So were most of the beaver and buffalo. But visions of the splendid shining mountains stood strong and clear in the aging trapper's mind.

Bridger's daughter, Virginia Wachsman, said that, by 1873, her father's health was failing. His vision became so poor that she had to lead him around. Or, stooped and slow-moving, he would take his cane and feel his way to the wheat field where he would kneel and run his hands through the rich soil, or check the heads of the ripening wheat for its progress. He also had a gentle horse that he still rode about his farm. Jim Bridger, king of the mountain men, died on his Missouri farm in 1881, at the age of seventy-seven.

Today, in Mount Washington Cemetery, in Kansas City, Missouri, there stands a monument to the memory of "James Bridger— 1804–1881—celebrated as a hunter, trapper, fur trader and guide. Discovered Great Salt Lake 1824. The South Pass 1827. Visited Yellowstone Lake and geysers 1830. Founded Ft. Bridger 1843. Opened overland route by Bridger's Pass to Great Salt Lake."

The monument's stone image of Jim Bridger shows a clean-shaven mountain man, serious and determined—his eyes facing west, as they always had.

· 10 ·

The Legend of Broken Hand

Trapper Tom Fitzpatrick was known to the Indians by two strange names, both of them earned the hard way. Sometimes they called him "Broken Hand," but after his miraculous escape in the summer of 1832, during which his hair was said to have lost its normal dark-brown color, the Indians named him "White Hair."

Fitzpatrick was born in Ireland, in 1799, and was still a teenager when he found his way to this land of promise. Stories coming from the frontier excited his imagination, and like many another young man of his time, he made his way westward over the mountains and along the rivers until he landed in St. Louis. There, he heard the excited talk of beaver and riches to be earned trapping them, and he joined William Ashley's crew in the spring of 1823, to go up the Missouri.

Although he was of medium height and slender build, he was strong for his size, and possessed natural traits essential to a leader among the trappers: self-assurance, decisiveness, and everyday horse sense.

These qualities soon brought him to the attention of Ashley, who needed dependable men. Fitz, in company with his good friend Jed Smith, was traveling westward with a small trapping party in the harsh winter of 1823–1824. Historians believe that Smith was in charge and Fitzpatrick was second in command. One of their party was Edward Rose, who had friends among the Crows. Rose had heard that across the Continental Divide, in the Green River country, there was an abundance of beaver still untouched by white trappers. Smith and Fitzpatrick, always searching for virgin trapping country, headed for the Green River.

On this trip, nature put them to the test. Game was scarce; the

93

men were hungry much of the time. Bitter, howling winds sapped their strength. Their horses grew weak. That March, they made their way along a broad, flat region that led upward so gradually that it scarcely seemed to be a climb at all. They noticed that the streams were now flowing toward the West instead of the East. The trappers had crossed the Continental Divide and found the South Pass over the Rockies. They had come down into the headwaters of the Green or, as the trappers knew it from the Indians, the Seedskeedee. Their route would become a thoroughfare for trappers and explorers, missionaries, and wagon trains of farmers.

In the Green River country, the beaver turned out to be as plentiful as the Indians predicted. The party split into two parts and began acquiring fat packs of fur. Then, Fitzpatrick's fortunes took a bad turn.

His group had been joined by a band of Shoshones who ate abundantly on the leftover beaver meat the trappers could not use. The Indians seemed friendly, but one night they slipped away and took with them all the trappers' horses. This put Fitzpatrick and his crew in an extremely hazardous situation, and they were hundreds of miles from help.

They had no way to transport their furs to the first summer rendezvous in 1825, so they cached their furs, traps, saddles, and other property, and set off in a somber mood, traveling on foot and hoping to avoid other troublesome Indians. Some days later the little file of white trappers rounded a bend in the mountain trail and came face to face with half a dozen Indians. Shoshones. The horses they rode looked mighty familiar.

Faster than the Indians could make the peace sign, Fitzpatrick's crew had the muzzles of their flintlocks covering them at point-blank range. They took back their mounts, then they forced their captives to guide them to the Indian village, where they reclaimed, at gunpoint, the rest of their horses. After the scowling Shoshones turned over all the horses the trappers could identify, there still remained one horse unaccounted for.

This wasn't going to wash with Fitz. He was plain damn angry and he instantly ordered his men to tie one of the Indians to a nearby tree.

While the bound Indian stood looking down the open end of a trapper's gun, Fitzpatrick explained to the Shoshones that unless the last horse was brought in promptly, they would have a funeral ceremony to conduct. The horse appeared.

The trappers now backtracked to their cache, exhumed their furs and traps, saddled and packed their horses, and set off at last for rendezvous. Fitzpatrick led his men back across the South Pass and down again where the waters flowed to the east. He had made his name as a leader of men and an explorer who could always find his way through the mountains. These were skills that would put him at the head of many expeditions in the years ahead.

Fitzpatrick, along with Milton Sublette, Jim Bridger, Henry Fraeb, and Jean Baptiste Gervais, bought out the fur company of Smith, Jackson, and Sublette in 1830 and renamed it the Rocky Mountain Fur Company. The real leader of the Rocky Mountain Fur Company was Fitzpatrick.

Later, as time for the 1832 rendezvous in Pierre's Hole approached, Fitzpatrick returned to St. Louis to bring back supplies for the trappers. His big problem was money, but Fitzpatrick arranged with Bill Sublette, older brother of his partner Milt Sublette, to supply The Rocky Mountain Fur Company. It was on this trip, as Fitzpatrick was returning to the mountains with the supply train, that he had his most famous brush with death.

There were other fur companies assembling in Pierre's Hole, and everyone knew that the first supply train to arrive would surely skim off the cream of the furs and beat the competition in the race for high profits. Fitzpatrick decided to hurry on ahead of his supply train with the news that it was coming. He took two swift horses, planning to ride them alternately, and set off at a gallop. He was traveling alone and he was traveling light.

When Bill Sublette arrived at Pierre's Hole with his train of supplies, including the coveted casks of corn whiskey, he figured that Fitzpatrick would already be there waiting. But Sublette was wrong. Old Fitz hadn't shown and this fact alone put a damper on the rendezvous hilarity. Seasoned trappers looked at each other and shook their heads. Old Fitz knew his way sure enough. Couldn't lose him blindfolded in these here mountains. Something must have gone amiss and about the only thing it could have been was Indians, more than likely the danged Blackfeet again. This conclusion wasn't far wrong, but the Indians had to get in line because first Fitzpatrick tangled with a giant grizzly bear.

After leaving the supply train, he rode hard for four days or so and all went well. In the cool mountain air he and his horses made excellent time. Then, he stopped one day to rest his horses. While his horses grazed, Fitzpatrick sat on a rock gnawing at the last of his little store of jerky.

Suddenly, he heard a bear scrambling across the rocks toward him at what he called "double quick time." Fitz sprang to his feet. He stood his ground as the bear skidded to a halt six feet from him and rose up on its hind feet to investigate. For what seemed a mighty long time, the grizzled mountain man and the towering bear stared each other in the eye. Fitzpatrick understood grizzlies well enough to know that trying to run would bring the animal down on him in an instant. "After discovering that I was in no ways bashful," Fitzpatrick is quoted as saying, "he bowed, turned and ran—and I did the same, and made for my horse."

He should have given the grizzly a little more time. The bear glanced back, saw the man running, and wheeled about. Fitzpatrick calculated that he had enough of an edge to mount and race off ahead of the bear, but his horse, seeing a giant grizzly approaching at full speed, ignored the man grabbing for the saddle, bolted, and threw Fitz flat on his back in front of the chuffing bear.

A less experienced person might have scrambled away trying to escape the bear, but Fitzpatrick kept his senses. Leaping to his feet, he confronted the grizzly. Once more the bear turned and ran off. But it made a mistake: it stopped to eat what was left of Fitzpatrick's lunch, which probably attracted it in the first place. "I crept to my gun," said Fitzpatrick, "keeping the rock between him and me, having reached it, took deliberate aim and killed him on the spot." The trapper feasted on bear steaks, then moved on and covered another three miles or so before making camp for the night.

The next morning he followed a small mountain stream into a beautiful little valley and had the bad luck to be spotted by a band of Gros Ventre trophy hunters who coveted his scalp. The best description of what happened next comes from the writings of Zenas Leonard, a trapper who heard it in Fitz's own words at rendezvous.

Fitz began slipping away, thinking that the Indians might not have seen him. He was wrong. The young braves swung in behind him, bottling him up in the canyon where he was surrounded on three sides by precipitous walls and towering peaks. A man could deal with bears, and maybe even enjoy the excitement of it, but this latest problem was more serious business. Fitzpatrick figured he still had a good chance because his spirited horse could outrun anything the Indians rode. He turned one horse free and set spurs to the other one. It bounded up the steep rocky slope lunging over rocks and slipping in the loose soil. But the horse was soon winded and the Indians, who had left their horses behind to pursue the trapper on foot, were closing the distance rapidly. Fitzpatrick leaped from his saddle and, carrying minimum equipment, began climbing the mountainside on foot.

He soon realized that he would lose this race. There were too many warriors after him, and they were too fast on their feet. They had slowed temporarily while securing his horse, probably reasoning that now the white man was theirs anyhow.

The white man, meanwhile, was racing through a field of boulders and along rock ledges. He momentarily passed from the Indians' sight, and in that instant, found a crevice between the rocks, slid into it, and began stuffing leaves and grass into the opening to hide himself.

The job was barely finished when the first of the Indians came screaming up in mad pursuit. The band passed within a few feet of the silent Fitzpatrick. As Zenas Leonard quoted him, Fitzpatrick is supposed to have said, "What a moment of intense anxiety was this! All chance of escape cut off. No prospect of mercy if taken! Hope began to die—and death inevitable seemed to be the very next incident that would occur."

The Indians, apparently unable to believe that the white man had escaped, continued to search. They clambered over the slope the rest of that day. Finally, they began retreating back down the mountain. But little bands would suddenly stop and begin talking loudly and motioning until, deciding that they might not have looked hard enough in a certain spot, would scramble back up the slope to search some more. Night came. The Indians, accompanied by their newly acquired horse, went back down the valley.

Fitzpatrick began to breathe easier. Long after darkness filled the valley he crept from his cramped refuge to inspect the scene. He thought he saw a way out of his dilemma. In the blackness, he began a long sneak play down the mountainside, believing that he was slipping around the Indians by a wide margin. He had miscalculated. He suddenly appeared on the edge of the Indian camp. But the weary Indians, and even their dogs, slept on, while Fitzpatrick crept back up the mountainside and settled into his hiding place again.

He awakened early the next morning. So did the Indians. Refreshed by their sleep and driven by their lust for scalps, they attacked the hill again, sending blood-curdling war calls up the slopes as they came. The warriors eventually grew weary of this sport and began amusing themselves by racing their new horse against their own ponies. Fitzpatrick, peering down on them from behind the bushes, was pleased to see that his horse acquitted itself nobly.

By the second night Fitzpatrick thoroughly understood the lay of the land. Once more he slipped down the mountain and this time made it around the Gros Ventre camp. He followed the creek for the rest of that night, then hid and stayed out of sight throughout the day. Occasionally, a few Indians passed his hiding place, studying the ground for the slightest sign of the white man.

The next night Fitzpatrick followed the creek to its confluence with Pierre's River. Now he was sure where he was. There were still too many hostiles around so he decided to cross the river. He built a raft of logs, loaded it with his remaining possessions, gun, powder, possibles bag, and shot pouch, climbed aboard, and shoved off into the current. He moved steadily toward the far shore.

Then the current swept the little raft into fast water and carried Fitzpatrick downstream farther than he expected to go. He bounced into a field of rocks. The raft was picked up by the turbulent whitewater and slammed against a boulder that tore it apart, dumping man, gun, and everything else into the rushing stream. When the trapper reached shore, after a tiring fight against the current, he was far poorer than when he started. All he had left now to protect himself against man or bear was the knife in his belt. Weary, wet, and hungry, he ". . . stood on the bank in the midst of despair."

During the days that followed, Fitzpatrick, like a wounded animal, moved with extreme caution, staying hidden as much as possible. For two more days he followed the river, living on roots and plants.

As the days dragged on, Fitzpatrick grew steadily weaker. He wasted time wandering from place to place, searching for food. Finally, he grew so weak that he could scarcely walk, and he saw little hope that either trappers or friendly Indians would rescue him.

Meanwhile, Bill Sublette's supply train had arrived at the rendezvous site without Fitzpatrick. The anxious partners sent out a small party to search for Old Fitz. One story says they found him and gently brought him into camp. Another account holds that he was rescued by two Iroquois hunters. It may be that he came into camp on his own. Whatever the truth, he arrived in a dazed condition, nearly starved, clothes mostly ripped off, his feet bare, his body bleeding and bruised, his cheeks hollow.

It was also said that during the ordeal his hair turned white. From this he gained his new name among the Indians—"White Hair."

Precisely how Old Fitz acquired the hand injury that gave him his other Indian name is still debated among historians. One explanation may be found in the archives of the Missouri Historical Society in St. Louis. In a small room at one end of the archives stand files of drawers containing microfilmed editions of Missouri newspapers of long ago. One of these newspapers, *The Jefferson Inquirer* for December 25, 1847, tells what really happened to Fitzpatrick's left hand.

Again Fitzpatrick, according to this story, was scouting alone when discovered by Blackfeet. Fitzpatrick, as usual, was on a strong, young horse and soon gaining distance on the Indians.

The Indians headed him directly toward a cliff below which the Yellowstone River flowed. There was no time to hesitate, no way to turn back or change course. Fitzpatrick put spurs to his mount and off the cliff they went to splash into the river below. There, while trying to remove his rifle from its cover, Fitzpatrick shot himself in the hand. The accidental shot mutilated his hand, but even then he managed to reload and shoot again, killing two of his pursuers and giving himself time to hide in the woods. During the following days he eluded the Indians and came, eventually, back to his friends. Now the Indians called him "Broken Hand."

Through those years when the fur business flourished, then faded, Fitzpatrick was at the heart of the trapping industry. As a partner in the Rocky Mountain Fur Company he continued to explore and trap. But he saw new trapping companies crowd into the already heavily worked valleys. The wildness of the mountains was feeling the pressure of the growing human presence. Soon there would be lines of covered wagons heading west.

The first of these was ready to move in 1840, and out in front leading the way was the rawboned Fitzpatrick. The following year he led others westward, and his presence probably spelled the difference between success and disaster for the newcomers moving through that vast open land.

When the nationally known John C. Frémont set off on his second western mapping expedition in 1843, his guide was Tom Fitzpatrick. Later Fitzpatrick served as a scout for the army.

These experiences brought the respected Fitzpatrick to the attention of government officials. They appointed him agent to the Indian tribes of the Upper Platte and Arkansas, and in this role he dealt successfully with Arapahoes, Cheyennes, Kiowas, Shoshones, and Sioux, conducting treaty negotiations and dealing with land claims.

The Irish boy who made good in the western mountains was married to a woman whose father was white and whose mother was a member of the Snake tribe. They had two children.

He was off to Washington on official government business in 1854, when pneumonia took him at the age of fifty-five. He had lived well beyond the life expectancy of Rocky Mountain beaver trappers.

The Mountain Man's Guns

The beaver trapper roaming the wilderness was never far from his rifle. When he slept, the long gun was beside him, loaded and ready. When he set his traps or cooked his food, the rifle was within reach. When he traveled, "Old Betsy" rode much of the time across his saddle where she could be brought to instant action.

There was pride in what the gun would do. "Old Betsy shoots center, she does, and knows fat cow from bull." The trapper expected his rifle to drop a buffalo at two to three hundred yards, stop a charging grizzly, and settle all conflict with Sioux, Crow, or Blackfoot—in the trapper's favor.

With his life riding on his marksmanship, the trapper became a remarkable shot. He was young, his hand was steady, and his eye keen. He could put a lead ball into a two-inch mark at one hundred yards and put the next one, and the one after that, right beside it. His practice games, testing his skills against those of his friends, included snuffing candles at thirty yards, driving nails, and cutting a bullet in two by hitting the sharpened blade of an ax.

The earliest trappers heading west carried with them the rifles they had used in the eastern forests. They did not yet realize how inadequate these guns would be in the land where they were going. But they had no choice. The rifle the early trapper carried was known as the Kentucky rifle, but more than likely it was built in a shop in Lancaster County, or elsewhere in Pennsylvania. Typically, it was a full-stock flintlock with a 44- to 46-inch barrel, bored to about .40 to .45 caliber.

By forcing a hickory rifling rod with steel teeth through the barrel, the gun maker had worked the inside of the barrel into a system of lands and grooves. The seven or eight grooves were given about one complete twist in the length of the barrel, which was enough to set the bullet to spinning and help it hold its course.

This gun was an excellent choice in eastern forests where the largest game was the whitetail deer or the black bear, taken at relatively short range. But in the West where a man—or wild animal—can see for hundreds of yards, and the target is more likely to be a half-ton buffalo or an angered grizzly, the squirrel gun that served so well in the woods of Kentucky was out of its class. The problem, as explained by firearms historians Louis A. Garavaglia and Charles G. Worman in their book *Firearms of the American West 1803–1865*, was ". . . a simple matter of ballistics." As the range increases, the velocity of the smaller caliber ball diminishes and its shocking power falls off. The smaller ball was also more likely to be pushed off course by crosswinds than was the heavy ball.

Word came back to the gun makers in Pennsylvania, Ohio, and St. Louis that the trapper and trader in the West needed a heavier gun. Some older guns were rebored; others were replaced. Out of this came the Plains rifle. Typically it was a .50 to .55 caliber percussion rifle, weighing ten or eleven pounds, and had a barrel 36 to 42 inches long. Brass mountings were replaced by steel, which was lighter weight and also reflected less glare to disturb the shooter or flash a warning to wild game or Indian adversary.

The Plains rifle with its heavy barrel and chunky stock was not a gun of beauty or grace. But it had not been made for pretty. It was fashioned for heavy work, which it did admirably. In 1920, Horace Kephart wrote of tests made with his Hawken rifle which was typical of the guns carried by the Plainsmen. "For ordinary shooting," he wrote, "the customary charge of powder was only half the weight of the bullet and the recoil then was almost unnoticeable. With this load it would shoot practically flat up to 150 yards and with extreme accuracy. By adding more

Model 1803 Harpers Ferry Rifle. This was the gun chosen by Lewis and Clark for the members of their expedition to the Pacific in 1804. All photos courtesy the Winchester Arms Museum, Cody, Wyoming.

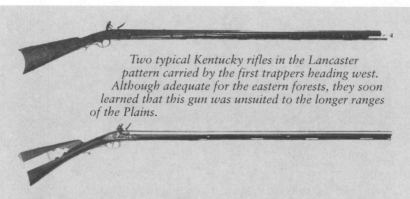

Two typical Kentucky rifles in the Lancaster pattern carried by the first trappers heading west. Although adequate for the eastern forests, they soon learned that this gun was unsuited to the longer ranges of the Plains.

powder it would shoot straight and would kill at 200 to 250 yards with common round ball."

Even after percussion Plains rifles began to replace the flintlocks, the mountain men were often slow to accept the change. Although the Reverend Alexander John Forsyth, a Scottish minister and waterfowl hunter, obtained a patent on his percussion system in 1807, the American beaver trappers were still relying on their flintlocks through the 1820s. The trappers had grown up using flintlocks, and their reluctance to make the change is understandable. Those little percussion caps were easily dropped by cold fingers. Sometimes they refused to fire. Besides, a man could run out of caps and be in a tight spot indeed. On the other hand, if he lost a flint, he could usually find another stone that would do the job.

In these times prior to mass production, the busy gun shop might turn out a few dozen rifles a year. The St. Louis guns destined to become most famous were the rifles made by Jacob Hawken and his younger brother Samuel. The reputation of the Hawken rifle, and its role in the fur business, according to Charles E. Hanson, Jr., director of the Museum of the Fur Trade at Chadron, Nebraska, may have grown out of proportion over the years. In his book *The Hawken Rifle: Its Place in History*, Hanson says, "There is no doubt it was a fine gun but so were a dozen others in the same period." But whether it is fair or not, or even sound history, the Hawken became fixed in legend as the standard gun of the mountain man.

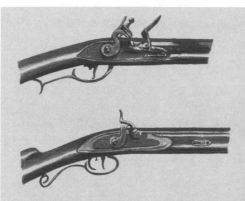

*Closeup of the lockworks
of a flintlock rifle (top) and
the percussion, or Plains,
rifle that succeeded it.*

In addition to his rifle, the trapper usually carried a pistol or two to provide back-up firepower for his single-shot rifle. Ideally, the trapper's handguns accommodated the same size lead balls he used in his rifle so he could cast a single size for both. In time, the single-shot flintlock pistols were replaced by multishot percussion systems, first the pepperbox with its revolving barrels, then the true revolvers, but these came late in the fur-trapping period.

Shotguns, especially double-barrels, were also common on the western frontier. The fur trapper ordinarily made a point of wanting nothing to do with a smoothbore. But by the 1830s the shotgun was becoming popular enough that St. Louis manufacturers, including the famous Hawken brothers, were making double-barreled shotguns for the western trade. The smoothbore had proved that it had at least two jobs at which it excelled. Loaded with shot or with a single lead ball plus a number of buckshot, it became a potent weapon for night guard duty around the trappers' camps. If the light was so poor the guard could not be sure of his mark, he could, if armed with the well-loaded smoothbore, fire in the general direction of the approaching enemy and stand a fair chance of at least disabling him. In addition, the shotgun was what was needed for taking grouse, waterfowl, turkeys, and other small game when buffalo, elk, and other large animals were unavailable.

Some mountain men preferred carrying a musket that discharged a heavy ball. They compensated for the lack of accuracy by limiting their shooting to close-range work. Zenas Leonard

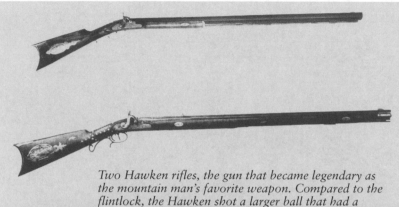

Two Hawken rifles, the gun that became legendary as the mountain man's favorite weapon. Compared to the flintlock, the Hawken shot a larger ball that had a flatter trajectory, greater range, and more hitting power.

told of an episode in which a companion used such a gun to settle an affair with a large California grizzly.

This hunter, and another trapper, were stalking a herd of elk across a pleasant meadow when they surprised five grizzlies, two adults and three cubs, resting in the grass. The adult bears charged the hunters. According to Leonard, one of the hunters, experienced in the ways of the grizzly, stood his ground and let the bears come. He held in his hands the gun which he called "Knock-him-stiff," and which carried a one-ounce ball. With Knock-him-stiff ready, he ". . . stood quite composed . . . until the bear came within reach of him when he discharged it with the muzzle in her mouth . . ." The hunter reported back in camp that this ". . . gave her a very bad cough." Following this example, the second hunter killed the other adult, after which the three cubs were dispatched, mostly because they were there.

Perhaps the strangest gun carried into the mountains in the early 1800s was an air gun used by Meriwether Lewis. Lewis used the air gun mostly to impress Indians. It had enough power to kill but made scarcely any noise. Strong medicine.

Shooting Bag

The size of the leather bag carried by the hunter varied with need and preference. It could be a simple single-compartment bag, or a complex one with partitions and pockets. The wide shoulder

strap supporting the bag frequently had gun tools, bullet mold, and other equipment attached by thongs. To make a simple single-compartment bag, the trapper marked the pattern on leather, then cut it out, folded and sewed it, and turned it right-side-out. A two-compartment bag could be made by sewing in a partition.

Shot Pouch

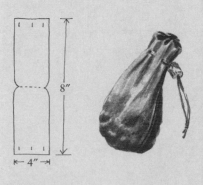

Although the mountain man customarily carried lead balls in the shooting bag, he might also put them in a separate and smaller pouch, making them easier to find in a hurry. The shot pouch was usually made from a single piece of soft leather stitched up the sides, then turned right-side-out. A leather drawstring with an antler slide was added for closure.

Ball Block

The ball block enabled the blackpowder shooter to keep a supply of lead balls, complete with patch, ready for instant use. Otherwise, he had to fumble in his shot pouch for them. The size and capacity of the ball block was a matter of personal choice. The wood was three-eighths-inch thick for carrying balls up to .50 caliber, half-inch thick for balls of larger caliber. Holes were drilled to allow for a tight fit for ball with patch. The ball block was carried on a thong attached to the shooting bag.

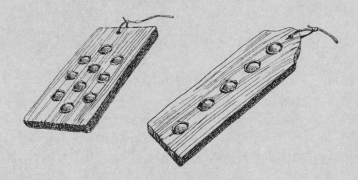

Flint Wallet

Trappers who carried flintlocks needed a supply of extra flints available. They generally carried them in special containers in the shooting bag. One common method was to store the flints in a leather, walletlike envelope with compartments sewn in for each flint. This helped prevent chipping and breakage, while keeping flints easily available.

Powder Chargers

The shooter in a hurry might measure the charge of powder into his hand, allowing just enough to cover the ball. But the safe method was to measure the powder charge in a section of bone or antler tip drilled to hold the precise amount needed. Also used was the hollow leg bone of a large bird.

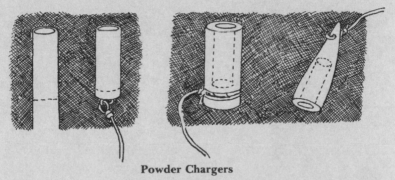

Powder Chargers

Percussion Cap Holders

Western trappers who changed from flintlock rifles to percussion systems devised their own methods for keeping caps secure and handy. One common style of carrier was made of rawhide (left), another of a small section of cow or buffalo horn. This was sometimes boiled and flattened somewhat. It was then equipped with a wooden end plug and a whittled stopper for the small end. It was carried on a short thong tied to the strap that supported the powder horn. The percussion caps carried in the rawhide capper could be fitted on the nipple and pulled free through the slot. Sometimes they were attached to a shoulder strap (center).

Patch Knife

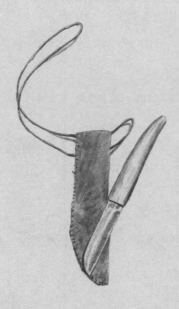

Trappers needed to keep a small knife handy for cutting patches when loading their guns. The miniature knife was often carried on a thong around the neck. Size was a matter of personal preference, but the blade was usually less than three inches long, with a handle about the same length. The handle was made of antler softened in boiling water so the tang, the metal extension of the blade, could be forced into position in it. As the cooling antler hardened, it locked the knife into the handle securely. A leather sheath, with attached thong, completed the outfit.

Blackpowder Gun Tools

The mountain man needed a wire and brush to keep the touchhole of his rifle clean. These tools were drawn from ones made by Ohio shooter Karl Wilburn. They have antler handles with holes drilled through the top to accommodate a leather thong. Boar bristles were selected for the brush because of their stiffness.

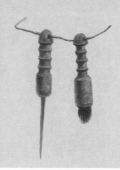

How To Scrimshaw

Adding names, dates, and pictures to powderhorns, as ancient sailors did on ivory, is easy if you follow the steps outlined by Karl Wilburn, who has made hundreds of powderhorns for customers across the country and teaches scrimshaw classes. Here are the essential steps to schrimshawing as he practices them in his shop.

1. Select what he calls a "scrimshaw grade" horn. It should have good curve and twist, white body, and proper size for the use to which you will put it.

2. Prepare the surface. Start by scraping the horn with a sharp blade, piece of glass, file, or all three.

3. Sand the surface using #220 sandpaper.

4. Go over it with 4/0 steel wool.

5. Hold it up against a strong light to inspect the surface for cracks, grooves, and rough spots. Sand these down and rub out with steel wool.

6. Sketch the picture or legend into the surface with a soft lead pencil. Pictures can be traced onto the horn with the aid of carbon paper.

7. Scratch or cut the design into the surface using a sharp knife point or needle.

8. Using fingers or a soft cloth, rub black India ink, available at stationery stores, over and into the design.

9. Wipe off the excess and go over it lightly with 4/0 steel wool. The permanent design now stands out boldly.

· 11 ·

Old Bill, Master Trapper

Maybe Old Bill Williams, cantankerous, ornery, unwashed, and a somewhat peculiar loner, could have traced the biggest tragedy of his mountain-man career, even his death, to Senator Thomas Hart Benton. After Missouri attained statehood, Benton became one of its first United States senators and held that seat for the next thirty years.

In the Senate he was in a position to influence government policy toward the West and he was a staunch believer in bringing as much western territory as possible into the union. He promoted the concept of Manifest Destiny, a loosely defined term, advanced to make the takeover of new territory in the West look like a holy crusade. The basic aim was to see the borders of the United States extend from the Atlantic to the Pacific. Benton wanted American soldiers stationed in the West to protect trappers and traders working in the beaver industry, and he wanted roads surveyed and opened to help move settlers to western destinations.

He was powerful enough in the Senate to get congressional approval for funds to explore these new routes west. The question then became one of who should lead such a journey of exploration, and Senator Benton also had the answer for this one. His vivacious teenage daughter Jessie had married a young officer in the Army's elite Topographical Corps. Although the senator had ranted and raved against the young man, he came to appreciate the symbiotic potential of their relationship.

His son-in-law was John Charles Frémont, bright, alert, and ambitious. Frémont had some army experience in mapping wilderness territory in the Minnesota country, and this helped Benton land the western plum for his son-in-law.

Although he knew his instruments, Frémont did not know his way around the mountains and valleys of the West. The "Great

Pathfinder" needed a guide, and there simply was no better place to look than among the old mountain men who knew by heart where the streams ran and the passes crossed the high places. Among the trappers who led his party at various times were Bill Williams, Joe Walker, Tom Fitzpatrick and Kit Carson.

Frémont was en route up the Missouri River on a steamboat when he met Kit Carson, also a passenger. Frémont and Carson became close friends. Frémont, who might have been called the great communicator of his day, had a flare for public relations. Carson was scarcely known outside the mountains where he was an exceptionally skilled trapper and frontiersman. Frémont's later writings, which were accomplished with his wife's considerable help, brought him added fame while catapulting Carson into national hero status.

Frémont carried out other expeditions, and in due time was planning to add to his fame with a trip on which he would seek the best route for a transcontinental railroad. Frémont apparently hoped to prove that rail traffic was practical to the West Coast the year around, so he deliberately planned his journey for the bitter weather of midwinter. He seems to have embarked from St. Louis without arranging for a competent guide.

When he reached Fort Bent, in southeastern Colorado, Frémont met Thomas Fitzpatrick, who had previously served as a Frémont scout but who was, by this time, an Indian agent. If Frémont hoped to sign Fitzpatrick on as guide again, he was soon discouraged. Fitzpatrick thought it was foolish to attempt crossing the mountains in winter, and said so.

Frémont soon had the impression that several other experienced mountain men agreed with Old Tom. In November the scene from Fort Bent was frightening. Unusually early snows were coming in on the wings of blizzards. There was already a foot of snow covering the ground, and the Sangre de Cristo Mountains, a hundred miles to the west, lay beneath snow cover heavier than anyone could remember for this early in the year.

Later that month, Frémont's group arrived at Pueblo where they found a handful of mountain men already settled in for the winter. Frémont could find nobody who was optimistic about the chances of getting across the snowpacked mountains in midwinter. One trapper, Dick Wootton, who had agreed to guide the party, had already resigned at Fort Bent after taking one look at the accumulated snows.

Among the mountain men at Pueblo was Old Bill Williams, and the determined Frémont finally talked Old Bill into serving as his scout. Old Bill did not think it would be easy. In fact, he thought it was going to be extremely difficult. "This hoss says that's a sight o' snow and I ain't aimin' to go under, but if that's the way yer stick floats, hyar goes." Williams did not fancy sitting around all winter doing nothing, but as affairs turned out, he would have done better to hole up and keep his feet to the fire.

Williams traced his origins back to Rutherford County, North Carolina, where he was log cabin born, in 1787, into a devout family. His mother taught him from books, with special emphasis on the Bible.

When young Will was seven years old, his parents sold their sizable farm and headed west. The journey over the mountains, through Cumberland Gap, across the Ohio River, and on through the forests to the St. Louis area must have been an adventure for Will. The family settled only five miles from the Missouri River and the Williams boys continued their education in hunting, fishing, trapping, and woodsmanship.

He had soaked up so much of the Biblical message that he discovered he had the calling. While still in his teens, the gawky Williams kid was announcing himself as Parson Williams and, performing the duties of an old-time Baptist circuit rider, began traveling from one community to the next on a bony mule, spreading the promise of heaven and the threat of hell, taking his pay in chickens, vegetables, mule feed, or whatever other goods the country folks might spare. Now and then he lived off the land.

Williams' preaching led him farther and farther from home until he came onto a village of Osage Indians. The life of the Indians appealed so deeply that Williams began mixing elements of Christianity and Osage ceremony to create his own dogma. Early missionaries, coming west to convert the Indians, employed him as an interpreter, but they could never be one hundred percent certain that Bill was relaying to the natives precisely their interpretation of what the Bible said.

Eventually, Williams rode the two hundred miles back to the family farm to break the news to his parents that he had joined the Osage tribe. He took an Osage wife and later, in the tradition of the tribe, another wife, or two, which did little to redeem him in the eyes of the missionaries.

There followed a series of trading ventures among the Indians. Williams obtained a permit and established a post to trade among the Osage people on the Grand River, a South Dakota tributary of the Missouri. Later the same year he became a free trapper on Clark's Fork in Montana.

Old Bill was about as well known as any trapper in the mountains, and to put the matter gently, he was known as a character. Some even said he had crossed the fine line separating eccentricity from lunacy, but the evidence weighs heavily to the contrary. He could talk intelligently among educated people.

He was a tall, gaunt, ungainly, hawk-faced man with leathery skin, a red beard, and shoulder-length red hair. He decked himself out in casually arranged beads and feathers, and wore oversized spurs. He possessed tremendous energy and stamina, and also ranked among the most skilled of all mountain men in the essential skills needed to travel, trap, and stay alive.

His secret for dealing with the Indians was to avoid being seen, and in pursuit of this aim, he became expert at traveling and setting his traps at night. He slept in his canoe whenever possible, tying it in the willows by a twenty-foot length of rawhide so he could cut loose easily and drift silently downstream in case of trouble. Floating downstream after dark, he watched for signs of beaver, set his traps, then checked them again at the first sign of dawn. He collected and skinned his catch and was again tied up out of sight when full light came.

Furthermore, he fired his gun as little as possible, often choosing to eat beaver, especially the tail and liver, rather than risk discovery by shooting a buffalo or deer. It wasn't that Old Bill was scared to fight. He was known as an excellent companion in a tight spot. When need be, he went on the attack and fought like a demon, speaking encouragingly all the time to his rifle and calling her by name. He shot with an uncanny marksmanship that was admired throughout the mountains.

Old Bill Williams, in spite of all precautions, had his share of encounters with hostile Indians, including the warlike Apaches that he met while trapping on the Gila River. He was off far from any help one day when a band of Apaches overwhelmed him and took his gun, knife, and tomahawk, as well as all his other possessions. Finally they began stripping his clothing off piece by piece until he stood stark naked in the desert sunshine. He was then given permission to set off through the cactus, which he promptly did. It was a long way back. Through valleys and over mountains, he limped for a hundred and sixty miles or so until the Zunis discovered him. These Indians, treating him much better than the Apaches had, outfitted him and sent him on his way. After traveling a total of perhaps two hundred miles, Old Bill came back into Taos.

He had acquired a reputation among the mountain men of often shunning the company of others. "This coon feels like caching," he'd say, according to George Frederick Ruxtons' *Life in the Far West*, and, loading his pack animal, he would disappear into the hills, sometimes for weeks or months. He had an uncanny sense of trouble when Indians were lurking about. "Injuns is all about, they ar'—Blackfoot at that. Can't come 'round this child, they can't—Wagh!"

Although we must remember that Ruxton was dealing in fiction, it seems probable, even to historians, that his description of Old Bill left a literal account of the mountain man. Ruxton also left what is probably a dependable version of the peculiar language that evolved in the conversations of the trappers.

> *Williams always rode ahead, his body bent over his saddle-horn, across which rested a long, heavy rifle, his keen gray eyes peering from under the slouched brim of a flexible felt-hat, black and shining with grease. His buckskin hunting shirt, bedaubed until it had the appearance of polished leather, hung in folds over his bony carcass, his nether extremities being clothed in pantaloons of the same material with scattered fringed down the outside of the leg—which ornaments, how-*

ever, had been pretty well thinned to supply "wangs" for
mending moccasins or pack-saddles, which shrunk when wet,
clung tightly to his long, spare, sinewy legs. His feet were
thrust into a pair of Mexican stirrups made of wood and as big
as coal-scuttles; and iron spurs of incredible proportions, with
tinkling drops attached to the rowels, were fastened to his heel,
a bead-worked strap four inches broad, securing them over the
instep.

    In the shoulder belt, which sustained his powder horn and
bullet pouch, were fastened the various instruments essential
to one pursuing his mode of life. An awl with deer-horn han-
dle, and the point defended by a case of cherry wood carved by
his own hand, hung at the back of the belt, side by side with a
worm for cleaning the rifle; and under this was a squat and
quaint-looking bullet mould, the handles guarded by strips of
buckskin to save the fingers from burning while running balls,
having for its companion a little bottle made from the point of
an antelope's horn, scraped transparent, which contained the
"medicine" used in baiting the traps.

It was said that Old Bill would arrive at rendezvous well supplied
with packs of beaver taken from secret trapping grounds, sell his furs,
spend all the revenue on drink and gambling, then head back for the hills
a free man. ". . . and nothing more would be seen or heard of him perhaps for months. . . ," wrote Ruxton.

    At other times he would travel with a party of trappers or a sin-
gle partner as struck his fancy, and sometimes take time to guide a party
needing the assistance of an expert. As the beaver business wound down
in the late 1830s, the innovative mountain man felt the need to seek other
sources of revenue. One such business was rounding up and selling Spanish horses that, although seemingly abandoned, did not really belong to
him. Old Bill Williams proved to be an expert leader in acquiring and
moving horses.

    He helped organize one of the largest of all horse raids in the
spring of 1840, when a mixed bag of trappers, friendly Indians, and others under his leadership descended on the missions of southern Califor-

nia. By the time they headed back east across the desert, they had gathered in some three thousand animals. They were bound for Bent's Fort near where the Purgatorie empties into the Arkansas in southeastern Colorado.

The Californians staged an organized pursuit. They cut out and recovered maybe half of the horses, but the raiders still arrived with a considerable supply of horses, for which there was always a ready market.

Williams was a distance traveler, always ready to put his moccasins to the trail again at the slightest whim. But Old Bill was sensible. He figured that the best way to deal with trouble was to avoid it and he had a knack for sensing hazardous situations ahead of time. In the winter of 1848, however, his system broke down. When Captain Frémont arrived at The Pueblo, Old Bill, although he had strong reservations and was going against all the advice of his fellow-trappers, agreed to guide Frémont on what most believed was an impossible adventure.

The thirty-three men and their long line of pack animals crossed the Sangre de Cristos in south-central Colorado and headed toward the Rio Grande. Frémont turned up that river, then swung straight into the La Garita Mountains—with Old Bill Williams advising against it all the way. But Frémont had a bad case of mind-set. He welcomed the difficult, perhaps reasoning that the bigger the challenge, the greater the glory. When Old Bill questioned whether or not they could make it over the mountains by the route Frémont insisted on following, Frémont sent him to the back of the line, replacing him with another guide who did not know the mountains.

Snow piled up in the valleys. It was so deep that the men had to lead their horses along the steep slopes. Temperatures fell so low the thermometer could not record them. Horses and mules slipped, rolled down the hill, and were lost. Snow blindness struck the men. Hands and feet froze.

Eventually the starved horses, then the exhausted travelers, began to fall. Men removed their boots and ate them, replacing them with strips of blanket. They ate their knife sheaths and other items of leather.

The survivors eventually made it into Taos. Behind them in the mountains, they had left all the party's scientific equipment, as well as eleven of their men—dead from starvation, cold, and exhaustion. This disaster was perhaps the worst ever suffered by a party guided by a mountain man.

The survivors, all in pitiful condition, were hardly safe before Colonel Frémont, who dreamed of becoming president, began shifting the blame off his own shoulders. He found his scapegoat in Old Bill Williams, claiming that the old trapper was the root of his trouble, the cause of the loss of human life, and the reason the "Great Pathfinder" had failed in his expedition. About the only thing that could be said for the expedition was that it proved that up and over the two-mile-high La Garitas simply wasn't the best route for a railroad.

Once in Taos, Old Bill, now sixty-two years old, regained his strength. By March, he and the expedition's physician, Dr. Benjamin J. Kern, were ready to go back into the mountains to recover the equipment and materials the party had abandoned. They were accompanied by a crew of Mexican helpers. Shortly after finding the equipment and starting back, they were both shot and killed, perhaps by the Utes, but nobody knows.

Old Bill Williams shaped his own image. As the unorthodox trapper, he may have been a role player for the fun of it. He was a superb mountain man, never stole horses when it seemed improper, and, except perhaps for signing on with John Charles Frémont, rarely made a mistake in judgment. He was proud of his skills as trapper and woodsman. He marked his beaver pelts "William S. Williams—M.T." The "M.T." stood for "Master Trapper," and danged ef he warn't or I wouldn't say so.

12

Trail Blazer

Captain Jedediah Strong Smith earned his high standing among the beaver trappers by an unusual combination of cool-headed leadership, attention to business, and a string of close calls that astounded his fellow trappers. There was frequent speculation on just when the Captain's luck would run out and leave Old Jed "lying wolf meat," his hair dangling from some Blackfoot warrior's lodge.

Smith was tall, over six feet, slender in build, and powerful. He had brown hair and blue eyes. His store of energy seemed boundless, and unlike many mountain men, he was quiet and serious by nature. His companions always figured they could count on Captain Smith in a crisis. He was long on courage and clear thinking in a tight spot.

He had another characteristic setting him apart from most of the beaver trappers: he was so serious about his religion that he always carried a Bible in his possibles bag. This might have labeled a lesser man as a mite queer out in country where it was said that God was always careful to stay east of the Missouri. Smith did not swear, smoke, get drunk, or chase women. His mind was on his work and his eye was on the horizon. For him, life was serious, exciting, and filled with challenges. There is often an element of luck in the background of the successful person, and Jed Smith had that going for him too—some of the time.

After his family moved west from his birthplace in south-central New York, first to Pennsylvania, then Ohio, Jed moved on to arrive in St. Louis in the spring of 1822 when he was twenty-three years old. He had the farm boy's knowledge of the outdoors but knew nothing of the western wilderness, except that it promised a fortune to anyone who could capture the animals and sell their skins.

In St. Louis that spring, Jed responded to General Ashley's call for young men to go to the mountains. He joined the party under the leadership of Ashley's partner, Andrew Henry. The boats made their way up the Missouri as far as the mouth of the Yellowstone, and there Henry and his party spent the winter. Jed Smith, however, journeyed on up the Missouri to the mouth of the Musselshell and hunkered down to wait out the winter. Here he began living in the fashion of the free trappers, subsisting on the meat he shot, and probably protected from the winter blasts by a shelter made of buffalo skins stretched over a framework of tent poles with both ends stuck in the ground.

By spring he was back down at the mouth of the Yellowstone where Henry needed a messenger to travel down the Missouri and meet General Ashley. The restless Jed Smith said quietly that he would carry the message to Ashley, and he was soon headed downriver again. This was how he volunteered himself right into that famous battle where the Arikaras waylaid Ashley.

Following the battle with the Arikara, Ashley and Henry sent Jed Smith out at the head of a dozen or so trappers to explore the untouched beaver country south of the Yellowstone River. It was during this trip that the trappers began addressing Jed Smith, their brigade leader, as Captain.

Indians were a constant danger. Nobody knew when a band of them would come racing down out of a rocky mountainside or across the plains, clinging to the sides of their ponies, arrows nocked, ready for the full draw. Scouts were kept out to give early warning in case the Indians appeared. From this trip, however, Smith would remember the grizzly bear more vividly than the hostile Indians.

His group traveled for days across a dry land of short grass and prickly pear. There were patches of timber in the draws, and along the streams grew bands of cottonwood and bushes bearing wild fruits. There were buffalo, prairie dogs, elk, antelope, and waterfowl. And there were grizzlies. Even if you didn't see the huge bears, you knew they were there.

One evening the trappers were pushing their way through a thicket toward a river to make camp for the night. They were leading their tired horses. Smith was out at the head of the line. Suddenly a huge grizzly rushed, chuffing and growling, out of the bushes near the middle of the line of men. She wheeled and ran along the line until she met Jed Smith face to face.

Trapper Jim Clyman, a member of Smith's party, later wrote down the events as he recalled them. "Grizzly did not hesitate a moment but sprang on the captain . . ." The huge bear took Smith's head in its mouth and tossed him to the ground. This ripped Smith's scalp open, leaving a flap of hair and bloody skin hanging down and exposing the white skull. The beast then grabbed the young captain by the middle, breaking, not only the blade off Smith's butcher knife, but also several of his ribs. Lead balls began thumping into the old bear's sides until the beast finally dropped, releasing Smith only in its moment of death.

The trappers stood around wondering what to do. Their captain lay bleeding on the ground. These wilderness travelers could treat simple cuts or bruises, boils, and snakebites, but they often depended on luck to see them through serious medical emergencies. None among them had any experience treating wounds of the magnitude the grizzly had rendered on the torn body of Jed Smith. The trappers kept passing the buck, each one suggesting that the next one do something for the captain. Finally, they did the usual and put the question directly to him.

Smith, with his head laid open, ribs shattered, and abdominal lacerations bleeding profusely, was still thinking clearly. He dispatched two men to the river a mile or so away to bring water. Then he told Clyman to get a needle and thread and begin sewing up his head wounds. Clyman found a pair of scissors and cut off as much of the captain's blood-matted hair as he could. Now he could see the tremendous task he faced; he began sewing the flap of scalp back in place.

With this done, he looked at Smith's dangling ear which he said was ". . . torn from his head out to the outer rim." The ear was hanging by a flap of skin and Clyman explained to the captain that there was no way he could save it. This was not what Jed Smith wanted to hear. He instructed the first-time surgeon to take his needle and do his best, and Clyman began putting the ear back on, after a fashion. "I put in my needle stitching it through and through and over and over."

Once he had been patched up, Smith got to his feet, mounted his horse, and rode a mile to the campsite. There his crew installed him in the party's only tent and tried to make him comfortable. He needed recovery time and while he rested in camp, his trappers scouted the surrounding hills. Within ten days Smith's raw wounds had healed sufficiently for him to travel. He rode off with his party, heading west once more toward the high beaver country.

As long as he lived, Smith carried the vivid red scars of his encounter with the grizzly. The missing eyebrow, the gash across his weathered face, the ear somewhat out of place, all marked him as a member of that tough breed of respected men who had tangled with a grizzly bear and survived. The story of Captain Smith and the grizz spread throughout the mountains. The captain wore his hair long to help hide his terrible new scars.

Eventually, after proving himself as trapper and brigade leader, Smith had the opportunity to become part owner of a fur company. General Ashley, for whom he had worked, was willing to sell out, and the men who purchased the outfit were three of the most capable of all the mountain men, Jedediah Smith, William L. Sublette, and David Jackson. As Ashley headed downriver toward St. Louis and civilization with his profits, the three new partners made their plans for the coming year. Sublette and Jackson would head back into the high country around the headwaters of the Missouri and its tributaries. But Smith had his eyes on an entirely new frontier.

Legend had it that a major river had its beginning somewhere south of Great Salt Lake and flowed on all the way to the Pacific. Here could be new beaver country, waiting for someone to open it, and Jedediah Smith wanted a chance at it. If all went well, he would bring his party back to the summer rendezvous of 1827, on the southern end of Bear Lake which today straddles the Utah-Idaho border.

To the southwest lay a vast expanse of mysterious country unknown to the white man. The map beyond Great Salt Lake was a blank. The Indians were unable to answer Smith's questions about his unmapped region. Jedediah Smith was dreaming of wild streams where the beaver had not yet met the trappers, but the lure of unexplored country was as strong in him as the promise of beaver pelts. He was driven by the knowledge that no one had yet blazed a trail across this strange land all the way to California where the great Pacific rolled in against the shores.

How much of this had been in Smith's mind as he and his partners made their plans during the rendezvous at Willow Valley in northern Utah, in the summer of 1826, we cannot know. But we do know that by the middle of August, seventeen men, led by Smith, set off toward the Southwest. Once more, Jed Smith's eyes were on the horizon. This time his longing to travel where no others of his kind had walked was going to lead him into one of the more incredible of all the mountain men's journeys.

The adventure started with Smith's trappers in high spirits. The line of buckskin-clad men moved south along the east shore of Great Salt Lake, then rode on down the west side of the Wasatch Mountains, a north-south range, stretching for two hundred and fifty miles across the heart of Utah. Then the trail rises sharply from its basins, through coniferous forests, to twelve thousand feet. As long as there was fresh "buffer cow to make meat of," there were good times around the campfires, and uncounted buffalo grazed in the grasslands where these trappers rode.

But as they moved south and westward, the buffalo gradually gave out and the party began munching on the seven hundred pounds of jerky that Smith had directed his crew to pack on the horses. There were still antelope, "black tailed hares," and now and then a bighorn for the pot.

They came to the Sevier River and followed that colorful valley deeper and deeper into the desert. The land offered spectacular colors and memorable sunsets, but one doubts that the beautiful desert landscapes were now much admired by hungry, thirsty mountain men. These were men who had trapped hundreds of beaver from cool mountain streams, then feasted in the evenings on buffalo. The scene had changed. The sweeping mountain views were gone. Now they moved deeper and deeper into the wasteland of the broad, barren Mohave Desert.

In this bone-dry land of sand and rocks, stretching out between the Sierra Nevada and the Colorado River, they traveled beneath the searing sun, buffeted by strong winds, plagued by hunger and thirst. Smith was searching for the great river that he felt must drain Great Salt Lake into the Pacific. But there was no such stream.

After two weeks in the Mohave Desert, the party topped the San Bernardino Mountains. A shining new green land was spread out before them. To the west stood San Gabriel, a prosperous Spanish Mission, its occupants protected from the east by the broad desert fortress no American had yet crossed. San Gabriel was then grazing thousands of head of stock, and producing a wide variety of fruit, including fine grapes that yielded hundreds of barrels of wine each year.

The surprised friars in charge of this wealthy mission treated the newly arrived mountain men well. Smith had his blacksmith fashion a bear trap and gave it to the mission because bears had been raiding the orchards. The friars gave Smith enough cotton cloth for all his men to make themselves new, and badly needed, shirts.

Meanwhile, Smith wrote to the Mexican governor in San Diego, explaining that they had come to California in peace simply to find beaver. They had, he added, run out of provisions and this had made it imperative that they come on into the California country. Now they asked permission to leave.

The Spanish interests extended mainly to agriculture and convincing Indians to abandon their ancient beliefs and embrace the white man's religion. Trapping was of minor interest to them. The governor knew so little about beaver, or trapping them, that he referred to the American hunters as fishermen, perhaps because they knew about trapping sea otters and the otters lived in the edge of the ocean. Furthermore, he thought the story being handed to him by the gangly young captain of the "fishermen" had the sure ring of falsehood. Perhaps these men from the East were soldiers and spies with a clever cover story. The governor eventually sent word to Smith that he and his men could leave California—providing they backtracked along the same trail they followed to get there.

This was not precisely what Jedediah Smith wanted to hear. He always preferred exploring new trails in his search for beaver to retraveling ones he already knew. He led his little party out toward the mountains over which the trappers had come and, some distance from the mission, changed course and headed north toward the San Joaquin Valley. This brought the trappers to green and beautiful valleys lined with trees among which wandered all the deer and elk they needed. Best of all, there were beaver.

But Jed Smith was thinking about the need to return to American territory in time for the summer rendezvous. North of San Francisco he came to the American River and turned his party toward the towering mountains to the east. He was again traveling where no white man had gone before him.

The higher Smith and his trappers climbed, the more difficult the trail became. In the Sierra Nevada they fought bitter weather and howling winds. They floundered in belly-deep snow. The horses were dying and Smith feared for his men. Reluctantly, he turned his party around and headed back down toward the valley. There they turned south again and backtracked to the Stanislaus River.

Smith still had to cross the mountains and the desert to reach the rendezvous site. His partners would be there waiting for a report on his explorations into the Southwest. He decided to try it with a smaller party. He set off again, this time with seven horses and mules and two men, Robert Evans and the blacksmith Silas Gobel. Historian Dale Morgan, who wrote *Jedediah Smith and the Opening of the West*, concluded that, this time, Smith went by way of Ebbetts Pass, altitude 8,731 feet.

They struggled toward the pass through snow that drifted to eight feet deep. They ran out of food and survived on the flesh of their remaining horses. Finally, they were over the divide and starting down out of the high country. The days grew gradually warmer. The trappers came into the desert again. Now their real enemies were heat and the lack of water. As the days dragged on they knew that they might die in this desert. On rest stops they tried to bury themselves up to their chins in the sand to conserve moisture.

Eventually, from that barren desert south of Great Salt Lake, they could see the Wasatch Mountains ahead. But the distance was too great for Evans. He fell to the ground unable to go farther. Smith and Gobel stumbled on, and after a few more miles came to a spring. They fell on their bellies and buried their faces in the shimmering water. Smith had no sooner slaked his thirst than he started back carrying a kettle with more than a gallon of water for his dying companion.

Evans drank the entire offering and wanted more. This revived him, however, and now the ragged little group moved on toward the shore of Great Salt Lake. They traveled around the lake's south end until they came to the Jordan River and found it flooded out of its banks.

Neither Gobel nor Evans was a strong swimmer so the three trappers began cutting reeds and tying them into bundles which they bound together into a raft. Smith tied a rope to the raft, took the end of it between his teeth, and set off swimming for the far shore. Behind him Gobel and Evans clung to the raft and kicked to help propel it across the sweeping current.

At Bear Lake, the 1827 rendezvous was getting underway. Free trappers, traders, and Indians arrived from the mountains, and there was drinking, bartering, yarning, horseplay, and bargaining with the Indian maidens. Many of the stories being told were of the now-famous Captain Smith who had been chawed so fierce by the grizz, and now hadn't been heard from for nigh onto a year. Speculation was that Old Jed had by now sure enough gone under.

Then, in the middle of the afternoon of July 3, there came into the rendezvous a large party of Snake Indians up from the South, and traveling with them were three Americans, as ragged and beaten a trio as you would find anywhere. They were soon recognized, especially the tall, thin form of Jedediah Smith. Word raced through the community. Trappers already celebrating were given new cause. The small cannon brought out from St. Louis was fired in a special salute.

While the other trappers made the most of the carnival-like atmosphere of the rendezvous, the businesslike Jedediah Smith solemnly spent his time putting together another crew of men and assembling horses for his next trip. After spending only ten days in rendezvous, and laying new plans with his partners, he set off again. Eighteen men were lined out behind him. Jed Smith was going back to see more of California and to pick up the crew of trappers he had left there.

He knew something of the route now. By staying closer to the rivers he reduced somewhat the terrible hardships suffered on his first trip to California. By the middle of August the party reached the Mohave villages on the Colorado. This had been a haven for Smith on his first trip to the coast. The Mohaves had been friendly. They had allowed the trappers to camp with them, to rest and regain their strength. The chief had even assigned two young guides to show the trappers the best way to San Gabriel where some of the Mohave Indians had once lived for a while before deserting the mission and rejoining their people.

What Smith didn't know was that, following the trappers first visit the year before, the governor of California had been in touch with the Mohaves. He had warned the Indians that the white men coming down the Virgin and Colorado rivers into California were a bunch of rascals and up to no good. As a consequence, the Mohaves' "hearts were bad."

These Indians were capable warriors known for their fierce and unyielding conduct of battle. They were famous as swift runners who could run all night while now and then taking a little water from the ring of animal intestine slung over their shoulders. They were also known for their poison arrows, treated with a lethal mixture of human blood and rattlesnake venom.

While Smith's party spent a few days building rafts to ferry their supplies across the Colorado, the Indians waited, giving the white men no hint of what lay in store for them. The Indians waited until the party was split. Smith, with eight of his men, had moved onto a sandbar that reached out into the water. This was when the Mohaves attacked, killing the ten remaining trappers within minutes. Then they moved in on Smith and the other eight.

Smith took a tally of the weapons they had—five rifles and their knives. They quickly hacked down some of the poles in the nearby thicket, clearing space from which to fight, and used the poles to throw up a flimsy breastwork. "We then fastened our Butcher knives with cords to the end of light poles so as to form a tolerable lance," Smith wrote, "and thus poorly prepared, we waited . . ."

A few of the Indians were beginning to venture within range of the sharpshooters. Smith gave his trappers orders to fire, two at a time, and they killed two Indians at remarkable distances and wounded one more. This awesome display of marksmanship made the Mohave hesitate and reconsider. As the Indians fell back, the Americans disappeared into the bush, then into the desert. Once more Jed Smith escaped, and in due time his little group reached California.

Here they faced new troubles. The governor held them for several weeks while Smith argued his case. Letters even passed back and forth between the Mexican secretary of state and the United States minister in Mexico City, because the travels of this man Smith were becoming increasingly disturbing to the Mexicans. They must have been well aware that Americans wanted to extend the boundaries of the United States from the Atlantic all the way to the Pacific. Jed Smith was the vanguard.

Smith found the California atmosphere unfriendly, and only when a group of sea captains, anchored offshore, interceded for him was he allowed to depart. He rejoined his trappers left here from his first trip, and the combined group eventually headed north toward the Columbia on a trip certain to be as difficult as any Smith ever made. In the tangled, rocky wilderness of northern California, horses slipped and fell into turbulent mountain streams. Rain fell for days at a time. Men clambered over rocks where there was no trail. ". . . the Mountain over which I was obliged to pass," wrote Smith in his journal, "was so exceedingly Rocky and rough that I was four hours in moving one mile." There were also frequent skirmishes with the Indians, as well as attacks by grizzly bears.

Two of these bear attacks were aimed at Jedediah Smith, who still bore the terrible scars dealt him by the grizzly five years earlier. Smith escaped the first bear by making a high dive into a stream. The next bear charged Smith's horse. The captain wheeled his horse sharply, but the bear grabbed the panicked animal's tail and hung on. The bear tried for fifty yards or so to drag the horse to a halt before giving up and watching horse and rider race away.

But the greatest trouble came to the party in Oregon in July 1828, after Smith and two of his crew set off to scout a route for the main party to follow. Before the party could leave its camp, a large group of Kelawatset Indians attacked and almost wiped the trappers out. One trapper escaped into the forest. He eventually made his way across one hundred and fifty miles of wilderness to the Hudson's Bay outpost, Fort Vancouver, on the Columbia River. When Smith and the two trappers with him also arrived at this fort, they knew that the four of them were all that remained of the two parties of trappers Smith had led into the wilds of California. For the third time in his brief career, Jed Smith had survived an Indian massacre—the Arikara in 1823, the Mohaves in 1827, and now, a year later, the Kelawatset. The Hudson's Bay Company factor at Fort Vancouver quickly sent out a party to punish the Indians responsible for the massacre. Among the items recovered was Smith's journal, which is now safe in the archives of the Missouri Historical Society in St. Louis.

But Jed Smith's travels in the mountains were winding down. The following year he was back with his partners in Montana and spent a year trapping on the upper Missouri and its tributaries.

In October 1830, he returned to St. Louis. He had made money as a partner in his fur company and acquired fame on the frontier. He had come to know the West as well as any man. No other explorer, including Lewis and Clark, had seen as much of western America as Jed Smith had visited.

He wanted to take time out and complete his journals and maps for publication. However, he first agreed to help organize a large trading party to Santa Fe and the Mexican provinces.

This long line of wagons and horsemen moved out of St. Louis in April 1831. After crossing the Arkansas River, the Santa Fe Trail led them into a harsh, dry region. Furthermore, when the party arrived, the Southwest was suffering a severe drought. There were long days without water for man or beast. Hope of finding water was dim late in May, and one morning several little groups of men were sent off in various directions in a last-ditch effort to find a spring or stream.

Smith and one companion struck out southward. They came to a water hole but the hole was dust, so Smith told his companion to stay and try digging while he went on to check out a patch of green trees in the distance. His hunch was right. A few miles ahead he found the only water hole for miles around—and a dozen or more Comanche warriors hid beside the waterhole, waiting for thirsty animals to come.

As nearly as the story could be pieced together, Jed Smith happened onto the group suddenly. There was no hope of escape. As the Comanches rushed him, he had only time enough to get off one shot, which killed the chief. Jedediah Smith was immediately overwhelmed, and on these desert sands, his long string of remarkable escapes came to an end.

The unforgettable Jedediah Smith, who had come west as a kid, had blazed the trail soon to be tramped by thousands of westbound families headed for Oregon and California, had been the first white man to go overland to California, the first to travel the California coast north to the Columbia, the earliest to cross the rugged Sierra Nevada, and the first to explore the Great Basin. When he died that day beside the desert waterhole, Jedediah Smith was thirty-two. In eight years of trapping and exploring, fighting Indians and grizzlies, he had written his name indelibly into the legends of the American West.

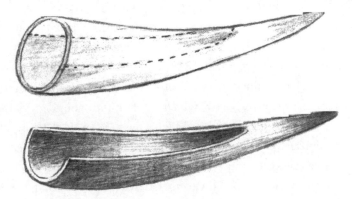

Horn Spoon
The mountain man needed few implements around his camp kitchen other than his knife and a kettle, but a large spoon came in handy. A spoon made from scraped and polished horn was lightweight and rugged. It was especially handy for dipping stew from the kettle.

13

A Grizzly Problem

*T*he first white man the wilderness grizzly bear saw was simply another animal, and the grizzly had never met the animal it feared. Even when the great bears learned that these newcomers could hurt them, they still attacked any man who surprised them or pushed them too far.

The mountain men, meanwhile, saw in the grizzlies an ultimate challenge to their skills and bravery—the highest test of manhood—so they sought the grizzly out in his native haunts and carried the challenge to him. Consequently, stories of the early trappers are laced with accounts of unforgettable conflicts between man and bear. Few, if any, of these encounters could match the legendary struggle that began one September day, in 1823, in what is now the northwestern corner of South Dakota.

Major Andrew Henry was leading a party of thirteen men in an overland shortcut away from the Missouri to go almost straight west up the valley of the Grand River toward the Yellowstone country. He always tried to keep his little band of trappers in the best position to avoid nasty surprises by Indians. There was security to be gained by staying within sound of your fellow trappers. But in Henry's party was Hugh Glass, an independent spirit who had a habit of straying away from the group whenever he chose. Trapper Jim Clyman was aware of this when he wrote in his journal for September 1823, that ". . . a Mr. Hugh Glass . . . who could not be restrained . . . went off the line of march one afternoon and met with a large grizzly bear which he shot and wounded."

Parts of the legend of Hugh Glass, born of that impulsive shot from a muzzleloader, remain fuzzy to this day. Some have speculated that the whole tale of his unfortunate encounter was the product of frontier imaginations. There is, however, widespread belief that the legend of Hugh Glass is true. It is admittedly the kind of bear story that could grow from campfire to campfire, and in the final analysis, one is free to make his own decisions on what he believes of this unforgettable frontier adventure. John Myers concludes his book *The Saga of Hugh Glass, Pirate, Pawnee, and Mountain Man* by finding the incredible story "thoroughly true."

The background of Hugh Glass, before his beaver-trapping years, is filled with questions. Glass may once have found temporary employment as a pirate. It is said that he sailed on a ship that was overwhelmed by the infamous privateer Jean Lafitte, who specialized in preying on Spanish ships in the Gulf of Mexico. Although Glass rarely spoke of those times, it seems probable that, in preference to execution at the hands of Lafitte, he chose to serve his apprenticeship as a pirate, biding his time, and reasoning that as long as he was alive and kept his wits, there was hope.

Glass's career as a pirate terminated one dark night off the coast of Texas when he and a buddy slipped over the side and swam for shore. On land, the big problem was staying alive in a world dominated by hostile Indians. The two men, slipping along northwestward, as swiftly as they could, while watching for signs of natives, made it all the way to Kansas before their luck ran out. There they had the misfortune to be discovered by a band of Pawnees, who were bad news anytime.

The Pawnees lived in lodges made of earth, and around their dwellings planted corn and squash to supplement the food taken by their hunters. They were proud and powerful warriors noted for their nasty tempers. They fought all the neighboring tribes at every opportunity and were recognized experts in creating unusual ways to torture their captives.

The jubilant Indians hustled their two white captives back to their village in high anticipation of the festive occasion ahead. The ceremony was soon in progress. The Indians chose Glass's companion for their first sacrifice. Instead of simply building a fire and putting him on it, they pushed numerous slivers of dry resinous pine into sensitive parts of his body and Glass was forced to watch his companion burn slowly. By intermission time, when this first act ended, Glass had a vivid picture of what lay ahead for him.

Instead of cringing and pleading, Glass forced himself to remain calm and appear unconcerned. This made a deep impression on the Pawnees, who considered bravery the greatest of virtues. Glass even offered the chief a gift. In the few trade items he had carried along was a small waterproof pack of vermilion, which was always considered of extreme value among the Indians.

The chief was impressed; he decided that this brave and generous white man would make an outstanding Pawnee, so he brought Glass into the tribe by the simple process of adopting him as his son. Once more, Glass the survivor was willing to make the most of this development and for the next couple of years lived as a Pawnee. He sharpened his survival skills. He learned the Indian techniques of living off the land.

His opportunity to desert the tribe came unexpectedly. When his "father," the chief, set out for St. Louis to confer with the Indian agent, Glass was taken along. When the rest of his tribe set off for home, Glass stayed behind.

He was still in St. Louis when Ashley and Henry began organizing their second historic trip into the mountains for beaver in 1823.

By this time, Glass was older than most of the mountain men, perhaps forty, but by any measure he was tough, resolute, and a most capable outdoorsman. He was also said to be something of a loner and independent by nature, but still a dependable partner in times of trouble. Here was the kind of man Ashley and Henry needed if they were to succeed in their new enterprise and deliver substantial payloads of furs back to St. Louis. Soon the party, including Hugh Glass, was deep into hostile country.

In autumn, the bears feed constantly, adding fat ahead of the coming winter. They eat all manner of foods, both plant and animal. One of their favorites is ripe fruit; they were especially fond of the wild plums growing in thickets along the streams. On this day, an old female grizzly and her husky cubs were busy gathering fruit in the heart of the thicket toward which Glass was headed.

He came upon the bear suddenly, or more accurately, she came upon him. She smelled him or heard him, or both, and his presence in her territory was an invasion of her space. She reacted in the only way she knew as she crashed through the brush toward the trapper. Glass waited as long as he dared, then gave her one in the heart.

The single shot lacked power to do the job and the grizzly came on without breaking stride. There was no time for reloading. The furious grizzly was on Glass almost immediately, her teeth chomping and claws raking whatever they could reach, while Glass made futile slashes at her with his butcher knife.

She was still at her job when the first of Glass's companions, responding to his loud calls for help, arrived on the scene out of breath. They shot the bear until she dropped and lay still beside the man she had mauled. One glance was all the trappers needed. Anyone could see that Old Glass was going under. He was torn apart and bleeding from numerous wounds and there was precious little anybody was going to be able to do about it.

They tried to make him comfortable in what they believed were his final moments. Then, after standing around quietly for a while waiting for him to die, it began to dawn on them that the tough old Hugh Glass was a long way from becoming wolf meat. He lived on through that night; then, according to George C. Yount, a mountain man who talked with Glass about the event, his companions moved on, carrying their silent and helpless companion on a litter. To this day people living in the wilderness far from help are drawn close together in case of emergency. They depend on each other. Yount spoke of this quality in the mountain men. "Among those rude & rough trappers of the wilderness, fellow feeling and devotion to each others wants is a remarkable & universal feature or characteristic."

For several days the trappers carried the litter. But Henry knew that the burden was eating into his crew's fall trapping time and that their slow progress increased the threat of Indian attack. He reasoned that he had little choice—he must leave Hugh Glass behind. But one does not abandon a helpless companion to die in the wilderness. Henry asked for volunteers who would stay with Glass until he died, see to it that he got a decent burial, then catch up with the main party.

This was not a detail for which anyone would volunteer lightly. Henry offered extra pay to any two men who would stay. Most accounts tell us that one who stepped forward was Jim Bridger, although events that followed seem out of character. The other was named Fitzgerald. They watched solemnly as the rest of their party struck camp, loaded their equipment, and disappeared in the distance.

They waited for Glass to grow weaker and die, but he lived on, day after day. Fitzgerald and Bridger grew restless. Perhaps Fitzgerald argued that Glass couldn't last much longer anyhow and that they should move out and save themselves. And perhaps the younger Bridger finally went along. Nobody will ever know the details of this conversation, but in the end the two trappers loaded up and departed. Glass, watching them make ready, was unable to speak to them because of injuries in his throat. He may have been conscious and awake when they took his equipment, including his rifle. Once Glass died, he would have no further need for the rifle and someone was certain to ask about it.

The two had not reckoned with the rawhide toughness of this man they abandoned. Here perhaps the most incredible story in the colorful history of the American West began. Glass had water within reach, and he may have managed to pick a few berries. He rested and regained some of his strength.

At first, he was so weak that he could not rise to his feet, so he began to crawl. Yard by yard, he worked his way back down the valley of the Grand River toward the Missouri. How far can a half-starved man, broken and bleeding, crawl in a day over rocky cactus-studded country? At first, Glass was marking his progress in yards.

Hunger plagued him. At one point, he killed a fat rattlesnake with a rock and dined on its flesh. There were sometimes berries to pick. His biggest break came the day a pack of wolves brought down a buffalo calf near him. The salivating Glass considered ways to take the treasure away from the wolves. Perhaps he hid in the bushes and waited until the wolves were sluggish on fresh meat, then chased them off with rocks. The meat strengthened him and he stayed beside it, resting and eating, as long as he could. Using his razor, he could have cut strips of it to dry in the sun and carried the jerky off in the pockets of his tattered clothes.

Eventually Glass was able to rise to his feet and walk. As his strength grew, his progress improved. He would probably find the culprits at Fort Kiowa where Henry's partner Ashley was headed, so he started back downstream planning to turn up the Missouri when he came to that river again. Eventually, a band of Sioux Indians befriended him and helped him reach Fort Kiowa.

He soon learned that the two who had abandoned him were no longer there, so he set off again following his party up the Missouri. One story says that he hitched a ride on a supply boat. The Arikaras were still attacking river travelers whenever they had the opportunity, and Indians scouts soon spotted the boat on which Glass traveled. In the attack that followed, the Indians killed everyone on board. Typically, Glass escaped; he was on shore at the time. Once more he was traveling alone.

When he finally reached Fort Henry, where the Bighorn River empties into the Yellowstone, the mountains were in winter's grip. Here he encountered Jim Bridger, the first of the two men he wanted.

Bridger might already have heard rumors that Glass lived. Or perhaps the old trapper, his frayed buckskins flecked with fresh snow and a satanic look on his scowling face, pushed open the heavy door and walked in out of the winter night like a ghost, to stand before the unbelieving trappers. Bridger was young and apparently Glass was more intent on finding the older man—Fitzgerald. It was sometimes written that Glass shamed the young Bridger and delivered an unforgettable tongue lashing. Nobody will ever know. But Glass was not done traveling yet.

Eventually, he tracked Fitzgerald to Council Bluffs, only to learn that he had joined the army. After tracking his former companion for hundreds of miles he took his satisfaction in confronting Fitzgerald with a shame that could not be lived down. Glass resisted the temptation to kill a United States soldier. But the trip may have been worth it to Glass.

To fur trappers, Glass had proved himself to be an iron man and his story, true or not, was repeated in trading posts and around campfires as long as beaver trappers worked the mountains. He began wearing his hair long to cover some of the scars the grizzly gave him. Other than that, he displayed little outward evidence of the attack, or his astounding campaign to survive. On a winter day, after Glass returned to trapping, he was surprised again by Indians. They caught up with him as he worked along the Yellowstone River. This time his luck ran out. The trapper who had survived Jean Lafitte, the Pawnees, a grizzly attack, and an incredible journey, died that day fighting his old enemies, the Arikara.

· 14 ·

Some Called Him
Thunderbolt

A fur trapper could always find more trouble than he needed, but Milton Sublette had a special knack for being where the action was. It was said that this son of old Kentucky, powerfully built and standing more than six feet tall, had the right attitude for a mountain man. He was bold and daring by nature. If a situation demanded physical action, Milt sensed it immediately and acted promptly. This was illustrated again one day in the spring of 1827 in Santa Fe, New Mexico, when Sublette set an example that must have made him the envy of his fellow trappers.

By this time he was a veteran trapper. Like many another famous mountain man, he had his start when he responded to General Ashley's call in 1823, along with his older brother, William. Both became famous trappers, traders, and leaders.

The interest in beaver trapping in the Southwest was growing, and when a group of trappers was recruited in St. Louis in the spring of 1826 by Ewing Young for a trip to the Southwest, Milt signed on. By traveling together, they brought added protection to each other in the land of the Mohaves and warlike Apache. Otherwise, the trappers were operating as free trappers who could work where they pleased and personally control the sale of their catch. By autumn Milt and his companions were setting traps along the Gila and its tributaries and taking enough beaver to make the venture highly attractive.

This was the kind of enterprise that would sooner or later get the trappers into trouble with the Mexicans, who were certain to resent the fact that these outsiders were coming into their territory and taking out thousands of dollars worth of resources. Not too surprisingly, the governor of Mexico clamped down on the fur trappers, declared their beaver harvest illegal, and moved to confiscate all the furs which the trappers had worked for through the year.

The trappers heard about this new order when they came into Santa Fe that year and promptly hid their valuable furs. This defiance caused the governor to order his soldiers to find the furs, bring them in, and tolerate no resistance. The furs were located, confiscated, and spread out to dry in the courtyard, where they were when Milt Sublette saw them soon after.

He promptly asked Ewing Young where his furs were and Young pointed them out to him. Milt was not one to stand idly by, allowing anyone to take the furs for which he had waded icy streams and braved death at Indian hands. Neither was he inclined to ask nicely that his furs be released to him. He dashed over, gathered up his bundle and made off with the furs before the startled guards were fully aware of what the audacious American was doing.

Although he had his furs, Milt was now an outlaw, and he went into hiding. The Mexicans never did locate him. By the next autumn he was ready to go back on the beaver streams and joined a party which is believed to have moved northward into Colorado, trapping as it went, still in defiance of the governor's orders.

There were the usual running battles with the Indians just about any time the trappers crossed paths with them. In one of these skirmishes Milt's friend Thomas L. Smith took a lead ball in the leg. The bone was damaged beyond repair. The suffering Smith and his friends discussed what they could do about the injury. If they did nothing, Smith would surely die from gangrene.

The answer was plain and, although it was not a job that Milt Sublette asked for, he slid his heavy butcher knife from his belt sheath and began rubbing its cutting edge back and forth on his stone, then filed saw-type notches in it. Trappers held the writhing Tom down as best they could while Milt cut his leg away.

Smith acquired two new identifying trademarks as a result of the operation. One was a personally whittled cottonwood leg on which he thumped around as he continued to trap, joking that this new leg seemed to tolerate the cold a mite better than the old one did. The other was his new name; thereafter he was known among the mountain men as "Peg-Leg Smith."

In 1829, Milt Sublette took an Indian wife. His friend Joe Meek later concocted a touching story of how Milt first met his wife. As the story went, there had been drinking, followed by a knife fight in which an Indian so severely injured Sublette that he lay for forty days recuperating under Meek's devoted care. Then they were taken prisoner by the Snakes, who planned to put them to death, but a beautiful princess of the tribe slipped them horses so they could escape. The girl's name was Mountain Lamb, and she became Milt's wife.

Historian Doyce B. Nunis, Jr., writing about Milton Sublette in *Trappers of the Far West*, edited by LeRoy R. Hafen, calls this story "pure fiction." Little is really known about Milton's wife except that she bore him two children who, as the trappers' children often did, probably bounced along happily on the pack animals as their parents worked the mountain streams for beaver and, once a year, made their way toward the summer rendezvous.

Milt was a leader and businessman as well as a trapper. In 1830, when the Rocky Mountain Fur Company was assembled for the summer rendezvous on the Popo Agie, at its junction with the Wind River near to-day's Riverton, Wyoming, Milt Sublette and four friends, including Bridger and Tom Fitzpatrick, bought out the company. Milt led trapping parties in the Indian country but the company, faced with growing competition and scarcities of beaver, did not make spectacular profits. Milt was also destined for a prominent role in one of the all-time historic battles between the trappers and the Blackfeet.

During the summer of 1832, the trappers gathered for rendezvous on the west side of the Teton Mountains at Pierre's Hole, a beautiful, flat valley of green fields and gurgling ice-water brooks. As the rendezvous wound down in July, Milt set off with his band of trappers for the Southwest. Washington Irving, in *The Adventures of Captain Bonneville*, tells what happened then.

The party made only eight miles that first day before settling
down in the south end of Pierre's Hole for the night. With Milt were fourteen trappers plus fifteen free trappers, as well as a party of eleven inexperienced New Englanders headed for the Southwest—a total of forty
people in camp.

The camp was quiet and uneventful all night, and the next morning the party made early preparations for a full day on the trail. Before
they could depart, however, one of them spotted a long line of people
winding out of a narrow passage on the sweeping mountainside across
the valley. "That be Fontenelle," speculated one of the trappers. "Could
say he's comin' into ronnyvoo a mite late."

All through the rendezvous that year, Lucien Fontenelle, of the
American Fur Company, one of the most skilled brigade leaders working
the mountain fur trade, had been expected in Pierre's Hole daily with his
train of supplies. This column of people and horses coming into the valley could be the American Fur Company train at last.

But some of the more experienced free trappers in the group cau-
tioned against hasty conclusions. "Yep, and could be Injuns too, and us
outnumbered plenty." One of the leaders brought out a telescope for a
closer inspection of the strangers a mile or so distant. What he saw did
not look good. Some of the Indians were on foot, others on horseback.
The trappers could now see plainly that they were facing a band of Gros
Ventres of the Blackfoot confederacy.

Sublette did some fast thinking. These Indians probably were un-
aware of the concentration of whites and friendly Indians up the valley at
the rendezvous site. But seven or eight miles was a considerable distance
to send for assistance and if they were going to get the word back to Milt's
brother, Bill Sublette, and others at the rendezvous site, the messengers
best be on their way. Two horsemen soon raced off up the valley to spread
the word.

Meanwhile one of the war chiefs of the Indian party rode out
from his group, half-closing the gap between the Indians and trappers.
The veteran trappers in the group probably did not take heart at this display of willingness to negotiate, because the Blackfeet had demonstrated

repeatedly that negotiation was a waste of time that might better be spent fighting. The chances were excellent that the Indian leaders were trying to gain time so their warriors could psyche themselves up for battle with their special medicine bags, paints, and incantations.

This distrust of the Indians may have had something to do with the pair of negotiators who rode out to talk with the chief. The two were not the ambassadorial types that cautious leaders would normally select for a peacekeeping mission. One of them was a half-breed member of Sublette's brigade named Antoine Godin whose bitterness toward the Blackfeet stemmed from the fact that they had tortured and murdered his father. As Godin rode out to greet the chief, riding beside him was a Flathead Indian whose people were traditional enemies of the hated Blackfeet who had so often defeated them.

The chief who came to confer with them had left his weapons behind. The band had obviously not been a war party, but instead an entire village on the move. The chief's trusting attitude was more evidence of this. He now held out the peace pipe he carried, presumably expecting the two who had come from the white man's camp to be equally friendly. That was the biggest mistake he ever made. According to Irving's record of what he heard from Captain Bonneville, who talked with various people present at the event, Godin asked the Flathead accompanying him, "Is your piece charged?"

"It is."

"Cock it."

As they drew near, the chief held out his hand and Godin grasped it. At the same instant he yelled to the Flathead to let the chief have one from his rifle which, according to Irving, ". . . brought the Blackfoot to the ground."

Some accounts say that the two "mediators" lifted the chief's scalp before racing back to the group of watching trappers, but it seems more plausible that, surrounded as they now were by flying lead, they settled for snatching the chief's beautiful scarlet blanket and waving it over their heads, counting coup, as they turned tail and departed at full gallop.

Both sides now prepared for the inevitable battle. The Indian children, accompanied by some of the women, moved back into the hills while the remainder of the group, probably taking some comfort in the numerical margin they held over the trappers, moved into the willows and cottonwoods at the edge of a swamp. This was an excellent tactical move. The Indians worked feverishly to throw up a fortress of logs and deepen a trench behind their barrier.

The trappers, meanwhile, tried to keep the Indians occupied by shooting at them from the ravine they occupied. They also saw to the safety of their horses and began using their packs to make a fortress of their own, all the time trying to calculate how long it would be before help came from the camp.

Back at the rendezvous, the riders raced into camp shouting, "Blackfeets got Old Milt pinned down." Things began to happen fast. Milt's brother Bill, along with perhaps every other experienced Indian fighter in camp, saddled horses, slung on powder horns and possible bags, grabbed up rifles, and rode off down the valley with the wind making their long hair fly. It was said that as they raced along beside each other, many a trapper made his verbal will, appointing a friend to make proper distribution of his effects, in case he went under by the weapons of the Blackfeet.

The Blackfeet, in their snug little fortress, soon saw the odds change dramatically. The whole valley seemed to come alive with trappers riding in through the sagebrush. But the Indians were still secure. Their best protection was the fact that the sharpshooting trappers simply could not see any marks at which to aim. Shortly after arriving, Bill Sublette did spot one Blackfoot warrior peering through a small hole in the brush and shot him through the eye, but this was the exception.

Bill Sublette apparently wanted to bring the whole thing to a head immediately by organizing a direct charge against the Indian stronghold. Ride in, have it out, and be done with it. ". . . but all hung back," as Captain Bonneville reported, "in awe of the dismal horror of the place, and the dangers of attacking such desperados in their savage den." Those hanging back might have been wiser than the brash souls urging frontal attack. A direct attack would surely have increased the number of trapper casualties. A small group of the bolder trappers did begin moving in on the Indians, but Bill Sinclair was promptly shot. He fell fatally wounded while Bill Sublette took a bullet in the shoulder.

One estimate placed the number of trappers and allied Indian fighters at five hundred after those coming from the rendezvous arrived. But the Blackfeet apparently never considered surrender. The shooting, and yelling of insults—"You count coup on butterflies—white dog wear squaw moccasins"—continued through the day.

There was an eventful interlude when it appeared that the trappers might attempt to fire the fortress and burn the Blackfeet out. The Blackfoot chief issued a stirring speech that carried across the battlefield to the ears of the trappers. "You may burn us in our fort but stay by our ashes," shouted the chief, "and you, who are so hungry for fighting will soon have enough. There are four hundred lodges of our brethren at hand. They will soon be here—their arms are strong—their hearts are big—they will avenge us!"

The trappers looked at each other and began repeating what they thought the interpreters of the chief's message had said. "That's some, that is." If they had heard right, a major force of Blackfeet warriors was about to overwhelm their lightly protected rendezvous camps eight miles up the valley and rob them of all they possessed. Within minutes, a large share of the trappers had mounted their horses and were retracing their steps as fast as their lathered steeds would carry them. A cloud of dust moved up the valley marking their progress.

Behind them were enough fighters to keep the Indians pinned down in their fort, and as the long day gradually blended into the darkness of night, Pierre's Hole became quiet.

At first light the next morning the trappers listened for signs of life from the Indian fortress. The place was strangely silent. In the dark, the Blackfeet had made their escape, leaving some of their dead behind. They had lost twenty-six warriors while the trappers counted thirteen fatalities. Both sides had their wounded. This was the end of the famous Battle of Pierre's Hole. Milt Sublette and his trappers returned to the rendezvous site on the chance that the main party of Blackfeet would still descend on the camp and their help would be needed. But the revenge, of which the chief had warned, never materialized.

The final years of Milt Sublette's life were a mix of business pressures and personal health problems. Early in 1834, while leading a seventy-man party westward from Missouri for the Rocky Mountain Fur Company, Milt had to turn back after only ten days out because of pain in his foot.

By 1835, Milton's leg was in worse condition than ever. He made a trip back east, and in St. Louis his doctor amputated the leg. This still did not keep him out of the mountains. His last trip was as an escort for a large party of Oregon-bound settlers, traveling through the mountains with several hundred horses, as well as wagons drawn by six-mule teams. There was also a smaller cart pulled by two mules, and this cart eventually became the ambulance for Milt Sublette, who could no longer ride his horse.

He died at Fort Laramie in April 1837, at the age of thirty-six, and was buried there. Modern doctors see symptoms of cancer in the condition that claimed his leg, then his life.

· 15 ·

From Apprentice to
Pathfinder

George Brewerton, a young Lieutenant in the U.S. Army, had settled himself in his chair to record his personal observations of the mountain man who had become a national hero. Before they met, Brewerton had his own preconceived notions of what the legendary trapper would be like. He expected him to stand more than six feet tall, be "... a sort of modern Hercules in his build—with an enormous beard, and a voice like a roused lion, whose talk was all of 'Stirring incidents by blood and field.'" But Brewerton admitted to his readers in *Harper's Magazine* that he was dead wrong about Christopher H. "Kit" Carson.

To Brewerton's surprise, Kit Carson turned out to be a quiet, unassuming little gentleman, standing only five feet four inches tall and weighing perhaps a hundred and twenty-five pounds. He was, in many ways, the opposite of the legendary buckskin-clad beaver trapper. "The real Kit Carson," Brewerton admitted to his readers in 1853, "I found to be a plain, simple, unostentatious man rather below the medium height, with brown curly hair, little or no beard, and a voice soft and gentle as a woman's."

One can understand how Brewerton, and others meeting Carson for the first time, might wonder if this could really be the swashbuckling hero of the wild adventures about which they had read so much. Since he first guided John C. Frémont through the western wilderness, Kit Carson had been marked for fame. Frémont wrote glowingly of Carson in his government reports, and this brought the soft-spoken mountain man to public attention.

Writers of dime novels found the public hungry for a new hero.

The adventures of Kit Carson, some of them real, some fantasy, were described on page after page of exciting copy. Although Carson had been in the right place at the right time, and this played a role in his rise to fame, he was also among the most skilled and intelligent of all the trappers, an outstanding woodsman, and an unbelievable marksman. He had more than his share of courage. Beaver trappers would say of him, "Old Kit's some, he is, or I wouldn't say so."

Kit Carson was born on a farm near Richmond, Kentucky, on the day before Christmas, 1809. When Kit was still a toddler, his father moved the family to Howard County, Missouri. Anyone would have predicted a rather ordinary life for the youngster.

When Kit was fourteen, his father, thinking the kid would need to know a trade, apprenticed him to the local saddlemaker. Kit, who never did warm up to making saddles, worked in the cluttered room with the odor of new leather in his nostrils, and learned to cut and sew, while his thoughts ranged far beyond the dark walls around him. Kit envied the travelers visiting the saddlery on their way to distant mountains. After a couple of years of working and dreaming, young Carson slipped away and joined a party headed for New Mexico.

His master, who looked upon this as the act of an ingrate, marched off to the office of the local newspaper where he inserted an advertisement describing Carson and offering a one penny reward to anyone who would fetch the boy back, thereby freeing himself of all contractual responsibilities.

The lad eventually made his way to Taos, which was by then the southwestern center of the fur industry. Here he met mountain men and the talk was of Indians, but especially beaver plews and the prices paid for them. During the next three years Carson traveled through what is now Arizona and southern California working for the celebrated mountain man Ewing Young.

Young, an excellent businessman and leader, had been a farmer back in Tennessee where he was born into a frontier family. He believed in rough treatment for Indians and was so quick to resort to gunfire when threatened that he was often accused of excessive killing. He was a noted shot who once, seeing a Mohave chief shoot an arrow into a tree, promptly split the shaft with a bullet from his muzzleloader. He quickly saw the promise in Kit Carson, and young Carson found service with him to be an apprenticeship more to his liking. The quick-witted youngster was soon mastering the trapper's trade while memorizing all the routes they followed through the mountains.

He next joined a party led by Tom Fitzpatrick and set off to trap in the Rocky Mountains. His courage was tested often. He recalled one of these events in *Kit Carson's Own Life Story*. In January 1833, his party was camped for the winter on the Arkansas River when fifty or so Crow Indians slipped into camp and stole nine horses. This was a serious loss and one that no self-respecting mountain man could ignore. "In the morning," said Carson, "we discovered sign of the Indians and twelve of us took the trail of the Indians and horses."

They rode for forty miles, unraveling the trail and separating horse tracks from those left by herds of buffalo. The snow was knee-deep and, by the end of the day, the horses were plodding along with their heads drooping.

Two or three miles ahead, in the gray evening light, stood a grove of trees and the little party headed for it, intending to make camp. From the trees, they could see the smoke of several campfires three or four miles distant. The trappers forgot about making camp, tied their horses in the grove, and settled down to wait.

Once darkness was upon the land, the trappers circled the Indian encampment and came on it from the other side. They worked themselves into position, a few steps at a time, until they could plainly see the entire camp from a hundred yards out. They had advanced so quietly that no horse or dog had given the alarm. The Indians were now celebrating the acquisition of their new horses as the trappers waited in the shadows.

Eventually, the Indians lay down to sleep. The last fires burned down to a red glow. Nothing moved. The trappers lay in the snow, shivering and waiting until absolutely certain that the Indians were sleeping soundly. They could see their horses tied near the sleeping warriors.

"When we thought they were all asleep," Carson said, "six of us crawled, toward the horses." The other six stayed in reserve, rifles ready in case of need.

But deep snow muffled sound and the stealthy trappers, taking advantage of every log and rock, slipped up to their horses and severed the rawhide lines that tethered them and turned their horses free. The animals were reluctant to move away from the camp. Carson reached down for a handful of snow and thumped a snowball into the ribs of the nearest horse. The animal began to move out, and they drove the horses away from the Indian camp into the night by throwing snowballs at them until they were back to where the six waiting trappers caught them. The trail weary Indians slept on.

In the dead of night, the trappers then held a whispered conference. They argued about what to do next. Nine of them who had now recovered their horses voted to get out of there and put as much distance between themselves and the Indians as they could before dawn. The other three, led by Carson, who was following Ewing Young's example, had a different idea. These Indians had made them travel a long, cold trail. The argument continued for some minutes.

"We got what we come fur, and I figure we best get on back the way we come."

"This hoss ain't fer going back 'till we larn 'em a lesson."

No trapper wanted it said that he was skeered to chase Injuns, or that he refused to help his friends in a good fight. Soon all twelve agreed that the proper course of action was to take full advantage of this opportunity, as Carson is quoted as saying years later in something less than typical mountain man jargon, "let the consequences be ever so fatal."

Three of the men slipped off into the night, leading the recaptured horses toward the woods where the trappers had tied their mounts. The remaining nine moved in on the sleeping Indians. They marched straight toward the camp. A restless dog awakened his masters and the Indians reached for their weapons. "We opened a deadly fire," said Carson, "each ball taking its victim." The Indians returned fire. But their marksmanship could not equal that of the trappers working from behind trees, coolly shooting only when sure of a mark.

Daylight came and the Indians discovered that they outnumbered the white men five to one—so they charged. The mountain men waited until the Indians were almost on them, then quickly killed five more.

The Indians withdrew, then attacked again. The trappers were drawing back toward the grove where their three companions waited with the horses. The Indians broke off their attack and departed, and the trappers mounted their horses and started the long ride back to their camp. "Our suffering," said Carson, "was soon forgotten." The fact that they had not only recovered their horses, but also "sent many a redskin to his long home," put them in high spirits.

The running skirmish with the Indians was not always so one-sided. In the fall of 1834, in a party of fifty mountain men, Carson was trapping deep in the Blackfoot country on the headwaters of the Missouri. Beaver were scarce, but Indians were plentiful. "A trapper could hardly go a mile," said Carson "without being fired on." Trapping under these risks was a constant battle of nerves. The trapper moved as silently as possible, watching for sign of all kinds, a strange moccasin track, the warning cries of jays and crows, the movement of leaves where there was no wind, the sudden silence, the nervousness of his horse. Stepping into the shallow stream with his set trap in one hand and his rifle in the other, the trapper never knew whether or not dark eyes watched from the shadows. During this autumn trapping season, Indians killed five members of the party. The remainder withdrew to their winter camp on the Snake.

The following February a band of thirty Blackfeet stole eighteen of their horses. This time, a dozen trappers tracked the horses and the Indians through the snow for fifty miles and eventually caught up. They could see their horses tethered on the hillside.

They were outnumbered. A frontal attack would be foolhardy. All they wanted this time was to get their horses back. They sent a message asking the Indians to parley, and the Indians agreed. Each side sent a representative midway to talk over the situation. The Indians brought five of the poorest captured horses and refused to give back any more.

All members of both parties were in a fighting mood, so the battle was soon in progress. Carson and a friend were advancing on two Indians when Carson turned and saw a Blackfoot warrior about to shoot his companion. While Carson engaged in shooting this Indian, he forgot the others. He turned in time to see one with a gun leveled on his chest. Carson, his gun now unloaded, dodged, but the Indian's bullet grazed his neck and passed through his shoulder.

The trappers withdrew a mile or so and spent a cold night without fire or robes to keep them warm. The blood from his wound ran down Carson's neck and froze there. In the morning the Indians were still present. This time the trappers gave up. They set off for their camp, and never did recover the remainder of their horses.

The following summer, while in rendezvous on the Green River, Kit Carson had another test of his raw courage when he became embroiled in what some have labeled a duel. If this was a duel it was not one of those formal sunrise ceremonies in which two cultured gentlemen stand back to back, count twenty paces, turn, and shoot at each other's hearts. It was instead a garden-variety western shootout.

Brigade Captain Andrew Drips had in his trapping party a monstrous French-Canadian who was as nasty as he was oversized. He was also a loudmouth bully. His name is given as Shunar, and there is some belief that Shunar was especially despised by Carson because Shunar had been trying to seduce if he could, and rape if he had to, the beautiful Arapaho maiden that Kit Carson was courting.

Most trappers simply stayed out of the giant's way. According to Carson's autobiography, Shunar, ". . . made a practice of whipping every man he was displeased with—and that was nearly all." Carson was on hand one day when Shunar, after pummeling two or three others, began announcing to the world that he could do the same to anyone, anywhere. The French trappers, he shouted, were easy to take and he had proved it already. And, as for the Americans, well, he'd just take a switch to them children.

"I did not like such talk from any man," says Carson. Kit marched up to Shunar and, looking up into the giant's face, announced that Shunar was now looking at the worst American in camp, and did he want to make something of it. For good measure, the straight-talking Carson added quietly, "If you keep on talking that way, I'll rip your guts."

Shunar wheeled silently and went to his horse. He mounted and charged out in front of the camp. Carson knew a challenge when he saw it, so he grabbed "the first arms I could get hold of," which happened to be his pistol, mounted his own horse, and galloped up so close to the burly Shunar that their horses were touching. Carson said, "Am I the one you're fixin' to shoot?" Although Shunar said "non," he was, at the same instant, drawing the cover from his long gun.

Carson allowed Shunar to draw his gun, then they both shot. Bystanders swore that the shots came so close together they thought it was the report of a single gun. Carson's shot hit the giant in his shooting arm, putting him out of commission, while Shunar's ball, as Carson described it, "... passed my head, cutting my hair and the powder burning my eye."

Carson's report says that nobody had any more trouble with the Frenchman. Bernard DeVoto, in *Across the Wide Missouri*, speculates that this might have been due to the fact that, while Shunar begged for his life, Kit Carson fetched another gun and finished the job. It seems probable, however, that Carson, after treating the man for a bad case of loudmouth, allowed him to live. The Arapaho girl in question is believed to be the one that became Mrs. Kit Carson.

Kit Carson had the kind of mind that locked into a subject until the matter was settled. He once tracked an Indian horse thief for a hundred and thirty miles, killed him in a gun fight, and returned with the horse.

The one instance in which he confessed to having been genuinely frightened occurred when a couple of grizzlies chased him. He had just killed an elk so his gun was unloaded. "There were some trees a short distance," wrote Carson in his autobiography. "I made for them, the bears after me. As I got up one of the trees, I had to drop my gun, the bears rushing for me, I had to make all haste to ascend the tree."

Carson shinnied up the nearest aspen when the bears were within a dozen feet of him. One of the bears soon wandered off, but the other one was more persistent. He repeatedly attacked Carson's tree, growling, biting, and shaking the tree, but he failed to dislodge the trapper. Carson admitted to ". . . never having been so scared in my life."

Except for the sequence of events set in motion when he returned to St. Louis briefly in 1845, Kit Carson's name never would have become famous. He completed his business and headed back to the mountains, making the first leg of the journey up the Missouri River on a steamboat. Also on board was John C. Frémont, who was planning to make his first mapping journey into the western part of the country. Frémont needed a guide. Over the next two years Kit led the party across the South Pass and on to California, Oregon, and many parts of the Rocky Mountains. His riverboat meeting with Frémont had changed his life.

Carson later became a scout for the army and a courier, carrying dispatches between California and the President's office in Washington, D.C. George D. Brewerton, reporting for Harper's Magazine, was with him on one of these rides. Brewerton wrote of Carson's caution in Indian country. "While arranging his bed," said Brewerton of Carson, "his saddle, which he always used as a pillow, was disposed in such a manner as to form a barricade for his head; his pistols half-cocked, were laid above it, and his trusty rifle reposed beneath the blanket by his side, where it was not only ready for instant use, but perfectly protected from the damp. Except now and then to light his pipe, you never caught Kit exposing himself to the full glare of the campfire."

He served as an Indian agent and was a successful commanding officer during several years of army service. Kit Carson died a national hero Mary 23, 1868. Brewerton wrote of Carson, "A braver man than Kit perhaps never lived."

· 16 ·

The Happy Mountain Man

Joe Meek was a big man who smiled easily and liked a good time. He sometimes played jokes on his friends just for the hell of it. One fine day Meek and three other trappers were up on the Pryor's River in Yellowstone Country setting their traps when Meek had what he thought was a clever idea.

As they approached a narrow pass known as Pryor's Gap, where prudent men might logically expect an Indian ambush, Meek dashed ahead on his spirited white horse. He was only a short distance into the pass when he wheeled about, lowered his large frame close against his mount's neck, and, in a cloud of dust, raced back at breakneck speed, his horse under spur and quirt. Meek's companions knew the signals; old Joe had sure enough run into a passel of Injuns and the time had come to vacate this place if they hankered to keep their hair.

Meek had cried "wolf" without saying a word and was having a big chuckle watching the other trappers race off down the trail at top speed, until he glanced over his shoulder. There, sure enough, came a Blackfoot war party, whooping and yelling, and trying to get within range.

The Blackfeet, who had been waiting in ambush, were on foot, however, because their common practice in close-quarter fighting was to hide their horses, slip about in the thick vegetation, and take their enemies by surprise. This tactic came within moments of working and, except for Joe Meek's love of a joke, the Blackfeet might have shot him from their ambush.

Meek's encounters with Indians sometimes took on a more serious complexion. On a May morning in 1834, when he and five other trappers were trespassing on Comanche hunting grounds near the Arkansas River in southern Colorado, they saw in the distance, across the open plain, a large party of Comanches riding hell-bent toward them. Meek and his party, a hundred and fifty miles from the main body of their group, knew they could expect neither help nor mercy.

Their problem was compounded by the fact that they were out in plain view and there was not a bush or ravine to hide them. Running would only delay the inevitable torture and death. The Comanche, known as excellent horsemen, were mounted on powerful animals.

Meek glanced at his companions, one of whom was Kit Carson. Almost without a word they leaped from their frightened mules and formed the animals into a tight circle. Then, holding the reins tightly, each man slipped his butcher knife from his belt and cut his mule's throat. The weakening animals soon slid to their knees and fell in a ring around them. Then, digging as fast as possible with their knives, the trappers prepared the best fort they could of dirt and warm horseflesh.

The screaming Comanches, more than a hundred strong, their head medicine man in the lead, drew closer, weapons waving above their heads, feathers flying in the breeze. Then, before they could get into range with their spears, their horses slid to a halt and milled about. They had caught the scent of the mules' fresh blood and would come no closer—which was exactly what Meek and Carson expected.

The Indians had made the mistake of coming within reach of the trappers' deadly rifles. According to plan, three of the trappers shot while the others held their fire until the first three could reload. This put three dead Comanches on the ground, among them their medicine man. The Indians drew back, reformed, chose a new leader, attacked again, and three more Comanches were added to the dead.

All day the little party, surrounded by its dead mules, repulsed the Comanche attacks. According to Joe Meek's story, which was written down for him in 1870 by journalist Frances Fuller Victor in a book entitled *The River of the West,* "The burning sun of the plains shone on them, scorching them to faintness. Their faces were begrimed with powder and dust; their throats parched and tongues swollen with thirst, and their whole frames aching from their cramped positions, as well as the excitement and fatigue of the battle."

This was simply the price of survival. They knew their enemy well enough to understand the kind of death awaiting them if they were overrun. Time and again throughout that bright May day, the Indians repeated their attack. And time and again they left dead warriors behind. As darkness settled over the plain, the Indians drew back. Their women, who came to drag away the dead, had now recovered forty-two bodies, taking time meanwhile to taunt the mountain men for fighting like women behind dead mules.

That night the trappers slipped away, leaving behind their packs of furs. They carried only their guns and blankets as they started for camp a hundred and fifty miles away. Their task now was to put enough distance between themselves and the Comanche that the Indians would give up the pursuit. They settled down to a steady dog trot, and ran all night, then kept on going. According to Victor, they ran seventy-five miles before coming to water, then, after refreshing themselves, ran another seventy-five miles into camp.

This escape supplied fresh material for Meek's stories around the campfires and at rendezvous. Meek could hold an audience spellbound, for in a frontier society that developed storytelling to an art form, Joe Meek was a master.

Most mountain men came from poor backgrounds, but Joe Meek grew up on a Virginia plantation. He had resisted schooling but he had some education. He was tall, powerfully built, and considered handsome with his broad shoulders and dark eyes. As a young man he was filled with a longing for adventure and, unhappy under the stern eye of a stepmother, he left home for the frontier. Before long he was across the Mississippi and headed for the mountains and the headwaters of the Missouri. He spent the next eleven years in the mountains.

His frequent encounters with grizzly bears figured heavily in Meek's stories. The tale that brought the biggest laughs was Joe's account of the bear that he and another trapper spotted one day across the Yellowstone River. The temptation was too strong to resist. The two trappers took careful aim and shot the bear, dropping him on the spot. The only problem then was getting enough of the animal back to camp to prove that they had really shot another grizzly.

They tied their horses, stripped off their clothes, leaned their guns against a cottonwood, and wearing nothing but their belt knives, stepped into the frigid waters of the Yellowstone. They came dripping out on the far side, climbed the steep bank, and approached the bear just as it recovered its senses. The beast rose to its feet and, as Meek told Mrs. Victor, "took after us."

With the injured bear on their heels, the two naked trappers bolted for the river. "The bank war about fifteen feet high above the water," said Meek, "and the river ten or twelve feet deep; but we didn't halt. Overboard we went, the bar after us, and in the stream about as quick as we war."

The bear tried desperately to get at one of them, but the trappers went in opposite directions and came out on the side of the stream where they had begun their swim, while the confused bear landed on the opposite shore. The strong current had carried the trappers a mile downstream, and they picked their way back barefoot through the cactus to their well-rested mules. Even then, they brought back nothing to prove their story.

An even closer call came for Meek on the late winter day that he and his companions discovered large grizzly bear tracks in front of a mountainside cave. It had been a harsh winter. Meat was scarce in the trappers' camp. The buffalo had moved out ahead of winter and other game was rare. Little bands of trappers scoured the surrounding countryside for meat to feed themselves, with perhaps some left over to bring back to camp. The hunting parties were sometimes out for a week or more at a time.

The trappers frequently faced hunger, even in summer. On one occasion, Meek, traveling with a brigade led by Milton Sublette, crossed an extensive plain where they could find no food for man or beast. As Meek later told Mrs. Victor, "I have held my hands in an ant-hill until they were covered with the ants, then greedily licked them off. I have taken the soles off my moccasins, crisped them in the fire, and eaten them." They also captured the large, black crickets, tossed them into a kettle of hot water, then ate them as soon as they stopped kicking. Or they would bleed a mule and sup on the blood, taking care not to drain too much because the mule was as weak as they were. On this day Meek and his companions climbed a long slope watching for bighorn sheep. They found no wild sheep, but along a rocky ledge discovered the footprints of the "enormous" grizzly. The bear sign told them that the grizzly had taken refuge in a nearby cavern after a brief appearance in the open, as wintering bears will sometimes do.

One of the trappers suggested that somebody should go into the cave and drive the bear out, and he would be waiting on a rock above so he could shoot the beast when it appeared. Meek said, "I'll send old grizz out or I wouldn't say so." Two other trappers, willing to prove their courage, joined him and they headed for the cave.

The entrance was high enough for them to walk in upright, and they moved slowly into the shadows, senses at full alert. As Meek told the story, their eyes adjusted to the dim light, and they saw an extremely large bear standing in the middle of the cave, staring at them. As the rest of the scene came into focus, they realized that two only slightly smaller bears flanked the big one. There were grizzlies enough to go around.

Inching closer, Meek's story claimed that he struck the big bear with his "wiping stick." This made it run past the trappers toward the entrance and as it emerged, the first trapper shot the bear, but not too well, so it wheeled about and dashed back into the cave where, in the half-light, the trappers finished it. The young bears were chased from the cave and promptly fell to the concentrated shots of the other hunters. That night there were fresh roasts over the fire for the whole camp—and a fresh round of storytelling.

Meek's most famous bear encounter occurred along the Yellowstone when he and two other trappers spotted a large bear busily digging roots beside the creek. Meek could not let the bear go its way without giving it one from Old Sally. His plan called for him to slip up and shoot the bear while his companions held his horse in readiness, in case he had to make a fast escape.

As he told Mrs. Victor, he slipped to within forty paces before bringing his gun up, but when he pulled the trigger, the cap burst. The sound was enough to alert the feeding bear. Baring her teeth, and growling from deep in her throat, the old bear rushed down on Meek, whose legs were pumping as fast as they could in his frantic effort to reach his horse, while attempting all the while to put another cap on the nipple of his gun. He was almost within reach of his jittery horse when all the horses and their riders bolted, leaving Meek alone with a maddened grizzly. The bear promptly ripped his belt off.

By now Meek's story is going very well. He explains that he had managed to put a new cap on his gun so he stuck the muzzle into the bear's mouth and pulled the trigger, but found that he had failed to set the double-triggered gun. The bear was angrier than ever. Just as Meek managed to set the triggers, the grizzly gave the gun a swat, knocking it from her mouth.

In that instant the gun fired but the bullet struck her well clear of her vitals, and this new injury added fuel to her anger. Then two large cubs, learning by example, joined their mother in attacking the trapper. The old bear knocked Meek's gun out of his hands, and he drew his knife. He stabbed her deeply behind the ear before she whipped a paw up, with lighting swiftness, and swatted that weapon from his hand also.

She was so angry that she next began abusing the cubs, which mother bears will often do under similar stressful circumstances. While she was engaged in this disciplinary action, Meek had time to get his tomahawk, his last weapon, into action. The bear now had him backed up against a rock ledge from which there was no escape. He was weaving and swaying like a boxer, following every movement of the old female grizzly until he saw his opportunity. With all his force he brought the tomahawk down behind her ear and sank the sharp blade into her brain. The mighty grizzly slumped to the ground and lay dead at his feet.

Another time, on Pryor's River, Meek and a companion went to run their beaver traps where the high banks above the river are lined with thickets of wild plum and willow. Meek had an uncanny feeling that there were strangers nearby. Two or three times he saw wild game running from the thicket. Osborne Russell recorded the event in his *Journal of a Trapper*.

Meek and his companion Dave Crow, a quiet little man who had been fifteen years in the Rockies, rode into Jim Bridger's camp where Russell was one of the brigade, and Russell heard Meek tell Bridger about the experience.

> *I have been, me and Dave, over on to Priors Fork to set our traps . . . Gabe, do you know where Prior leaves the cut bluffs going up it? . . . Well after you get out of the hills on the right hand fork there is scrubby box elders about 3 miles along the Creek up to where a little right hand spring branch puts in with lots and slivers of Plum trees about the mouth of it and some old beaver dams at the mouth on the main Creek? Well sir we went up there and yesterday morning I set two traps right below the mouth of that little branch and in them old dams and Dave set his down the creek apiece, so after we had got our traps set we cruised round and eat plums a while, the best plums I ever saw is there. The trees are loaded and breaking down to the ground with the finest kind as large as Pheasants eggs and sweet as sugar the'l almost melt in yo mouth no wonder them rascally Savages like that place so well—Well sir after we had eat what plums we wanted me and Dave took down the creek and staid all night on a little branch in the hills and this morning started to our traps we came up to Dave's traps in the first there was a 4 year old 'spade' the next was false lickt went to the next and it had cut a foot and none of the rest disturbed, we then went up to mine to the mouth of the branch I rode on 5 or 6 steps ahead of Dave and just as I got opposite the first trap I heard a rustling in the bushes within about five steps of me I looked round and pop pop pop went the guns covering me with smoke so close that I could see the blanket wads coming out of the muzzles. Well sir I wheeled and a ball struck Too shebit [Meek's horse] in the neck . . . and we pitched heels overhead but Too shebit raised runnin and I on his back and the savages just squattin and grabbin at me but I raised a fog for about half a mile till I overtook Dave.*

Even on his injured horse, Meek outdistanced the Indians, and he and Dave made it in to Bridger's camp.

In 1835, Meek's good friend and "booshway" Milt Sublette came down from the mountains and went east to get medical treatment for an old foot injury that was growing steadily more painful. The problem eventually claimed Sublette's life. As Meek tells it, Milt left behind his beautiful Indian wife, whom he called Isabel, and who was known among her people as Mountain Lamb. Meek had long admired her, and he told Mrs. Victor that Mountain Lamb was "the most beautiful Indian woman I ever saw." He described the dapple gray on which Mountain Lamb rode, her fine decorated clothing, and beautiful, braided black hair. Once Sublette was gone, said Meek, Mountain Lamb became Joe Meek's wife. Her life thereafter seems so filled with turbulence that one suspects Joe of story enhancement again.

One day when the camp was moving, she failed to keep up and a dozen Crow warriors swooped in and captured her. The enraged Meek and half a dozen friends took chase. He rode right in among the enemy shooting as fast as he could load. He and his companions killed two of the kidnappers, the rest fled, and Meek proudly led his wife back to camp.

Another day a few Crow warriors were visiting the trapper's camp when one of them made a serious error in etiquette. The records do not tell us why it happened. We learn only that this Crow warrior slapped the Mountain Lamb on her backside and Meek, as anyone might have predicted, shot him on the spot. "Nobody slaps Joe Meek's wife," he said. But Mountain Lamb did not have much time left. She and Meek had been together for only one year when, as the story goes, she died from a wound inflicted by a Bannock arrow.

With the fur business winding down, Meek, after eleven years in the mountains, began looking toward Oregon. He moved out with a wagon train of settlers, preachers, and gamblers. With him was his new wife, Virginia, a Nez Perce. They arrived in the Willamette Valley late in 1840.

In Oregon, Meek's Indian wife and half-blood children met frequent prejudice, but the family became prominent and Meek became a frontier leader. He farmed for a while, was elected sheriff, and was appointed United States Marshal of the new Territory. He later held other offices. Joe Meek, the happy mountain man, died proud of the fact that, "I never tried to act like anybody but myself."

LEATHERWORK

Leather was the raw material from which the mountain man manufactured many of the essential items he needed. He converted hides to clothing, gun covers, knife sheaths, parfleches (see pages 166–176), and the various pouches needed for his possessions. He learned to work with leather, and knew which hides were best for various purposes. Most of all, he learned how to treat leather to preserve it. Much of what he learned of dealing with skins and tanning them came from the Indians and, if he had an Indian wife, she inherited these chores.

The Indian method was to brain tan the hide by rubbing cooked brains into it. To prepare the hide for this step it was first soaked, stretched over a fleshing beam, and fleshed by scraping away the adhering fat and flesh with the aid of a sharpened scraper made of bone or elk antler. The end of the scraper was beveled and notched. A thong was threaded through a drilled hole and wrapped around the wrist for added pressure. Then the hide was turned over and the hair removed using the same scraper. Hair was scraped off and the hide stretched or rubbed

over a board or taut rope until soft and flexible. When finished, the brain-tanned hide was soft and nearly white in color.

The Indian or mountain man who wanted buckskin to be soft, darkened in color, and water-resistant smoked the hide. The hide could be suspended from a crossbar held between two forked sticks (see page 165, 1). Or the buckskin was sewn along the top and side around a tripod of saplings so the open end could be staked down over a smoldering fire (see page 165, 2 and 3). The wood was rotted or wet so it would not break into flame and burn the leather. A fire was built beforehand and allowed to burn down to hot coals, then smothered with rotted dry wood to produce smoke. After the hide was smoked, it was rolled and allowed to cure for several days. The smoke carried oils that penetrated the hide, giving it a degree of water resistance. The longer it was smoked, the darker it turned, and it needed frequent inspection to catch it at the color desired. Finally, the bag was turned other-side-out and smoked on the second side.

Trapper's Awl

Early fur trappers used an awl for making clothing and leather equipment. Awls were also a major trade item with the Indians.

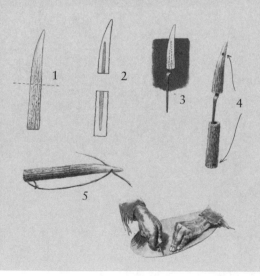

An awl was usually made from a forged cylindrical spike tapered at both ends and offset in the middle. For a handle, an antler was cut into two sections (1), each section drilled with a hole (2), and the pointed half forced over one end of the awl. The other antler section served as a kind of sheath (4), held in place by a leather thong (5).

Buckskin Shirt

Made of soft, tanned deerskin, the mountain man's shirt was worn long, usually halfway between his waist and knees, sometimes even longer. The front and back were cut as one piece to be draped over the shoulders. The shoulder area was reinforced by sewing in strips of leather from neck to sleeve. Then the sleeves were sewn in place, and the shirt turned inside out. Strips of leather were often added for fringe to both the sleeves and the sides of the shirt. The sides of the shirt were either laced or sewn.

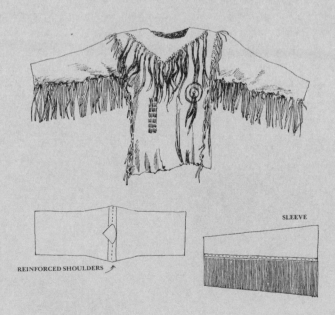

REINFORCED SHOULDERS

SLEEVE

Moccasins

Moccasins were made in many styles. Style shown here is one worn by northern plains Indians and also by fur trappers. Double and single thickness of rawhide could be sewn on the sole for added protection against cactus and rough terrain.

When the mountain man's footgear wore out, as it frequently did, he made himself a new pair of moccasins. The process was, as Rufus Sage, an early western traveler among the trappers, wrote, "a business in which every mountaineer was necessarily proficient . . ." In essence moccasin making consisted of wrapping a piece of leather around the foot, cutting the leather, and sewing it to fit.

The simplest moccasin of all may have been described by Hiram Chittenden. "The moccasin was made of a single piece of heavy dressed buckskin. A plain seam ran from the heel to the ankle, but the upper part, from the toe to the instep, was gathered. The shoe thread was the sinews of deer or of buckskin."

Rufus Sage wrote, "He merely takes two pieces of buffalo (or any other suitable skin), each being a little larger and wider than his foot, particularly towards the heel; these he folds separately, and lays them together parallel with the turned edges; then, rounding and trimming the sides, to render them foot-shaped, with an awl and the sinew of buffalo or other animal, or small strips of thin deer skin ("whang") he sews the vamps from end

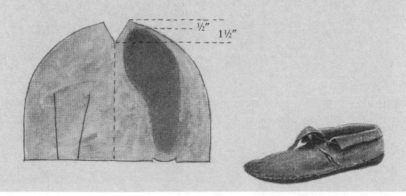

to end,—then after cutting a tongue-like appendage in the upper side, midway from heel to toe, and stitching together the posterior parts, his task is done."

Mittens

When setting traps or skinning and stretching pelts, the trapper could seldom wear gloves to protect his hands from the cold. But when he was traveling, hunting, or wood cutting, a pair of mittens could be valuable protection against the frigid weather of the plains and mountains. As he did for much of his equipment, the mountain man had to make his own mittens, or his Indian wife sewed them for him.

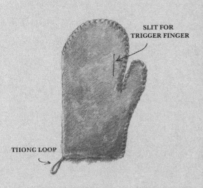

SLIT FOR TRIGGER FINGER

THONG LOOP

For this he usually chose deer or elk skin, well tanned, and made as soft and waterproof as he could get them but with the fur left on.

Leather Button

The mountain man had no store-bought buttons, so he ordinarily made his own. One common one was fashioned from soft, tanned deerskin, rolled tightly and held in shape by drawing the tapered end through a slit. The result was an easily made fastener that could be tied in position, and would hold a pouch shut, or light clothing in place.

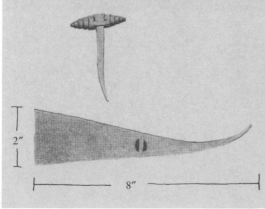

2"

8"

Leggings

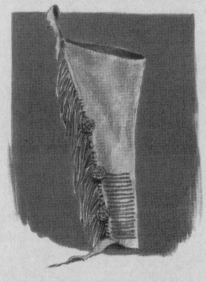

Mountain men sometimes wore leggings as added protection against weather, brush, and cactus. Leggings were made of heavy leather and individually fitted to the owner. The trapper measured the length of his leg from hip to ankle, the inside of his leg from crotch to ankle, and the circumference of his upper leg, allowing

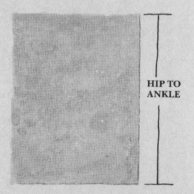

HIP TO ANKLE

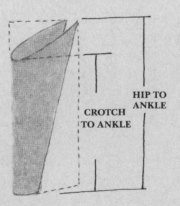

HIP TO ANKLE

CROTCH TO ANKLE

for a loose and comfortable fit. He cut two pieces, as shown, sewed or laced the sides, added leather for fringe, and sewed on a loop to attach the legging to his waistband.

Parfleche

Many trappers, especially those with Indian wives, adopted the Indian parfleche, a kind of leather envelope that served as a wilderness suitcase for carrying extra clothing and other property. The parfleche was also useful for carrying pemmican. The size varied, depending on the intended use, but the one shown here was highly popular and easily carried on horseback. The parfleche was normally made from buffalo rawhide. It was often highly decorated. Rawhide thongs held it shut and it could be stored either flat or hanging.

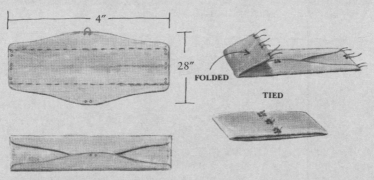

French Trapper's Pouch

French-Canadian trappers and boatmen often carried their possessions in this soft leather pouch equipped with a pucker string which was extended to serve as a shoulder strap. The pouch, measuring about 18 inches by 10 inches in diameter, was made of a single piece of tanned leather about 18 inches wide by 33 inches long. This allowed for an overlap to accept the stitching that converted the piece of leather to a cylinder. It

was fitted with a 10-inch bottom and a strong loop to which the shoulder strap was anchored. The pucker string was held shut by a slide made of a 2-inch section of bone drilled lengthwise so it could be threaded over the thongs.

Mountain Man's Knife Sheath

Common among the beaver trappers was a heavy knife sheath made so the belt held it securely in place. With the belt worn on the outside of the sheath the knife was not easily lost or grabbed by an unfriendly in case of hand-to-hand combat. The sheath was measured to fit the individual knife.

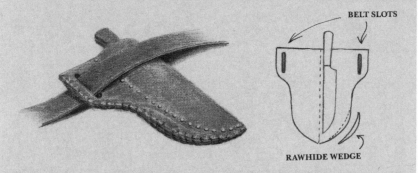

BELT SLOTS

RAWHIDE WEDGE

Tomahawk Sheaths

Mountain men commonly carried the tomahawk with the handle tucked down behind the belt, sometimes tying it in place with a thong to keep from losing it, while leaving it immediately available. Others made rawhide sheaths. The design of the sheath was a matter of personal choice. It may have covered the entire head of the tool or protected only the sharpened edge.

Horn Liner for Knife Sheath

A knife sheath lined with horn prevents the blade from cutting through the leather. Ohio buckskinner Karl Wilburn began this project by selecting a fairly straight horn. He chose one somewhat larger than the blade, allowing space to cut a slot for the belt. He removed part of the horn tip, but left the horn longer than the blade. Then he softened the horn by boiling it. Inserting the knife blade in the horn, he placed it between two smooth boards free of knots and prominent grain, and tightened the vise against the boards to flatten the horn and shape it to the blade. He left the horn in the vise overnight for thorough cooling and hardening. Then he used a drill and saw to cut the belt slot.

Using the horn liner as a pattern, Wilburn next cut leather for the sheath. He soaked the leather, fitted it to the horn liner, and laced the sheath along the open side while the leather was wet. After the leather dried, he removed the horn liner. Applying glue to the outer surface of the horn, he reinserted it in the sheath and let it dry under pressure.

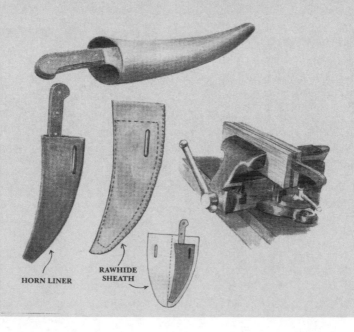

HORN LINER

RAWHIDE
SHEATH

Calf's Knee Gun Protector

The mountain man needed a method of keeping the powder dry in his gun. One common practice was to make a cover for the action of the flintlock from rawhide taken from a buffalo calf's knee. The shape of the knee naturally fitted it to the gun.

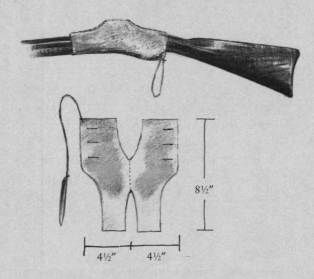

To make the calf's knee cover that he always uses when deer hunting with his 50-caliber percussion blackpowder rifle, Karl Wilburn of Ohio measured the gun and cut the leather to fit the pattern shown here. Using an awl, he punched holes and laced the calf's knee. Three sets of matching slots on the lower side hold a thin, flexible 4½-inch wand made of horn and secured to the cover with a thong. The cover is folded over the gun action and secured with the wand. For shooting, the horn wand is easily slid out so the leather cover can be removed quickly.

Buckskin Gun Case

Gun case design varied among mountain men. Some trappers used full cases elaborately decorated by their Indian wives. Others used plain cases and some used none at all. Materials commonly used were either blanket material or tanned buckskin that had been smoked and would stay soft. A major consideration in designing the case was always how fast the shooter could remove the gun. The partial case made without any flap to protect the end of the stock was popular because it could be stripped from the gun easily in an emergency when seconds counted.

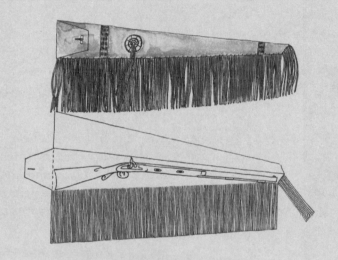

Pad Saddle

According to trapper Bill Hamilton, mountain men riding into skirmishes sometimes utilized the special lightweight pad saddle developed by the Indians. Indians used this substitute saddle, weighing perhaps three pounds, to give horses added speed and endurance in battle. The pad saddle, basically a leather cushion to be filled with dry grass or buffalo hair, was stitched through the center to divide it into halves. It usually measured about 20 inches long by 16 inches wide, and was equipped with girth and stirrups.

Rawhide Hobble for Horse

The mountain man faced the constant fear of losing his horse and being left on foot in the wilderness. To keep his horse from wandering too far as it grazed at night, the trapper secured the animals' front feet with a hobble. The hobble was sometimes made of woven buffalo hair but more often of heavy rawhide. The

strap was wrapped around one leg just above the hoof, twisted securely, then secured to the other leg. It was attached to the second leg by running the end of one strap through a slit in the other and holding it in place with a short stick. The 18-inch length of the hobble allowed the horse to move about enough to graze but kept it from leaving the area.

· 17 ·

To the End of the West

---

*T*he Green River rendezvous of 1833 was breaking up. The furs were sold, the earnings were gone, and the mountain men were once more loading pack saddles and heading out into the depths of the Rocky Mountains while maintaining a discreet silence about the secret creeks they intended to work. In this atmosphere, Joe Walker was supervising the assembling of men and the packing of supplies for a most unusual adventure.

Joseph Reddeford Walker was born in Tennessee in 1798 and was almost twenty-one when his family moved on to Missouri. Before he had been long on the Mississippi, his sense of adventure turned his eyes to the Rocky Mountains. Around 1820, he joined a party headed up the Missouri River, then westward following the Arkansas until the trappers turned southwest into New Mexico.

After Senator Benton and the United States Congress arranged for surveying the Santa Fe Trail, young Joe Walker signed on with the surveying party and helped lay out a wagon road as far as the Mexican border. Then he returned to western Missouri and joined in the early development of Jackson County. Independence, the county seat, was becoming a lively jumping-off place for anyone headed down the Santa Fe Trail.

Once local government was officially established, the frontier citizens of Jackson County began looking around for a sheriff. The towering Joe Walker, six feet four inches tall, dark complexioned, powerfully built, and even tempered, seemed just the man to maintain order in this rough frontier settlement. He served out his two-year term, then was reelected. By the end of his second term, the frontier was changing rapidly. The villages had regular streets with buggies and herds of moving livestock to keep the dust stirred up. This was no place for a man who dreamed of wide, clean land where a person could see no human or any of their works from one mountain range to the next. Each year the traffic grew and the restless Joe Walker knew that he had been long enough in one place.

He departed Independence early in 1831 for the Southwest, leading his own string of pack animals loaded with trade goods. On this trip he met Captain Benjamin Bonneville, a regular-army officer on special leave to organize an important journey of exploration into the Rocky Mountains. Bonneville signed Walker on to lead the party.

He had found a top man for the job. Joe Walker, a superb woodsman, excellent trapper, and fine marksman, was respected among the mountain men. He was a natural-born geographer, and all who traveled with him had confidence in his knowledge of the land. Walker was also restless, always ready for the next trip. Furthermore, in his quiet way, he had a knack for leadership. Zenas Leonard, the young adventurer from Clearfield, Pennsylvania, who signed on as clerk, and who kept a record of his experiences and observations, wrote of Walker, ". . . when our Captain was in the minority, and being beloved by the whole company, and being a man who was seldom mistaken in any thing he undertook, the men were very reluctant in going contrary to his will."

By summer rendezvous time on the Green River, Bonneville had a new plan, or perhaps he had it all along. There remains some confusion over precisely what Bonneville had in mind. Perhaps there were hush-hush instructions from Washington to send a party to probe the Mexican territory in California. Bonneville later said, when trying to explain away his own poor record, that he had instructed Walker only to go to the country around Great Salt Lake. However, it was common knowledge around the rendezvous that year that Walker's party was really headed for California, in Mexican territory. Joe Walker understood this all along. The California destination had been one of Leonard's reasons for signing on. Leonard had long wanted to enjoy the warm California climate and see the exotic sites of which he had heard. It was a feather in a mountain man's cap to say he had been all the way to California.

In the early part of Walker's trip all went well. There was abundant game, the travel was easy, and the line moved along in good spirits. As long as a mountain man could find buffalo to eat, he was content, but as they approached Great Salt Lake, the buffalo became increasingly scarce, and on the west side of the lake they found, and shot, the last buffalo they were to see on this westbound journey. After that the party sometimes ate sparingly—and sometimes not at all.

They passed Great Salt Lake and moved on west into Nevada following the Humboldt River, which lies within the Great Basin where streams do not drain to any sea but simply disappear as they sink into the sand. The unimpressive Humboldt became well known as the route of "The California Trail," and a major link between frontier settlements along the Missouri River and the California gold fields. The Humboldt gathers its waters from mountains whose peaks reach to almost twelve thousand feet. It flows westward, through north-central Nevada, then spreads out into the Humboldt Lake, commonly called the Humboldt Sink. There the thirsty sands swallow it.

Near the Humboldt Sink, Walker's party had its first serious brush with Indians. The area was occupied by the Digger Indians, a people known for their small stature and abject poverty. They were probably the most destitute people in North America, living on grass seeds and rabbits, as well as ants and other insects. Now and then, they took a fish with a spear, using for a point the sharpened leg bone of a sandhill crane bound to a pole.

These people might be excused for coveting the material goods that the seemingly wealthy white trappers carried into their land in such abundance. One trapper traded a member of the tribe a fishhook and two cheap metal awls worth a few cents for a robe made of perhaps forty dollars worth of beaver skins.

The traps used by the mountain men held such fascination for the Indians that they began following Walker's men and lifting their traps. This was viewed by some of the trappers as a capital offense, and they asked Walker's permission to shoot the Indians to "larn 'em some respect." Walker quickly and firmly drew the line. Permission denied. He preferred to deal with the Indians by peaceful means.

Many of Walker's group had never shot an Indian, however, and the opportunity seemed too good to pass up. ". . . some of our men were for taking vengence," Leonard wrote. One day, the trappers killed two of the Indians but did not let Captain Walker know of it. The next day they killed two more. This time Walker found out and dressed the offenders down properly.

But the damage had been done. Death chants sounded in the Indian camp. Day by day, the crowds of Indians following the party grew until there were several hundred of them. This worried Walker. These people, taken individually, were seemingly harmless. But the practical fact was that now several hundred of them were pressing the trappers and becoming increasingly bold in displaying their anger over the killings.

At one point the trappers, their backs to a lake, threw up a bulwark of equipment and luggage around themselves and their horses. The following day the Indians became bolder yet, threatening to overwhelm the white men. Large groups pressed in close to the trappers until Walker, deciding that the situation was explosive, gave his trappers permission to attack the Indians.

Thirty-two of the trappers now mounted their swiftest horses, checked their guns, and swept down on the Indians, killing thirty-nine of them within a few minutes. Those Indians not hit ran screaming for cover as the trappers moved among the victims "putting the injured out of their misery."

This massacre became the only lasting blemish on Walker's long career. People far from the scene condemned his action. Walker's defenders pointed out that he was hundreds of miles from help, that he could have been overwhelmed, and that he had to consider the threat to his mission.

As they moved west, Walker's men grew increasingly disheartened. Big game was scarce to nonexistent, and the trappers grew weary of eating the flesh of half-starved horses that died on the trail. They carried horse meat with them until it spoiled in the heat—and still ate it out of desperation.

Finally, they skirted the northern edge of Walker Lake in western Nevada. The desert, with its heat, hunger, and Indians, was not the last of the barriers faced by Walker and his men. Ahead of them now stood the Sierra Nevada, a towering range of snowy peaks blocking their way to the Pacific, and none of them knew a pass through the mountains.

After long days of tramping through the mountain snowfields, they came to what they believed to be the top of the range. Here they camped, but there was no food for the horses and only tough, stringy horse meat for the men.

Parties dispatched to search for both food and a pass across the mountains could find neither. Five days after reaching what they had believed to be the summit, the party was still climbing toward the snow-capped peaks. "Our situation was growing more distressing every hour . . ." Leonard wrote. At last, they came to the edge of the range and could look down on a spectacular distant valley with walls "almost perpendicular," and from this giddy height they began searching for an Indian trail that would lead them down through the rocks.

They came into an enchanted valley unlike anything they had ever seen before. Leonard described it. ". . . many small streams which would shoot out from under these high snow banks, and after running a short distance in deep chasms, which they have through the ages cut in the rocks, precipitate themselves from one lofty precipice to another, until they are exhausted in rain below. Some of these precipices appeared to us to be more than a mile high. Some of the men thought that if we could succeed in descending one of these precipices to the bottom, we might thus work our way into the valley below—but in making several attempts we found it utterly impossible for a man to descend, to say nothing of our horses." Joe Walker had discovered Yosemite, a scenic wonder that would become world famous.

Finally, one of the hunters shot and brought back to camp a small deer, and although this was not much food for the hungry trappers, it lifted their spirits. Then, they discovered a trail leading down toward the green floor of the valley far below. At one point they had to lower their baggage, and even their horses, over a cliff by ropes. That evening, shortly after dark, hunters brought in two large blacktail deer and a fat black bear.

Walker's party came to groves of giant trees higher than any they had ever seen before. They stared with disbelief at the astounding plants rising as high as three hundred and fifty feet into the air. Measuring them, they found trees with circumferences of a hundred feet. Walker and his men were standing beneath the towering redwoods of California, the world's tallest trees, some more than two thousand years old.

One evening in camp, some of Walker's men heard an unfamiliar rumbling. Lying down with their ears to the ground, they detected a constant sound like distant thunder and told each other that they were hearing the waves of the Pacific Ocean. The trappers were elated. ". . . we had stood upon the extreme end of the great west," Leonard wrote. The event filled them with a burst of patriotism, and they envisioned the United States as spreading her boundaries to the western ocean. "She should assert her claim by taking possession of the whole territory as soon as possible," Leonard wrote in his journal, "for we have good reason to suppose that the territory west of the mountains will some day be equally as important to a nation as that on the east."

Later, after reaching the shore, they had another totally new experience: they came upon the carcass of a ninety-foot-long sperm whale, perhaps the only time that Rocky Mountain beaver trappers found a whale. They also saw a ship anchored in the distance, and they raised a flag made of two white blankets. The ship moved in closer to shore, and crew members came ashore in small boats. The trappers learned that the ship was the *Lagoda* out of Boston.

Forty-five of the trappers then went aboard at the captain's invitation, and clad in their greasy buckskins, gathered around the ship's table laden with cheeses, bread, and other delicacies. The hospitable captain cracked open kegs of cognac, which the mountaineers drank from fancy glasses instead of cups made of tin or buffalo horn. The visit became still another high point in the Walker party's California experience. The ship's crew then came ashore with them and, during a party lasting through the night and into the next day, feasted on the first fresh meat they had eaten since shipping out.

Deer, elk, and bear were plentiful, and although the trappers still dreamed of buffalo steaks, they were living well again on the abundance of California's sleek big-game animals. Said Leonard, "These animals are the fattest of the kind I had ever eat."

Walker needed a place for his group to set up their tents for the winter, and found it at the mission of San Juan Bautista where the Spanish rulers and priests lived among several hundred Indians. In a region rich in grass, the Spanish raised cattle, splendid horses, bountiful gardens, and fruit, including grapes for the barrels of wine they made. The fur trappers had never before lived so well.

There were ceremonies, celebrations, feasts, bull and bear fights, and feminine company. Six of Walker's party, mostly carpenters and other craftsmen, decided to stay on in California where the living was good. The Mexicans offered Walker fifty square miles of land if he would stay and bring in fifty families of settlers. He decided, perhaps wisely, that a man with his wanderlust would always be discontented if he settled down in one location, especially one still beyond the borders of the United States. He turned down the offer.

Joe Walker moved his party out of its winter camp to make the long trip back across the rugged mountains, this time by Walker Pass. They returned in time for the 1834 summer rendezvous on Ham's Fork in southern Wyoming. Following the rendezvous, Walker led a trapping party north to the headwaters of the Missouri. Here he trapped, traded with the Crows, and was back on the headwaters of the Green for the rendezvous in 1835. After this he terminated his four-year relationship with Bonneville and became a brigade leader for John Jacob Astor's American Fur Company.

In the years that followed, Walker continued to trap and also serve as a guide for westbound parties. He was a guide for Frémont on his third expedition in 1845.

Walker's career took him over much of the West. Ardis M. Walker, writing of Joseph Walker's experiences in *The Mountain Men and Fur Traders of the Far West*, calls Joe's travels "fabulous," and they were. Even in a fraternity where all seemed to be in nearly constant motion, Joseph Walker was a phenomenon. His later years of cattle ranching in

California were still interrupted by frequent journeys to exciting parts of the West. As Zenas Leonard said of him, ". . . to explore unknown regions was his chief delight."

If you travel the West today, following the trail of Old Joe Walker, you will come upon places bearing his name—Walker Lake, Walker Pass, Walker River, and more. He died in the autumn of 1872, at the age of seventy-four, and directed that his headstone, in addition to the bare statistics, say, "Camped In Yosemite—November 13, 1833."

FIRE AND SHELTER

Fire was essential, and the trapper's most common practice was to start a fire using flint and steel. Fire-starting steels came in various designs. A common one was the C-shaped steel which fitted over three fingers. This was a popular trade item as well as an essential part of the trapper's outfit. In addition, the trapper carried flints against which to strike the steel. The shower of sparks produced was directed into a piece of charred linen, punk wood, a twist of dry grass, or tinder from the inner bark of grape or dead cedar. Once the spark caught, the tiny glowing spot was gently fanned or blown upon until it produced a small flame.

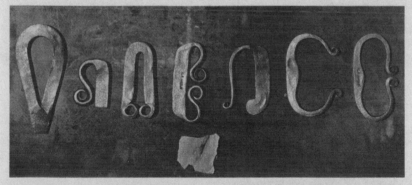

Seven types of strikers used by the mountain men to start a fire. These were made by blacksmith George F. Ainslie in his Prairie Elk Forge, *Lavina, Montana. From left: Voyageur, Crow, Mexican Chispa, English Trade, Colonial, Tom Tobins, French Recurve.*

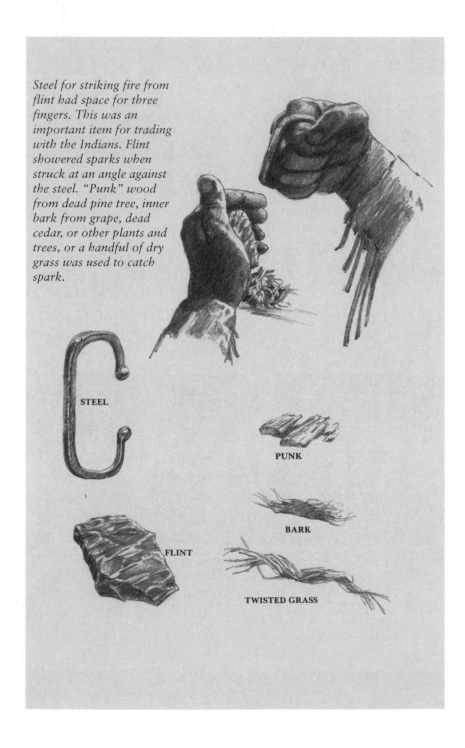

Steel for striking fire from flint had space for three fingers. This was an important item for trading with the Indians. Flint showered sparks when struck at an angle against the steel. "Punk" wood from dead pine tree, inner bark from grape, dead cedar, or other plants and trees, or a handful of dry grass was used to catch spark.

STEEL

PUNK

BARK

FLINT

TWISTED GRASS

The mountain man had alternate methods of fire starting. One was to use his flintlock. If the gun was loaded, as it invariably was, the trapper covered the touchhole, placed tinder in the pan instead of gunpowder, brought the

Mountain men carrying a flintlock also had a variation of the flint and steel in his gun. If the gun was loaded, he plugged the touch hole, placed tinder in the frizzen instead of gunpowder, brought the piece to full cock, and pulled the trigger. Then he put the burning tinder to his kindling.

gun to full cock, and pulled the trigger to send sparks into the tinder.

In addition to flint and steel, the mountain man often carried a "burning glass" with which he could start a fire on a sunny day. Lewis and Clark carried dozens of these small lenses for firemarking and trading.

Trappers traveling alone, or with one or two companions, were often caught away from their semipermanent camps in bitter weather. Weather permitting, the trapper slept beneath the open sky. He might take the trouble to place his buffalo robe on a mattress of leaves or pine boughs. Then he pillowed his head on his saddle and wrapped himself in his blanket for the night. If he was staying several days in the same area, or if the weather was especially threatening, he built a primitive shelter, usually near a stream where, in addition to water, he could find wood for his fire and grass for his horse. His hut would often be no more than a buffalo robe stretched over a framework of saplings stuck in the ground and bent over at the top. In front of this shelter he built a fire to reflect warmth on his bed.

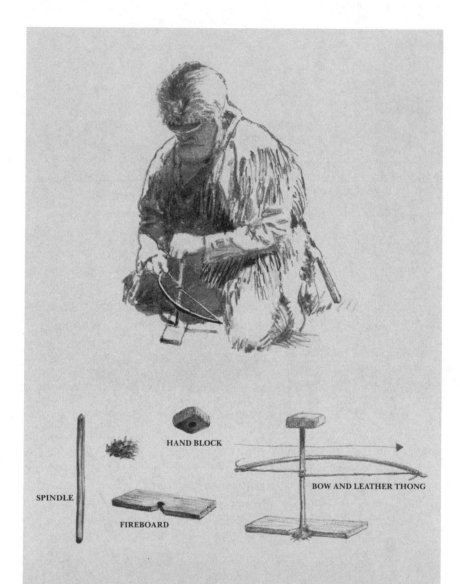

SPINDLE

HAND BLOCK

FIREBOARD

BOW AND LEATHER THONG

As a last resort, the trapper could use the Indian method of starting a fire with a bow and fireboard. He placed the fireboard on the tinder; put the spindle, blunt end down, in the hole; and braced the hand block against his knee. Looping the bowstring on the spindle, he moved it rapidly back and forth, increasing pressure and speed until friction brought the tinder to the kindling point.

To build a winter shelter, a trapper often formed a dome-shaped framework of freshly cut poles stuck in the ground. Willow poles were preferred. Then he covered the framework with skins sewn together.

Sometimes he erected an open-faced shelter with a fire in front for cooking and heat.

· 18 ·

The Marryin' Kind

Some years after James P. Beckwourth, a husky, medium-sized black man, left the fur business, he sat down and related his wild adventures to journalist T. D. Bonner. The result was, in some ways, the strangest of all the tales of the mountain men.

Beckwourth's mother was a slave on a Virginia plantation where his father was the plantation overseer. When young Jim was twelve years old, his father took him to St. Charles, Missouri. A couple of years later the boy was apprenticed to a blacksmith, but he had scarcely begun to force air from the leather pleats of the bellows before he knew that he definitely did not want to spend his life in a smithy's shop. Iron mongering wasn't his calling, and after a few years he decided to escape. After he and his master exchanged strong words about Beckwourth's staying out late at night chasing girls, the husky young apprentice, a brash, strong-willed, and by his own admission, volatile young man, let his master have one alongside the head and took his unauthorized leave.

Those were heady times along the Mississippi. The talk was of beaver trapping, and Beckwourth's introduction to the trade started when, at nineteen, he accepted a horse tending job offered him by General Ashley. Beckwourth left behind his sobbing sweetheart, Eliza.

He practiced his marksmanship and perfected other outdoor skills and soon became, by his own testimony, a first-rate trapper, hunter, scout, and Indian fighter, skilled enough in all to work as a free trapper.

Whatever we know about Jim Beckwourth, there can be no doubt that he was a gifted storyteller. Campfire storytelling was a popular entertainment form and stretching the truth to improve a story was more art than sin. Some who traveled with him just said plain out that Old Jim was an outrageous liar. But in recent years, historians have found

enough evidence to prove that many of his immodest claims were justified, even though he did have a compulsion for making himself the hero
of his own stories. To hear him tell it, Beckwourth was hell on Indians.
His account of his mountain adventures leads to the belief that the native
tribes were vanishing because of equal parts smallpox, disappearance of
the bison herds, and the arrival of Jim Beckwourth.

According to Bonner's *Life and Adventures of James P. Beckwourth*, published in 1856, Jim's life as an Indian began when he went
among the warlike Blackfeet to serve as a trader. This was risky business.
The Blackfeet knew that he had taken the scalps of their brothers. But his
reputation for bravery saved him. Courage in the face of extreme danger
was honored, and the fact that Jim would come among them to trade was
proof enough that he had backbone. The tribe's fights with neighboring
Indians became his fights too. "I soon rose to be a great man among
them," Beckwourth said with his usual modesty.

"One of the chiefs offered me his daughter for a wife." Beckwourth had been married only a few days when his temper and impetu-
ous nature brought him what he referred to as a "slight difficulty in my
family affairs."

The problem began when a jubilant war party returned to camp
holding aloft coup sticks on which dangled the bloody scalps of three
white trappers. Beckwourth seethed, but considering the company he was
keeping, there was not much he could do about it. His temper surfaced
quickly, however, when his new wife wanted to join in the fun during the
scalp dance. Surely, Beckwourth's words on that occasion have been san-
itized by his biographer, who has him saying, "You must not rejoice when
my heart cries out." What he probably said was more like, "Them's my
friends yore wantin' to dance over and you just stay out of it or this child's
gonna knock you on yore ass." Whatever his words, the meaning was
clear: he flatly forbade her to join the scalp dance.

A short time later, when a friend came into his tent to report that
his wife was the best of all the dancers, Jim lost his temper again, grabbed
his battle ax and ran out among the dancers. He pushed through the
crowd, stalked up to his bride, and using the side of his ax, rendered her

a thudding blow on the side of the head which, in his own words, "dropped her as if a ball had pierced her heart."

Silence settled over the stunned crowd. In the next instant the cry went up for Beckwourth's death. As his recently acquired relatives moved to place him on a huge bonfire, Old Jim knew he had a problem. Then, his new father-in-law, the chief, stepped forward and delivered a powerful oration. He had lost a daughter, he said, but "That thing disobeyed her husband . . . When your wives disobey your commands, you kill them; that is your right." His combination of logic and tribal law quieted the troops.

Later in the day, the chief gave the trapper a younger and more beautiful daughter, "in place of the bad one," and Beckwourth was married again, as he said, before he "even had time to mourn." But that night, when snuggled beneath the warm robes and just beginning to appreciate his new wife, someone crawled into his lodge, sobbing. His first wife had recovered. He now had two wives and claimed that, all the while, he was still pining for Eliza back in St. Louis.

Twenty days later, when he was thirty-nine packs of beaver pelts richer, Beckwourth left the Blackfeet and returned, with a large Indian escort, to Ashley's camp. To keep everyone happy, he sent some gifts back to his abandoned wives and father-in-law.

Beckwourth's Indian days, however, were only beginning. Later the American Fur Company dispatched him to establish trade with the friendly Crow Indians, and a new world opened for the young Beckwourth.

He fared better with the Crows than he had with the Blackfeet. The Crows accepted an unlikely story that one of Beckwourth's fun-loving friends handed them. With tongue in cheek, the trapper explained that Beckwourth was really the long-lost son of their chief, stolen as a small boy twenty years earlier by the Cheyennes and now a mighty brave. Before the tribal rejoicing could reach fever pitch, an aged lady emerged from her lodge. She walked slowly up to Beckwourth. She stared into his face. "If he is my son," the old lady announced, "there will be a small mole on his eyelid." Silence settled over the crowd and strong hands gripped tomahawk handles. Beckwourth's eyelids were pulled down and examined. His good fortune was holding; on one of his eyelids there was a small mole which, for the first time in his life, he fully appreciated.

The whole village erupted with wild dancing and singing while the prodigal son was hugged and kissed by crowds of relatives or, as he said, "welcomed nearly to death."

That first evening, his newfound father, the old chief, wanted to know if his son, now called Morning Star, wanted a wife. What could Beckwourth do? The next day one of the chiefs sent his three beautiful young daughters over so Beckwourth could take his choice. The trapper selected the eldest, in part because he liked her name—Still-water. They were exceedingly compatible. Beckwourth said the only thing troubling him now and then were his recurring memories of St. Louis and Eliza.

For the next several years, Beckwourth lived as a member of the Crow tribe, relishing the attention of the women, the opportunity to lead warriors to victory over other tribes, and the ease with which he could acquire furs from the Indians. He became a leader of the Crow warriors, and with repeated demonstrations of his skills, shooting, and battle strategy, his fame grew.

As a Crow chief he was naturally at war with the powerful Blackfeet. In one of these attacks, Beckwourth and a companion found themselves in a monumental footrace with a large party of antelopelike Blackfoot runners. Thoughts of St. Louis flashed through Beckwourth's mind. Would he ever again set eyes on the fair Eliza? "The Indians were close at my heels," he said, "their bullets were whizzing past me; their yells were sounding painful in my ears; and I could almost feel the knife making a circle around my skull."

He figured that he ran ninety-five miles that day before reaching the safety of his own party. Mountain men, listening to the story later, allowed that what Old Jim claimed would sure to hell be a full day of runnin', and no doubt "Old Jim *felt like* he run that fur. Wagh!" The Blackfeet ran him so hard that he needed three days to recover. His Crow companion, who had hidden among the rocks, came in on the third day. "Morning Star dead," he said. Then he saw Beckwourth grinning at him.

Off the battlefield, Jim's time was occupied with family matters. If a Crow maiden began to appeal to him he took her to wed. Eventually he had eight wives in separate lodges. There were, however, still two of the Crow women who fascinated him, perhaps in part because they seemed unavailable.

Pine Leaf was one of these. Jim Beckwourth admired her for her bravery and brains, as well as her beautiful face and the way her body moved beneath her buckskins as she walked around camp. But Pine Leaf was an angry woman. Her twin brother, a promising young man, had been killed, and Pine Leaf swore that she would kill a hundred Cheyennes in revenge before she would marry. In addition to her physical beauty, and other admirable qualities, Beckwourth liked the way she swung a battle ax and the wild abandon with which she could plunge her spear through an enemy warrior. Pine Leaf could count coup and take scalps with the best warriors of the Crow nation. Beckwourth told of the day a Blackfoot warrior swung his war ax down, aiming at Beckwourth's head. Pine Leaf dashed in and ran her spear through the enemy warrior, thereby destroying his concentration. The war ax missed Jim but killed his horse. Beckwourth looked longingly at Pine Leaf. "I began to feel a more than common attachment toward her," he said.

Not surprisingly, when they were riding one day across the prairie, Beckwourth asked Pine Leaf to marry him. She told him that he had too many wives already, but laughed and said, yes, she would marry him.

"When?" Jim asked.

"When the pine leaves turn yellow." Days passed before the jubilant trapper remembered that pine leaves don't turn yellow. The next time he asked her, she said she would marry him when he could find a red-headed Indian. Beckwourth was getting nowhere with this one.

Even more of a challenge was a beautiful Crow woman named Red Cherry who was secretly lusted after by a fair share of all the young warriors in camp. The major obstacle in any romance between Beckwourth and Red Cherry was that she was already the wife of Chief Big Rain.

According to his story, Beckwourth kept up his hot-breath pursuit until Red Cherry, obviously impressed, agreed to ride off with him and carry his shield into battle. For this, Chief Big Rain, following tribal custom, gave Beckwourth a severe public flogging. This happened two more times, each with similar results. If this was expected to teach somebody a lesson, it wasn't working, and finally Big Rain faced facts. Beckwourth rewarded the chief with an outrageous list of gifts, and Red Cherry became Beckwourth's latest wife.

About this time, Beckwourth took a trip back to St. Louis to see his family. His father was dead. When he went to look up Eliza, he found that she thought he too was dead, and had recently married.

Among the Crows, Beckwourth's fame as a warrior continued to rise. He became an important chief. But he was growing weary of the Indian life. His restless nature was telling him that the time had come to move on. One person among the Crows, however, thought she knew a way to keep Beckwourth in the tribal fold.

By this time, Pine Leaf had more than kept her vow to the Great Spirit and fully avenged the death of her brother. "I believe you love me," Beckwourth is quoted as remembering her words, "for you have often told me you did, and I believe you have not a forked tongue. Our lodge shall be a happy one."

"This was my last marriage in the Crow nation," Beckwourth said. After the ceremony, the newlyweds left for a few days of combination honeymoon and hunting trip.

A scant five weeks after his marriage to Pine Leaf, he announced that he must journey back to St. Louis on business. That was the last time the beautiful Pine Leaf, or any of his other Crow wives, ever saw Jim Beckwourth.

Although Beckwourth may have set something of a matrimonial record, the taking of Indian wives was a common practice among the mountain men. The wife had her own work. She made the camp, packed and moved, cooked, and sewed. She cleaned skins and searched for plants that added variety to the meat diet. Her heritage fitted her to the rugged outdoor life of the mountain man. Furthermore, as the wife of a trapper

Horn Cup
A large section of horn could be turned into an attractive and serviceable cup and carried in the mountain man's gear. The horn was cut with one side long enough to provide for a handle which could be bent to the desired shape after the horn was softened by boiling. The bottom of the cup was fitted with a wooden plug.

she gained prestige and wealth. The trappers outfitted their wives in the finest clothing and decorations they could buy at rendezvous.

Jim Beckwourth, back in St. Louis, joined a company of Missouri volunteers to go to Florida and fight the Seminoles for the U.S. Government. This too lost its appeal after some months, so Beckwourth returned to St. Louis. But his trail soon led back to the beaver country.

On a trip to the Southwest in 1860, he met a Spanish girl of considerable beauty and brought her back to Colorado as his latest wife. Four years later, when Beckwourth's wife ran off, taking along their daughter, he did not bother to follow. Instead, he took another Indian wife and settled down to ranch, mine, and trap.

Perhaps his last trapping trip, long after the large populations of beaver were cleaned out, was with three companions in 1866. The four trappers and Beckwourth's current wife headed off for a region that Beckwourth knew well—the Green River country. There the Blackfeet attacked them and only Beckwourth escaped to make his way back to Denver.

In one last journey, he returned to the Crows as an emissary to open negotiations between the Indians and the United States Army. While visiting the Crows, he became sick and died. In the Crow tradition, his body was wrapped and placed on a platform in a tree, ending the long and strange adventures of James Beckwourth, trapper, trader, Indian chief, and lover.

· 19 ·

Journal of a Trapper

The four buckskin-clad beaver trappers thought they had an idyllic campsite, but they didn't know yet about the war party of Blackfoot Indians peering at them through the underbrush. All around them were the towering lodgepole pines, and stretched out before the pleasant campsite was a bright green meadow, offering excellent grazing for their horses. Summer flowers dotted the edge of the meadow and a little stream of cold, clear water gurgled down past the camp. The stream wound through the meadow and carried the snowmelt into the broad blue waters of Yellowstone Lake near what is today Fishing Bridge in Yellowstone National Park.

The Indians were patient. No need to hurry. Besides, they harbored a deep respect for the long guns the white hunters kept close at hand. By the time the Indians crept up on the little encampment, the trappers were well settled. Two of them had set off into the forest to shoot an elk for camp meat.

Meanwhile, the trapper named White lay down on the soft mattress of pine needles to take a peaceful afternoon nap. The fourth trapper was Osborne Russell, who later recorded the events of that day in his already mentioned *Journal of a Trapper*. Russell had finished running his beaver traps and was spending a quiet hour working on his equipment. Then, taking his rifle, he started down the lakeshore, just enjoying the beautiful day and the mountain scenery. Russell was the rare mountain man with a sense of appreciation for the splendor of the landscape. "My comrades," he once wrote, "were men who never troubled themselves about vain and frivolous notions, as they called them. With them every country was pretty when there was weather and, as to beauty of nature or art, it was all a 'humbug' as one of them often expressed it." But Russell was known to climb a mountain all the way to the snow line simply to sit there on a granite ledge for two hours or more gazing out over the peaks, ridges, and valleys and contemplating the nature of the universe in all its Rocky Mountain splendor.

On this day, beside the shore of Yellowstone Lake, he stripped off his buckskins and laid them out beside his rifle, which he had leaned against a pine tree. He then spent a lazy half hour bathing in the icy mountain lake. He dressed and wandered back toward camp. It must have been at about this time that the Blackfeet came upon the little camp and hid in the bushes to reconnoiter and determine how to capitalize on their good fortune.

Hungry after his swim, Russell went first to the spot where they had spread out their stock of dried meat, perhaps forty yards from their bedding area. There, he removed his powder horn and bullet pouch and laid them out carefully on a log. Carrying the meat, he moved back toward where White was still sleeping, sat down, and ate until his hunger was satisfied. He then kindled a fire, removed his pipe and tobacco from his carrying bag, and, lowering himself onto the pine needles carpeting the forest floor, started to enjoy a smoke.

But as he lifted a glowing stick from the fire and touched it to the tobacco in his pipe, he raised his eyes to scan the campground and reassure himself that all was in order. But all was not in order. The Indians had begun to move, and Russell saw the heads of a few of them as they slipped through the underbrush toward the horses. Russell grabbed his rifle and yelled "Indian!" which brought White out of his sleep as few other words could.

Both trappers now had their rifles in hand, but neither was close enough to his powder and lead. In fact, one of the Indians was already escaping with Russell's powder horn and bullet pouch.

The two trappers were now completely surrounded by the yelling Blackfeet, and they were down to one shot each. They cocked their rifles, picked a spot in the circle of Indians, pointed their guns at the enemy, and began a desperate effort to stay alive. Said Russell, ". . . the woods seemed to be completely filled with Blackfeet who rent the air with their horrid yells."

The Indians, who were directly in front of the trappers' guns, wisely gave ground, opening a twenty-foot gap through which the mountain men plunged as they headed for the forest. White had taken only a few steps when he felt the impact of an arrow penetrating his right hip. Russell yelled at him to yank out the arrow but keep running, and even as he spoke, another arrow found its mark in his own hip.

Moments later, with both trappers still running at top speed in spite of the arrows they had taken, another arrow thudded into Russell's right leg and the pain was so severe that he stumbled. The floor of a lodgepole pine forest is often littered with downfall timber, lying at all angles, and now Russell was stretched across a log, in plain view of the Indian who had scored with the second arrow.

As the warrior leaped the short distance over the fallen logs and brought his war ax high above Russell's head, the trapper rolled swiftly to one side. The ax came down where his head had been, and Russell leaped to his feet. He and White resumed their mad scramble through the forest from log to log while arrows continued to whistle past them.

When the trappers had gained a little distance on the yelling Indians, Russell whispered to White. Both men whirled about and took dead aim at the Indians. The Blackfeet darted behind trees, giving the trappers time to put another fifty yards or so between themselves and the Indians.

They had now come to a place where they had to make a stand. Russell's leg gave him much pain and the loss of blood had weakened him. They dropped into a fortress of fallen logs which hid them from the Indians who were searching the forest everywhere around their hiding place.

Russell's plan now was to make a final desperate stand, die like men, and take at least two of the Blackfeet with them. He whispered to White to take the first Indian who turned his eyes on them and he would get the second one. They rested their rifles on fallen logs and tried to calm their breathing to steady their hands. The Indians apparently believed that the two trappers were still on the run. The first group of perhaps twenty warriors scrambled past without even glancing at their hiding place. A second line of Indians raced through the woods on the other side of the little nest of fallen logs, and even though they were within twenty or thirty feet of the trappers, they did not see them.

The two files of Indians came together again beyond the trappers hiding place and raced on through the woods and out of sight. As long as Russell and White could hear them running they did not move. Finally, they crawled out of the log pile and hobbled off toward the lake, a quarter of a mile distant. Russell had to stop and rest his injured leg frequently.

The Blackfeet doubled back and the trappers could hear them yelling as they took possession of the camp and everything they owned, including horses, food, skins, and personal items. After moving along the lake for a mile and a half, Russell called a halt. He could go no farther.

With some of the pressure off, and time to reflect on their chances, White began to come apart. He started whimpering and saying they would never get out of this situation alive. Russell was more experienced and a leader by nature. He had once been as green as his companion. But a person learned quickly in the wilderness or he did not survive. He felt somewhat responsible for the safety of White. The kid had come from a Missouri family that pampered him and never gave him much to do beside "horse racing and gambling." Russell gave White a verbal lacing that went something like, "If you think you're going to die, you'll die sure enough. But I'll tell you this—I'm not going to die. I can crawl from this place on my hands and one good knee. And I can kill two or three elk [he didn't say how without powder or bullets], make a shelter of the skins, dry the meat and live on until I'm able to travel again."

White was in better shape than he thought. His wound was superficial. After spending a miserable night beside the lake, they moved quickly into the pine forest just in time to escape the Indians now coming in their direction. They watched from the pines as sixty Indians came on the scene, singing and talking. But the Indians were interested in a herd of elk swimming in the lake. The Blackfeet killed four of the elk and spent the next several hours dressing them out and packing the meat so they could carry it with them.

Now, the trappers began their long journey back toward Fort

Hall, which is eight miles or so north of Pocatello, Idaho. First, however, they returned to their campsite and there found one of their companions. The Indians had chased the other two men when they came back searching for Russell and White. The trappers had escaped but the fourth member was now lost in the forest. He eventually made his way back to Fort Hall alone. The Indians had left behind nothing but a bag of salt.

In the following days Russell and his little party, trying to get back where Russell could get medical attention, traveled lean and hungry. They made miserable little camps and shivered through the nights. In spite of Russell's injuries, they covered twenty miles the first day and thirty the second. Their return route took them across the towering snow-capped Grand Tetons, probably, as historian Bernard DeVoto believed, by way of Moran or Cascade Canyon, down the west slope, then through miles of sagebrush flats. The last two days of their journey they covered more than sixty-five miles through country where game was so scarce that they were completely without food. Russell's condition grew steadily worse until he finally had to stop every few minutes to rest. With several miles remaining to go, the party met a trapper from the fort who took Russell the remainder of the way on his horse, bringing him finally to Fort Hall.

Once in the fort, Russell rested, ate well, applied salve to his wounded leg, and, after only ten days of recuperation, was back setting beaver traps in that glorious season when autumn turns the aspens yellow on the mountainsides.

Russell was leading life as he preferred it. This Rocky Mountain splendor through which he wandered was a world apart from the life he once knew. Beaver trapping was his deliverance from the known and predictable, his escape route from the dull life into which his boyhood friends had drifted. The adventure, scenery, freedom, and promise of riches from fur justified the hours of hardship and risk of life.

He had come here from Maine, and Oz Russell began to dream of more exciting adventures in distant places.

His first plan was to go to sea, and at the age of sixteen he ran away from home and shipped out. But the life of a sailor confined to his ship bored young Russell, and when his ship tied up at the harbor in New York, he jumped ship and turned inland. The next we hear of his travels he was, according to Aubrey L. Haines, who edited the best-known edition of Russell's famous *Journal of a Trapper*, in the fur business. He was working for the Northwest Fur Trapping and Trading Company in the Minnesota and Wisconsin area.

From there his trails led westward, and after some years he appears in the Rocky Mountains ready to begin his career as a beaver trapper. Unlike many of the mountain men, Oz Russell could read and write and, unlike most, he began keeping a journal of his travels. That journal has since become one of the most valuable of all records telling us how these wilderness trappers lived and worked in the Rocky Mountains.

"At Independence, Missouri, on the 4th of April, 1834," wrote Russell, "I joined an expedition fitted out for the Rocky Mountains and the Mouth of the Columbia River, by a company formed in Boston under the name and style of the Columbia River Fishing and Trading Company." Russell agreed to work for this company for eighteen months for two hundred and fifty dollars.

He was excited by the promise of adventure that lay ahead as a line of forty men, each leading two loaded pack horses, moved out across the prairies. His company was loaded with supplies slated for delivery to the Rocky Mountain Fur Company during one of the last of the mountain-man rendezvous on Ham's Fork in southwestern Wyoming.

But the fur industry was beginning to lose its vitality, and by the time the supply convoy reached its destination, the Rocky Mountain Fur Company, which had contracted to buy the supplies, was out of business. A good stock of the supplies remained unsold, and this prompted Russell's employer to build a fort for supplying trappers. This was the beginning of Fort Hall in southwestern Idaho, where he was left to work, as the main body of the party moved on toward the mouth of the Columbia River.

Now he was dreaming of becoming a free trapper. But he had lessons to learn. Unlike many, he had not brought a lot of outdoor skills west with him. He knew that he was green, and he was not one to gloss over his lack. His early fumbling efforts make all the more remarkable his eventual proficiency as a hunter and wilderness survival expert.

Less than a week after the main party of his company pulled out for the mouth of the Columbia, leaving Fort Hall in the care of the twelve-man team, Russell and three others were dispatched to find and shoot some buffalo. This was a totally new experience for the young man from Maine. Some distance from the fort they began to see bands of buffalo. "I now prepared myself," wrote Russell, "for the first time in my life to kill meat for my supper with a rifle."

He lowered himself to hands and knees and began crawling toward the grazing animals, carefully moving the gun with which he had so little experience. He came to a point some eighty yards from the animals, slowly stood up, and took what he believed was careful aim. His choice was an impressive bull, although a cow would have provided better fare.

At the crack of Russell's rifle, the bull ran off a short distance with the rest of the herd. But the bull was wounded, so Russell reloaded and took a second shot, after which the bull was still on his feet. He stayed on his feet as Russell sent bullet after bullet in his general direction. As fast as he could reload and shoot, Russell continued trying to bring the bull down until, as he admitted, "I had driven twenty-five bullets at, in, and about him which was all that I had in my bullet pouch. Whilst the bull stood apparently riveted to the spot I watched him anxiously for half an hour in hopes of seeing him fall, but to no purpose." When the party returned, Russell helped pack in the two buffalo the others had killed.

Russell's early inexperience could have ended tragically. Shortly after his first buffalo-hunting fiasco he was again sent into the field to hunt. This time he and his companion encountered a grizzly bear feeding peacefully on roots dug from the soft earth near a patch of willows. Here was Oz Russell's first opportunity to graduate into the ranks of the bear killers.

The two men moved in on the bear, their guns cocked and ready. The bear roared in pain and surprise when Russell's companion shot it through the shoulder. It dashed into the willow thicket, and the hunters advanced on it, guns again ready. They came within about ten feet of the bear without seeing him. Then the beast shook the willows with his roaring and charged, mouth open and "eyes flashing fire."

Instead of shooting, the two hunters took to their heels. They ran in opposite directions, and the bear selected Russell, chasing him to the edge of a swamp. There, Russell had no choice. He wheeled and faced the animal, which slid to a stop ten feet away and stood on his hind feet towering over the trembling hunter.

In that instant Russell pointed his rifle and pulled the trigger because, as he said, he didn't know what else to do. He claimed that his rifle just happened to be pointed toward the bear. But it was pointed very well: the bullet went through the giant bear's heart and it "uttered a deathly howl and fell dead." Russell claimed that it took him half an hour to control his trembling so he could help butcher and pack the hide and meat on the horses for the trip back to the fort. Afterward Russell made a secret promise to himself that never again would he pursue a wounded grizzly into heavy cover.

Other than that, any grizzly would remain fair game. One November afternoon while hunting the high country for sheep, Russell took time out to rest on a rock ledge from which he could view the broad mountainside. Soon he spotted a sluggish grizzly resting outside its den. Russell began his careful stalk, and while still a hundred and eighty yards from the bear, he took careful aim, shot, and missed. The bear glanced around, then moved into its den.

No bear was going to escape a mountain man this easily. Oz Russell reloaded, slipped up to the mouth of the den, rolled into it a five-pound rock, and stood back with his gun at the ready. But the bear chose to ignore the provocation. Next, Russell began tugging and straining at a rock that weighed perhaps three hundred pounds. As it began rolling down into the den, Russell leaped back, waiting to see what would happen. He did not have long to wait. The annoyed bear charged from its den, mouth open, and rushed the hunter, who promptly shot it through the left shoulder. The grizzly dropped on the spot and rolled down the hill. The following day Russell returned to camp with his load of bear meat ready for salting and storage for winter.

After his service at Fort Hall, Russell signed on with Jim Bridger's brigade. These bands of trappers, sometimes a hundred strong, offered company and protection. But the elite of the mountain men were the free trappers.

Before long Russell became a free trapper and soon proved that he was among the best of them. There was an everlasting element of uncertainty in the daily life of the mountain man and this may have been a large part of its appeal. Russell was sharply aware of the hazards in this Rocky Mountain world. He liked to say that the earth would lie as heavily on the monarch as on the hunter. Then he would speculate that perhaps the earth would not lie upon his bones at all, but that at any time they might well be "... bleaching on the plains in these regions like many of my occupation, without a friend to turn even a turf upon them after a hungry wolf has finished his feast."

He had come to the profession later than some and was reluctant to leave. Finally, in 1843, after nine years as a mountain man, Russell moved out of the Snake River Country, away from Fort Hall, and headed for Oregon. He found his way to the fertile lands of the Willamette Valley. There, he was working for a contractor when an explosion blinded his right eye. He next went into politics, served on an early governing body overseeing the affairs of the Provisional Government of Oregon, then served as an appointed judge.

Judge Russell later moved to California where some of his business dealings turned sour and his health failed. Nobody can say whether or not the years of wading icy mountain streams, living in rain, snow, and bitter weather contributed to his rheumatism and the paralysis that afflicted him from the waist down. He died in 1892, when those years of wild mountain living were a fading memory.

Trappers Who Fished

Mountain men often carried fishhooks in their gear and, given the opportunity, caught and ate everything from trout to catfish. There was nothing fancy about their fishing gear. Hook and line were attached to a willow stick cut from the stream bank, and the hook was baited with whatever live bait was available—worms, minnows, grasshoppers, grubs. These offerings often yielded large, unsophisticated trout from the wilderness waters.

According to research done by the Museum of the Fur Trade, fishhooks carried by the early trappers were handmade hooks from England and looked much like today's hooks. The major difference was that the end of the shank was flattened and not shaped into an open eye. These hooks were popular trade items among the Indians when dealing for furs.

In an emergency the mountain man could take fish by more primitive methods. Some doubtless used bone hooks as the Indians had long done. Trappers could also capture fish in basket traps made of willow sticks.

One trapping brigade, after weeks of near starvation in the southwestern deserts, arrived at the Snake River where trout were plentiful. They had no hooks but one of them, while working with his saddle, discovered a large pin the saddlemaker had left in the saddle by mistake. When fashioned into a hook, it caught enough large trout on live bait to feed the brigade. Furthermore, there were enough left over for the trappers to ride off the following morning with large trout tied to their saddles.

Bone Hooks

The mountain men learned to make bone hooks from the Indians. Selecting a hollow leg or wing bone of a turkey or other large

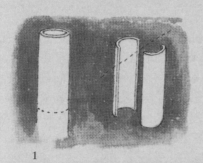

1

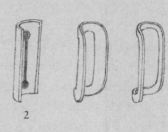

2

bird, the trapper sawed off a small piece and then cut it in half, lengthwise (1). He bored two holes in one of the blanks, scratched a line between them, and widened it until it became a hollow ring (2). Then he cut the ring (3) to get two hooks, which he sharpened on a stone (4), and went fishing.

3

4

· 20 ·

The Bones of Old Black Harris

Successful mountain men were often naturally gifted with tremendous strength and stamina. They survived days and nights that taxed their bodies and souls beyond the average man's tolerance level. Such a phenomenon was Moses "Black" Harris, whose name was known wherever fur trappers went. Harris had two specialties, one of which was storytelling. Jim Beckwourth, no slouch as a yarner himself, labeled Black Harris as one of the western mountains' premier dealers in tall tales. Harris probably created stories for which others, including Jim Bridger, were sometimes given credit.

Most famous of all these tales was a harmless yarn that traced its origins to a field of petrified logs found by a trapper in a lonely canyon in Wyoming. The story was a natural for those who specialized in elaborating on yarns they'd heard around the campfires, and every time it was repeated it grew a little bit. Frederick Ruxton wrote that Black Harris, the campfire raconteur, might even repeat the story back in St. Louis.

In Ruxton's story, Black Harris returns from the hills after three long years of trapping on the Platte and beyond. Once back in civilization, he decks himself out like a "Saint Louiy dandy," and is ready and willing to make social contact.

He sits down to dinner one day in a tavern, and a lady says to him, "Well Mister Harris, I hear you're a great traveler."

"Traveler, marm," says Black Harris, ". . . I ar' a trapper, marm, a mountain-man, wagh!"

"Well, Mister Harris, trappers are great travelers and you goes over a sight of ground in your perishinations, I'll be bound to say."

"A sight, marm, this coon's gone over, if that's the way your stick floats. I've trapped beaver on the Platte and Arkansa, and away up on Missoura and Yaller Stone; I've trapped on Columbia, on Lewis Fork, and Green River; I've trapped, marm, on Grand River and the Heely [Gila]. I've fout the Blackfoot (and d—d bad Injuns they are); I've 'raised the hair' of more than one Apache, and made a Raphaho 'come' afore now; I've trapped in heav'n and airth, and h——; and scalp my old head, marm, but I've seen a putrefied forest."

"La, Mister Harris, a what?"

"A putrefied forest, marm, as sure as my rifle's got hind-sights, and she shoots center. I was out on the Black Hills . . . whar was green grass, and green trees, and green leaves on the trees . . . and this in Febrary, wagh!"

Harris, with straight face, continues his travelogue, explaining how he shot the head off a singing bird and the head rolls across the ground and just keeps on singing and when he picks it up—"I finds it stone, wagh!"

In various versions of the story, by Harris and others, the tree in which the petrified bird rested had turned to stone. So had the grass and sagebrush around it. The whole valley was petrified. And why were the trees green in February? "Why, marm, raise this child's scalp if it ain't so, them sunbeams was putrefied too, wagh!"

The mountain storyteller's popularity hinged, in part, on the fact that he was forever adding to his repertoire of tall tales. On occasion, Jim Bridger, normally a quiet and serious man, joined the storytellers. A traveler once asked him, "Mr. Bridger, how long have you been in these mountains?"

"See that big hill yonder?" Bridger is quoted as answering. "When I first come to these parts, that hill warn't nothin' but a hole in the ground."

Mountain man Warren Angus Ferris wrote of the trappers, in *Life in the Rocky Mountains*, "They told as extravagant yarns as they pleased and we believed as little as we liked." One hunter would tell of coursing an antelope for a full week over the Wind Mountain Range without pause for food or drink, then the next one would try to top him with a wild account of how he rode a grizzly bear, full tilt, through a village of Blackfeet.

Although his stories made Harris welcome around the campfires, this wiry, sinuous mountain man spent most of his time off in the hills, making his own trails into distant and silent valleys, weathering a climate as bitter and threatening in winter as any on earth. In fact, Harris became known as a specialist in solitary winter travel.

One who trusted this trapper's skills on the snowy trails was William L. Sublette, older brother of Milton. The Kentucky-born Bill Sublette went up the Missouri with Ashley's second expedition in 1823 and was there for the famous Arikara attack, escaping with his life by swimming to his boat through volleys of lead and arrows. Sublette then went with Jedediah Smith's overland party headed for the beaver streams in the Rockies, as well as the group that first crossed the South Pass, opening the way to work the beaver-rich waters of the Green River and the Southwest. He later joined Smith and David E. Jackson to buy out Ashley's company.

Most mountain men were content to sit out the bitter mountain winters, huddled around the fires in their skin lodges. There they did such work on traps, saddles, and firearms as they considered essential, gathered fuel for their fires, hunted for meat, played euchre and did not risk lightly a lonely death by freezing or the blow of an Indian hatchet. But if the winter trip had to be made, they were ready to go. In the heart of the winter, Sublette knew that he had to get a message back to St. Louis, across several hundred miles of frozen wilderness. Their agreement with General Ashley called for informing him by March 1st, 1827, if they wanted him to supply their rendezvous in the coming summer. Unless they could arrange this with Ashley, their trapping season, and therefore the continued existence of their fur company, might suffer a fatal blow.

Sublette, who was the partner in charge of business arrangements, decided to make the journey personally, and looked around for one of his men to go with him. Two travelers could protect each other and stand a better chance of getting through than one person might, and a traveling companion would take the edge off the loneliness during the long weeks of hiking through the white wilderness. Sublette's choice for a partner was Moses Harris.

He had several reasons for selecting Harris. First of all, the iron-tough Harris could probably stand the trip if any man among them could. Harris, born in the Appalachian foothills southeast of Spartanburg, South Carolina, had come to the mountains in the awakening years of the fur industry. He soon demonstrated that his remarkable stamina kept him on the trail when others could not hold up.

Harris had rawhide for muscle and steel for nerves. Artist Alfred Jacob Miller, who sketched Harris, in 1837, described the famous trapper. "He was of wiry form, made up of bone and muscle, with a face apparently composed of tan leather and whip cord, finished off with a peculiar blue-black tint, as if gunpowder had been burned into his face." Harris was of medium height and had black hair and whiskers and brown eyes.

He may have first met Sublette after signing up with Ashley for the general's ill-fated boat trip up the Missouri in 1823. Some historians consider it probable that Harris also was in the first Ashley crew the year before.

Sublette and Harris, carrying their message to Ashley, left winter camp in Cache, or Willow, valley and headed east for St. Louis on the first day of January 1827. Sublette allowed two months for the trip, planning to reach St. Louis by March 1st.

They set off on foot. Horses would have found the going impossible in the deep snow, and besides, there would have been a serious problem finding forage for the horses. The only animal accompanying the two travelers was a pack dog on which they arranged small packs of provisions, Indian fashion. The dog could travel easily across the crusted snow.

In addition to their supply of dried buffalo meat, blankets, rifles, and lead and powder, the two trappers carried snowshoes, which they frequently needed where snow drifted in the valleys.

For days they pushed eastward, over ridges and along the slopes, two dark spots inching across an endless white winter landscape. Sharp wind buffeted them. Biting cold numbed hands, feet, and faces. At night they dug down into the snow, kindled a small fire, melted snow for water, chewed on their supply of cold jerky, then wrapped themselves in their robes and slept fitfully with the arctic winds whistling over them.

Summer or winter, the mountain man on the move was constantly alert for signs of wild game, but Harris and Sublette found little game to supplement their slender rations. Among the animals they did take during those two long months of walking were a rabbit and one deer. One day they shot a raven and ate it. Another day they came upon some wild turkeys, killed four, and feasted.

When they were still a couple of hundred miles out of St. Louis, they ran out of food and could find no game. Night came and Sublette snuggled down in his robes trying to sleep on an empty stomach. Then, Harris made a suggestion that almost sickened him. Harris had been watching the dog that had trotted along with them for hundreds of miles. The dog, also hungry, continued to carry its pack. It limped badly. Harris suggested that they eat the animal. Sublette finally agreed, but killing the dog was not easy.

Harris tried to dispatch the animal with a single blow of his hatchet but, weakened by lack of food and long days of walking, only struck it a glancing blow in the neck, and the dog ran whining off into the night. Sublette and Harris scrambled after it and soon recaptured it, and, while one man held the dog, the other finished the grim job. Harris threw the body on the fire to singe off the hair and roast the meat, and dog meat renewed their strength for the next couple of days.

Indians were also a threat. The trappers had been under way only a short time when they cut the trail of a large band of Indians. An experienced mountain man could easily identify Indians by the style of moccasins worn; these tracks were left by Blackfeet, and no doubt about it. The trappers slipped away, making a long detour, and avoided the warriors. They also came upon a band of Pawnees and, because of the advanced stage of their hunger, followed the Indians and asked their help. The Pawnees were as destitute as Sublette and Harris were. Sublette did succeed in trading his valued butcher knife for a single buffalo tongue, which was eaten at once. Harris had injured an ankle and Sublette, still hoping to stay on schedule, traded his pistol for a horse, which lent some speed to the last miles of their journey.

The messengers limped into St. Louis in early March and, in spite of all their problems, they were only three days late, still in time and able to make their arrangement with Ashley for rendezvous supplies.

This winter journey had to be repeated three years later when Sublette and Harris once more traveled to St. Louis in midwinter from their winter camp on the Wind River in Wyoming. This time they traveled for six weeks. Harris, the specialist, continued to make difficult winter trips as long as he was in the mountains.

Later, as the settlers looked to the west, and wagon traffic picked up on the Oregon Trail, Harris was among the mountain men whose guide services were in demand. He led the eastern farmers, merchants, and miners over trails he had memorized in two decades of mountain travel. At night, around their campfires, Harris' stories of wild adventures with wild animals and wild Indians mesmerized the travelers. He was setting out at the head of a wagon train from Independence, Missouri, in 1849 when he contracted cholera and died.

Moses Harris, known as Major Harris, and sometimes called "The Black Squire," left no family in the East that anyone knew about. A Missouri reporter of the day wrote that, as he lay dying, Harris whispered that ". . . among some unknown tribe of Indians he had a wife and two children . . ." and asked that word of his death be spread along the route west so his family would know that he had gone under.

Behind him, Moses Black Harris left his legacy—a man of special skills, not only in beaver trapping, but also in winter travel and, perhaps most of all, in brightening the travels of others who heard, then repeated, his fantastic stories, keeping his memory alive long after he was gone.

The *St. Louis Reveille*, in an 1845 story, proclaimed Harris, ". . . as fearless as an eagle, strong as an elk, preferring the wild haunts of the Indian and the buffalo to the tameness of civilized life."

James Clyman once wrote a brief, inelegant poem to the memory of his friend Moses Harris.

Here lies the bones of old Black Harris
who often traveled beyond the far west
and for the freedom of Equal rights
he crossed snowy mountain heights
was free and easy kind of soul
Especially with a Belly full.

· 21 ·

Trappers in the Southwest

As America pushed westward there lived at the leading edge of the frontier a breed of restless hunter always longing to leave the settlements and move deeper into the wilderness. Just as this longing drove Daniel Boone and Simon Kenton over the hills and into the forests of Appalachia, it drew men of James Ohio Pattie's nature off on their grand adventures.

Pattie came honestly by his wanderlust. His father Sylvester, driven by the same urgency, had brought his family out of Virginia to the Kentucky frontier, then farther west to Missouri. There, Sylvester operated a sawmill on the Gasconde River, and his boy, James Ohio, doubtless sawed logs in his father's mill.

When young James's mother died of tuberculosis, Sylvester Pattie looked at his brood of nine children and began parceling them out among relatives and friends. Then he and the oldest son, James Ohio, now twenty, struck out for the western mountains. Sylvester Pattie never saw the rest of his children again.

His plan was to go up the Missouri, into the Rocky Mountains, and set himself up as a fur trader and trapper. The fur business was flourishing and others were leaving for the mountains. Pattie found three other men to join the party, and the five future beaver trappers set out with ten horses, carrying their traps, blankets, guns, ammunition, knives, tomahawks, utensils, and other goods essential for trading with the Indians.

They were scarcely under way up the Missouri, however, before they ran into their first serious trouble. At Council Bluffs the commanding officer called Pattie in and asked to inspect his permit for going into Indian territory as a trader. The fact that they needed such a permit came as a complete surprise to Sylvester Pattie, and he had to make a hard decision. He had already talked with others headed southwest toward the Spanish territory of New Mexico, so they altered their course and turned toward Santa Fe.

This was the beginning of several years of incredible adventures. We know much of what happened to Sylvester Pattie and his son James Ohio during those years because James Ohio Pattie left one of the most interesting journals of any of the mountain men. *The Personal Narrative of James O. Pattie* makes it plain that this young trapper and adventurer led a life filled with hazards. Although serious historians must make allowances for Pattie's flair for storytelling, his book leaves us a valuable look at the life and wanderings of those mountain men working at the southern edge of the beaver country.

The route led the party westward from Council Bluffs through what is now Nebraska, Kansas, the southeast corner of Colorado, and on toward Taos, in northern New Mexico. Taos was then an important center of fur trappers working the southern part of the Rocky Mountains. Here trappers could replenish supplies and live in relative comfort between trapping seasons. Taos was much closer to the beaver country than St. Louis was. Eventually, James Ohio Pattie's travels would take him across Arizona, where he trapped heavily, deep into Mexico, and on to the Pacific Ocean in Spanish territory as far north as San Francisco. He also made at least one long swing into the heart of the northern Rockies.

Life would have been simpler for Pattie if he could have trapped beaver without becoming involved in so many side issues. By his own account, life in the Southwest was one conflict after the other. When Pattie and his father arrived in Santa Fe, they requested of the governor that he grant them a license to trap the Gila River. This stream showed high promise because the Spanish, although they sat on top of this rich resource, never bothered to take many beaver.

From the first, the Patties' chances for obtaining the needed permits were slight. But the night before they were to hear the governor's decision, all manner of alarms suddenly awakened the entire town. A messenger brought news that the daring Comanches had robbed and murdered a number of people on outlying farms, and had taken four women off as prisoners. One of them was Jacova, the beautiful daughter of a former governor. The following morning the fully armed mountain men joined Spanish troops and set off to rescue the captives.

About noon of the fourth day, they spotted the Indians and put themselves in a position to intercept the column. "Every man was ordered to prime and pick his gun afresh," wrote Pattie. The risky plan was for the American sharpshooters to drop the Indians closest to the prisoners before the Comanches could kill their captives.

At the head of the column were the women, driving the stolen sheep and horses. The women were without clothing and Pattie immediately noticed the beautiful Jacova. The riflemen allowed the column to come within thirty or forty yards, and as they commenced firing, three of the captive women were speared. Jacova ran straight for Pattie, so he wrote, and he gallantly stopped shooting just long enough to wrap her in a blanket. Young Pattie was thanked and praised by Jacova for his bravery, and later the governor and his daughter took him to their lodging place where he was given a room. The episode cost him his buckskin hunting shirt, however, because Jacova said that she wanted to keep it as a remembrance for the rest of her life.

Predictably, they were granted their trapping permit, and soon set off to trap the Gila.

They stopped over on the way at the Santa Rita copper mines where Sylvester Pattie would eventually become the manager. They had soon trapped two hundred and fifty beaver. They stretched and dried the skins on hoops made of saplings, as they feasted on the meat.

Grizzly bears seemed to be almost as common as beavers, and Pattie looked upon bears about as he did Indians; they always needed to be taught a lesson. Besides, chasing and killing grizzlies was rare sport for this Missouri squirrel hunter. One morning, while out tracking down the horses on a small tributary of the Gila, Pattie and a companion came upon a cave at the foot of a cliff. They stood studying the scene. "Them bushes looks mighty beaten down," Pattie said, and the tracks in the snow convinced him that the cave harbored a bear. Pattie never hesitated or questioned the wisdom of disturbing the bear in its slumbers. As he must have explained his plan to his companion, "Way I figure it, we both go in together. This way we kin confuse him and stand a better chance at shootin' Ole Grizz before he kin get us."

"Wagh," says his hunting buddy, "I tell you true, Jim, this child's not aimin' to go in any cave with a grizzly bear and git hisself kilt or mortal wounded."

"Now Hoss, we bin through a lot of hard times together," Pattie argues, "and you ain't never seen *me* let *you* down when there was danger." But none of his arguments could bring his companion closer to the cave, so Pattie explains that he prepared to handle the bear alone.

He began cutting pine knots and fashioning a torch. His plan called for confronting the bear head-on. He tied pine knots to a pole and struck a fire to light his torch. Holding the flaming sticks out in front of him with the same hand that cradled his gun, he moved slowly into the cave. Some distance into the darkness, a huge grizzly bear stood up about seven feet in front of him and the chamber echoed with its roaring. Said Pattie, "I leveled my gun and shot him between the eyes and began to retreat."

As the trapper whirled in his haste and headed for the exit, he stumbled and fell. This put his torch out. Behind him the wounded bear thrashed about and bellowed. Pattie scrambled from the cave, his face pale and his legs bleeding from the rocks. He had dropped his gun in his rush to escape.

Somewhat later, carrying a new torch and a borrowed gun, he edged back into the cave, only to find the bear dead. The bear was so heavy that they had to go for help, and four trappers had all they could manage to drag it out of its cave. Pattie claimed this was the largest grizzly he had ever seen. They rendered ten gallons of oil from it.

There were days in the mountains when the trappers could find no wild game for food. When the trapping was good, they could live on beaver, but sometimes their traps waited empty for days at a time. Pattie reported that on one of these days of scarcity, his party of seven trappers had a raven for breakfast and, later in the day, shot and ate a vulture.

They made their way back to the governor's house where the beautiful Jacova greeted the unwashed young American trapper as if he were a prince. But the good times were not to last. They next went to recover a cache of beaver skins they had hidden, only to find that someone had discovered the furs and made away with two hundred and fifty skins. Indians got the blame.

Pattie's father accepted an offer to stay and work the copper mines, but James Ohio said, "I had a desire which I can hardly describe, to see more of this strange new country." He set off on another long trapping journey down the Gila. He soon encountered a band of Indians who had his father's horse, still recognizable by the halter it wore. The young trapper and his companions discussed the matter with the Indians. While they talked, they held their cocked guns pointed at the Indians' chests, and the Indians not only returned the horse but also gave back a hundred and fifty of the beaver hides they still had. The trappers and Indians parted friends—of sorts.

But Pattie seemed unable to maintain friendly relationships with any Indians for long. He spoke often of killing them, sometimes scalping them, and even cutting off their heads, with no twinge of conscience. Once more he visited the beautiful Jacova, who urged him to cease his running about among the dangerous Indians and bears. But that was not to be; his answer was to organize another trapping trip with fifteen other American trappers.

They tramped along the shores of the Del Norte, then turned up the Pecos, through wild and rugged country. All was proceeding well enough, and the trappers were finding wild game to eat and beaver to trap when they suddenly met a war party of Mescaleros. The shower of arrows sent the trappers dodging behind the trees. Arrows were the only weapons this tribe possessed, but the Mescaleros proved themselves to be exceptionally capable bowmen. Pattie reported that their bows were powerful instruments fashioned of "elastic and flexible wood, backed with sinews of buffalo or elk." Apache arrows were made from lightweight hollow reeds in which they inserted pieces of hardwood plus a flint point. The shaft had a tendency to shatter, and when pulled out, it sent sharp splinters into the flesh of the victim while the point often separated and also stayed in the victim.

In this kind of skirmish the trappers drove off the Mescaleros but lost one of their companions and had two more injured, one of whom was Pattie. One arrow was deeply embedded in his hip, another in his chest. One of the trappers succeeded in cutting the arrow point out of his chest with his butcher knife, but part of the point in his hip had to be left there.

They soon met a band of Navajos searching for Mescaleros to kill. The Navajos were elated by what these white brothers had done to their enemies. They were overjoyed when they saw the Mescalero scalps. The Navajos accompanied the trappers for some time, while a medicine man treated Pattie with a healing salve that made his injuries bearable. Pattie had reached a new level of friendly relations with at least one group of natives.

After some more trapping, and killing "plenty of bears" to show them that they "should mend their rude manners," Pattie arrived at the settlement of San Tepec. Here he met a few of the trappers who had come to the Southwest with the original party. Pattie asked about men he knew from that earlier trip. He was told that of one hundred and sixteen men who came into the Southwest together, only sixteen remained alive.

Pattie continued his adventures in the Southwest. In one fight with an enraged female grizzly, he waited until the bear was within six feet and fired at her head only to have his gun "flash in the pan." Leaping over a precipice, he cracked his jawbone and knocked himself out on the rocks below. He awakened to find that his companion, following the current medical treatment, was in the process of bleeding him although his chin was still bleeding profusely. Within an hour he recovered enough that the two trappers decided they could now finish what they had started with the bear. They found her, and taking aim, both fired at the same instant and killed her.

Neither bears nor Indians, however, presented the Patties with as serious a threat as did some of the Spanish officials. Upon their arrival from one of their journeys, the current governor seized all their valuable furs, claiming that they were taken without the proper permits. He then locked the trappers in the stone jail where they stayed week after week. The elder Pattie died in his cell during this period, and a platoon of soldiers escorted James Ohio Pattie to his father's burial.

Pattie might also have died in jail except that word arrived of an outbreak of smallpox approaching the city. Pattie knew how to vaccinate people against this scourge. He was released and promised payment to travel up and down the coast of California dispensing vaccine to both white people and Indians in the missions.

He then learned that he was to be rewarded with a thousand head of livestock and the land to graze them, providing he would convert to Catholicism and become a Spanish citizen. The short-tempered Pattie, who saw no virtue in silence, said in effect that he would as soon be dead as belong to the band of robbers and murderers living along this coast. Then, to avoid being hanged for his insolence, he made a rapid departure.

In time, he took passage on a ship bound for New Orleans. From there he made his way up the Mississippi, then up the Ohio. He had no money to show for his six hazardous years in the Southwest, but he hoped to sell his story.

In Cincinnati, he met Timothy Flint, an educated man and noted editor and writer of the times. Flint was absorbed by the story of this twenty-six-year-old man who looked old beyond his years. He listened to the tales of Indians, bears, Spanish missions, and beaver trapping. Flint then recorded *The Personal Narrative of James O. Pattie*. He had saved an important segment of the wild adventures of the mountain men, tales that would otherwise have been lost for all time.

At last, after wandering over more of the West than most of the mountain men ever saw, James Ohio Pattie was back in Kentucky. But his boyhood world had changed. The forests were disappearing to make way for corn. The little stream he once fished for sunfish and Kentucky bass was no longer shaded by giant trees, and was almost dry. He scarcely recognized his enfeebled old grandfather who had once been a vigorous hunter and proud soldier. James Ohio sought out his brothers and sisters, but they were now strangers to him.

For a time he remained, visiting one relative after the other in their homes. He was saddened because he could never fit back into this picture. "If there is a lesson from my wanderings," he wrote, "it . . . counsels the young against wandering far away . . ."

But did he mean this? Would he truly have advised the hunter living in the days of the mountain man to stay at home and hoe corn? Pattie would surely have ignored such counsel himself, even if he could have seen what lay ahead of him.

Back in Missouri, his own wanderlust still would not let him rest. Little more is heard of James Ohio Pattie, but he apparently was drawn back to California during the years of the gold rush. There is some belief that he was caught in a devastating snowstorm high in the Sierra Nevada. Years later, one of his sisters would say this was the last she had ever heard of him, and that he had apparently died either in the storm or at the hands of the Indians.

THE MOUNTAIN MAN'S CACHE

When his bundles of fur became too heavy and bulky for the trapper to carry in his normal trapping operations, the mountain man stored them so, if all went well, they could be reclaimed later. The furs had to be kept safe from moisture, gnawing animals, and human eyes. His storage place was known as a cache (pronounced *cash*). Once stored in a properly constructed cache, as Captain William Clark explained in his journals, "... the skins and merchandize will keep perfectly sound for years."

First, the trapper selected a dry area, safe from flooding. Then he began digging. He cut out a two-foot circle of sod and carefully placed the removed earth on a buffalo robe or blanket. He dug straight down for twenty inches or so, depending on the firmness of the soil. Then he began widening the hole. As the hole deepened, it gradually took on a bell or jar shape. Depending on the amount of goods to be stored, digging might continue until

Beginning to dig the cache. Depending on the amount of his goods, the trapper might dig until the excavation was six or seven feet deep.

Lining the floor with cured buffalo or deer skins. Dry sticks formed a barrier between the packs of fur and the pit walls.

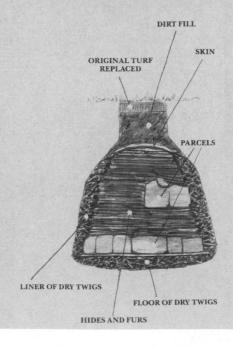

the excavation was six or seven feet deep. As an added precaution against water, the bottom was dug slightly deeper in the center.

Care was always taken to make the site as natural looking as possible. "As the earth is dug," wrote Clark, "it is handed up in a vessel and carefully laid on a skin or cloth, in which it is carried away, and usually thrown into the river, or concealed so as to leave no trace of it at all." Digging deep pits calls for special care because of cave-ins. There is a record of one mountain man dying when buried in one of these holes.

Next, the bottom of the hole was floored with a layer of dry sticks three or four inches thick, and finally covered with a cured buffalo or deer skin. This made a dry base for the cached goods.

The stored materials were arranged so they did not touch the sides of the hole. Dry sticks formed a barrier between the packs of fur and the walls of the pit. Only thoroughly dried material was stored in the pit.

Once the hole was nearly filled, the trapper covered his stored goods with a skin. Then he completely filled the hole with earth put aside for the purpose. He tamped the earth down thoroughly to prevent the settling that might give away the location or create a low spot to collect water. Finally, he replaced the plug of sod so it was level with the surrounding ground, brushed away all loose dirt, and used twigs to erase tracks in the grass.

One additional step was essential. The trapper took exact measurements from landmarks that would resist decay or erosion. Months might pass before he returned to collect his furs, and he must be able to find them. Almost certainly, furs and tools cached by mountain men lie buried to this day.

The Old Trapper
and the Kid

Although by 1840 both the supply of beaver and the demand for their furs were falling off, hopeful young trappers still flocked to the mountains in search of adventure. Among these latecomers was Billy Hamilton, who arrived in the West in a rather strange fashion. He had the good fortune to meet Old Bill Williams, one of the best known of all the trappers and one of the most expert of wilderness travelers. Williams was among those old-timers not yet ready to give up the mountain man's enviable, free-wheeling lifestyle.

Others of like mind still roamed the hills in little bands of free trappers, prospecting for beaver in valleys that had been tramped time and again. They took enough fur to supplement their trading with the Indians and keep them in the mountains they had come to love. By this time, they were, as Bernard DeVoto wrote in *Across the Wide Missouri*, "historical curiousities." They were also turning to the harvest of other natural resources, especially buffalo parts. Eastern people were buying buffalo robes, which were shipped out of the West by the bale. Old records tell us that in the early 1840s, some ninety thousand buffalo robes a year were shipped. Charles E. Hanson, Jr., writing in the quarterly publication of The Museum of the Fur Trade, says, "By 1840, the tanned buffalo robe had completely supplanted the beaver skin as the prime resource in the western fur trade." In 1848, a hundred thousand of these robes reached St. Louis, along with twenty-five thousand buffalo tongues, which were salted down and shipped by the barrel.

Old Bill Williams, who still signed himself "Master Trapper," sometimes interrupted his roaming long enough to show up at one of the forts, or even make a trip back to St. Louis to see his family, while outfitting for his next trip into the mountains. It was on one such visit in 1842 that he met the kid, Billy Hamilton.

Old Bill must have harbored serious reservations about young William T. Hamilton when the lad's father first approached him with his request. Hamilton senior, who had brought his family over from Scotland and eventually landed in St. Louis, explained that his twenty-year-old son William was having medical problems. Coughing. Fevers. Lethargy. His doctor, at a loss for any better suggestion, said that the young man should have a change of climate, and now William's father was suggesting that Old Bill and his free trapper partners take young William along to the Rocky Mountains.

If Old Bill hesitated about wet nursing a green kid through a land infested by hostile Indians and ill-tempered bears, his reluctance broke down when Mr. Hamilton offered to buy his son's way into the partnership. The offer came just when money was needed badly to purchase trade goods for the coming journey. The kid turned out to be an eager, clean-cut youth, seemingly alert and companionable, so Old Bill said yep, he reckoned Billy could tag along.

This was the beginning of an adventure that lasted through most of Bill Hamilton's long life. Even though he did come into the fur trapping business late, he was soon building a reputation as one of the more able mountain men ever to ride the trails. Later he wrote of these wild adventures in a book he called *My Sixty Years on the Plains*. His book is the source of most of what we know about his remarkable skills and adventures.

From the first, Hamilton was called "The Kid" by other members of the party. Although inexperienced, he was a natural shot, excellent hunter, and master horseman. Most of all, he possessed a hunger for the woodsman's knowledge, and was now surrounded by men whose years of trapping in the mountains had taught them every trick of survival. Perhaps the most skilled of all, and surely among the most famous, was the group's leader, Old Bill Williams.

This combination of old mountain man and young greenhorn was a happy one. Old Bill, who was fifty-five when the party left St. Louis in the spring of 1842, was thirty-five years older than Hamilton. He soon discovered that he liked this energetic kid. Wrote Hamilton, looking back on the occasion, ". . . few fathers ever gave their sons better advice." Before long, Hamilton noted with pride that the mountain men quit calling him "Boy" and began addressing him as "Bill."

He soon displayed an aptitude for learning the universal Indian sign language by which people of the Plains tribes could understand each other. Successful white traders and trappers managed to learn enough signs to get by in basic dealings with the Indians, but Bill Hamilton became a master at "hand talking," his dexterous fingers flying through the signs so swiftly that Indians frequently asked him which tribe he came from. He was often called in whenever other trappers needed to deal with Indians. Of one of these times Hamilton wrote, "The chief was a fair sign-talker but he was somewhat astonished to see a smooth-faced boy who could excel him."

The big adventure for Old Bill's party, and therefore for Bill Hamilton, began with stories told them by a former Hudson's Bay Company trapper named Duranger who spoke highly of the Walla Walla country where there was abundant beaver for the taking. Old Bill allowed that was one section of the country he always wanted to see anyhow. Others in his group soon voted in favor of the trip, even though the journey would require thousands of miles of travel and keep the party out for two years or more.

The group that set forth in March 1843 for the Blue Mountains of the Pacific Northwest included forty-three trappers, well equipped for trapping and also leading five horses packed with goods to trade with the Indians for furs. The trappers were divided into four subgroups. Each of these, called a "mess," shared duties as well as income from the furs it took.

The first serious problem with unfriendly Indians occurred in Oregon when the trappers came upon a village of Bannocks, one hundred lodges strong. The chief, flanked by his highly painted sub-chiefs, rode out to meet the trapping party. Hamilton fully understood every sign the Indians made and knew what the chief meant when he demanded to know what they were doing on his tribe's lands. He also understood when the chief demanded ponies in tribute and insisted that the trappers open their packs for inspection.

Hamilton's signs made it immediately clear to the chief and his scowling entourage that Old Bill's party had no intention of giving away their ponies or opening their packs. Nor did they intend to depart from the area or even stop trapping. At Williams' direction, Hamilton told the chief to have his people clear the way, that the white trappers were going forward. The chief was "thunder-struck" by this boldness.

The trappers had already made a close appraisal of the weapons the Indians carried and seen nothing more threatening than old Hudson's Bay flintlocks, spears, and bows and arrows. Old Bill's quiet orders were all that kept his trappers from attacking the Indians immediately.

That night the trappers camped a dozen miles or so beyond the Indian village. The camp guard soon spotted a few Indian spies slipping around studying the layout of the camp. Everyone knew what was coming, so Old Bill and his trappers made preparations for the inevitable.

Around four o'clock the next morning, the guards saw wolves lurking around camp. Two of the wolves that were shot through the head turned out, as the guards expected, to be Indians wearing wolfskin disguises. Said Hamilton, "Before the smoke had cleared from the rifles all of us were at the breastworks."

Dawn came. The chief's wolves had not returned, so the chief turned his eager warriors loose in a three-pronged attack. Half of the yelling Indians came on foot from two directions. The remainder were mounted warriors.

The trappers were heavily armed. In addition to their rifles, they were equipped with seven double-barreled shotguns, each barrel loaded with a half-ounce ball and five buckshot. Each man also carried a pair of Colt six-shooters which by this time were becoming common in the mountains.

Furthermore, they were deadly accurate marksmen. At close quarters their Colts were particularly effective because of the system they used in practice. They frequently conducted contests in which they rode at full gallop past six-foot-high posts, ten inches in diameter. The top foot of the post was stripped of its bark and squared, and into this area the rider was expected to put two bullets as he rode past at full speed, shooting equally well with either hand.

Hamilton was an expert rifleman in any company. Once, in a single bout of gambling at Fort Bridger, he challenged the old-time mountain men to a target-shooting match at five dollars a shot and walked off with two hundred and thirty-five dollars in winnings.

The trappers waited impatiently for the attacking party of Bannocks to come into range. They were still smarting about what the chief had said the preceding day. "What did that coon say again, Bill?"

"What he said," Hamilton repeated, "was 'You white dogs, I will wipe you out.'"

"This child don't take kindly to such talk. Wagh! I get half a chance I'll take that sonofabitch myself."

At seventy-five yards the trappers opened up with their rifles. "Almost every shot counted," wrote Hamilton. "Many Indians fell from their horses, and ponies fell pinning their riders."

"Then, seven double-barreled shotguns poured in their fire on the Indians, who had halted and were somewhat clustered. The shots created havoc and with a yell of despair, they fell back, leaving many wounded."

Then, leaping onto their fastest horses, more than thirty of the trappers, with a Colt in each hand, charged the Indians, who were breaking for cover. "The trappers' Colts," said Hamilton, "told with deadly effect."

The Indians, unable to understand how that number of men could shoot so many times, and with such uncanny accuracy, retreated with heavy losses. But even as the Indians tried to escape, Old Bill's party, according to Hamilton, continued the merciless attack, following the Bannocks and firing on them for more than a mile. The trappers lost one man and several horses. Their booty included sixty Indian ponies, a pile of flintlocks, and enough scalps for every man to have at least one of the gory trophies.

Hamilton applied the same vigor and dash to Indian fighting that he did to sign language, horsemanship, and fine shooting. Seeing the Bannock chief riding off at the head of his thoroughly defeated band, Hamilton, who rode an exceedingly fast pony, told Old Bill, "I can catch him."

"Let him go," Old Bill said, quietly.

Whites and Indians alike were frequently guilty of overkill, with the number of enemy killed dependent on what the opportunity offered. As word of this one-sided battle spread over the West in the following months, Indian and white man alike frequently asked Old Bill and his party why, once they had the Bannocks on the run, they still charged and continued to kill them. The trapper's answer always was that they wanted to teach them to respect the white man.

If there were enemies among the Indians, there were also friends, and Hamilton's favorites were the Shoshones with which Old Bill's trappers had associated earlier in the Wind River country. They visited and traded with Shoshones, led by the famous chief Washakie, who managed to retain his position of leadership among his warriors even as an old man.

As many before him had done, Bill Hamilton came to love the life of the mountain man, the freedom of movement in which an outdoor man lived close to the edge of danger, the promise of adventure around every bend in the trail. He was proving to himself, and others, that he had the skills and strength needed to survive beyond the frontier. "The American mountaineer," he said, referring especially to marksmanship, "had no equal on earth."

The more timid might question the wisdom of exposing oneself to constant danger, but Bill Hamilton had a ready response. "My answer has always been that there is a charm in the life of a free mountaineer from which one cannot free himself after he once has fallen under its spell."

Whatever else he did in his later years, Hamilton always remembered those wild free days in the mountains. He eventually became a professional guide, piloting settlers and adventurers. He was also a professional Indian fighter, U.S. Army scout, county sheriff, U.S. marshal, and trading post operator.

He finally settled at Billings, Montana, where he lived until he was eighty-six, known to all friends and neighbors as "Uncle Bill," the last of the real mountain men.

Even into his eighties he hiked each year into the mountains to trap. There, he surveyed again the sweeping mountain scene, and in his mind saw a distant line of riders moving across remote and beautiful valleys where beaver lived, and men, white and red alike, breathed the air of freedom.

THE MOUNTAIN MAN'S BOATS

For crossing rivers and traveling on them, the trappers employed rafts, dugouts, and boats covered with skins.

These skin boats, called bullboats because they were fashioned from the hides of large bull buffalo, were copied from the Indians. These were shaped like a round tub, or half a grapefruit, and were difficult to control. Indian women often used a bullboat made from a single bull skin for crossing streams. Larger bullboats were canoe-shaped and designated as two-, three-, or four-skin boats, depending on the number of skins needed to cover them. The large bull boat could haul several people, plus supplies and packs of furs.

Mountain man Thomas James, writing of one nine-man trip, said, "Here we made three canoes of buffalo bull's skins, sewing together two skins for each canoe, then stretching them over a frame similar in shape to a Mackinaw boat. Our canoe contained three men, about sixty steel traps [weighing five pounds each with chains], five hundred beaver skins [another seven hundred and fifty pounds], our guns and ammunition, besides other commodities." Each of these boats carried an estimated one ton with crew and goods aboard. Another writer tells of bull-skin boats twenty inches deep carrying two and a half tons with a four-inch draft.

The common single-hide bullboat took various forms. Some were round boats built with flat bottoms and straight sides. Others were curved from the gunwale to the bottom in a true bowl shape. The hair was generally left on the hide used to cover a bullboat and, according to Charles E. Hanson, Jr., Director of the Museum of the Fur Trade, was normally on the inside.

The framework of the trapper's bullboat was fashioned from sturdy willow sticks at least an inch and a half thick at the butt end. These could cross in the bottom of the boat, then be bent and bound to a stout ring formed of bent willow poles at the gunwale. Cross pieces connected these main parts of the frame, and the whole structure was tied together with rawhide thongs.

One method was to stick both ends of willow sticks into the

ground to form a framework of arches. After enough of these were bound together with crosspieces, the frame could be turned over and the bullhide fitted to it.

Green or wet rawhide was then stretched over the framework. The hide was bound tightly to the gunwale. It shrank as it dried in the sun, or overnight by the heat of a low fire. The hide was bound tightly to the gunwale with heavy thongs all around. If more than one hide was needed to cover the frame, the skins were laced together and caulked with tallow or bear grease. Elk tallow and ashes were sometimes mixed to make caulking.

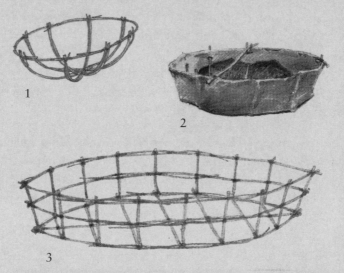

Three types of bullboats: (1) a single-hide bowl, framework only; (2) a single-hide flat-bottom; (3) a two-skin boat, framework only, capable of carrying two men and their equipment.

A bullboat was not maintenance-free. Trappers bound downstream for St. Louis with loads of fur had to unload their bullboats every night and haul them onto shore to dry. Constant caulking was needed, and even then, the hides were good for a limited time before they began to rot and come apart. The single-hide tubs used by Indian women for stream crossings lasted longer because they saw less frequent use.

Trappers occasionally used rafts. The secret of building a strong raft, when time and tools permitted, was to notch the logs, brace them with notched cross-logs, then bind all parts together firmly. Otherwise, the craft might suffer the fate of a raft once built by mountain man Zemas Leonard. "Supposing the Indians were not so numerous on the opposite side of the river," Leonard wrote. "I resolved to cross over—for which purpose I built a raft of old logs, laid my shot pouch, gun, blanket, &c. on it, and pushed for the opposite shore." Leonard nearly made it across, but his raft struck a rock and came to pieces. Leonard, his gun, blanket, and all other possessions were committed to "the watery element." The loss of his gun left him alone in the wilderness with only his knife for protection or food gathering.

The fur trapper and trader's favorite watercraft was often a canoe, made by hollowing out a large cottonwood log. This dugout canoe, although heavy and clumsy, was sturdy and capable of carrying a heavy load. Two large dugouts, lashed together and covered with a platform of poles, made a primitive pontoon boat that could haul ten tons or more.

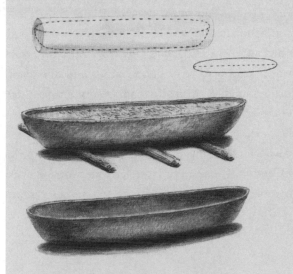

To make a dugout canoe, mountain men cut the top and bottom of a cottonwood log square, using a saw or ax (top). With an adz, they hollowed out the log and rounded the bow and stern (center). The finished boat (bottom) was a sturdy craft that could carry a heavy load.

· 23 ·

Long Shadows

*T*he years pass and the old man, sitting on a log to rest, struggles to recall the details. He remembers the long-ago day of the battle with the Rees on the Missouri, other close calls with little bands of warriors, and with grizzlies surprised in their business. He recalls the bitter winters in the mountains, the idyllic cool summers in the high places. He remembers friends lost in those days, and still wonders at the marvel that he, James Clyman, Virginia-born of sharecropper parents on George Washington's land, had gone west to join up with General Ashley so long ago, yet kept his scalp and lived on all these years.

When he went to the mountains, the rawboned Clyman stood more than six feet tall. He had dark-brown hair, blue eyes, and in spite of the fact that he was a bit round-shouldered and walked with a slight stoop, he was noted for his strength and endurance. The trapper who could outrun or outwork Jim Clyman was a rare individual.

Jim was a skilled woodsman, an excellent hunter, and among the finest rifle shots in the West. He was known for remaining cool under pressure—a good man to stand beside in a fight. Charles L. Camp, who edited Clyman's journals, published under the title *James Clyman, American Frontiersman*, said Clyman was a kind person, of good humor and abundant common sense. Unlike many mountain men, Clyman seldom exaggerated and was rarely critical of others. He read Shakespeare, Byron, and the Bible. But above all, he loved the wilderness.

He was fifteen when his family moved to northeastern Ohio, near the present site of Canton. Those were troubled times and it was here in Ohio, around the time of the War of 1812, that young Clyman had his first taste of fighting Indians.

On his own a few years later, he went first to Pittsburgh, then down the Ohio River and across southern Ohio into Indiana. There, fifty miles or so southeast of Indianapolis, he became a farmer for a while.

But Clyman, young and restless, never stayed long in any one neighborhood. After working for some time with a surveyor, he moved on to St. Louis, arriving in time to go upriver with General Ashley in the spring of 1823.

By the following year Clyman was a free trapper and a member of Jedediah Smith's little group that discovered the famous South Pass. They came to the Green River where the trapping was excellent, and they put together valuable packs of beaver furs.

The group split up to take maximum advantage of the wealth of furs in this beaver-rich country. Smith, with half a dozen or so other trappers, continued to work the Green. Clyman and Tom Fitzpatrick, meanwhile, worked their way back up across the South Pass and down the Sweetwater. Their plan was to regroup on the east slope in time to bring their fur harvest back to St. Louis the following summer.

Finally, with Smith and his group not yet in sight, Clyman began working his way downstream, around a long stretch of shallow, rough water, searching for water deep and smooth enough to carry bullboats loaded with furs and men. Fitzpatrick, meanwhile, hung back waiting for Jed Smith so he could bring them all together again downstream along the Sweetwater where Clyman was scouting the route.

Clyman, now on foot because Fitzpatrick apparently had his horse to help transport the packs of furs, was in no hurry. His companions were behind him. He ambled on downstream for three days or so, along the Sweetwater, to its junction with the North Platte in south-central Wyoming, and still the other trappers failed to catch up.

Meanwhile, Jed Smith was out searching for Clyman. They would likely have found each other if Clyman had not run into Indian trouble, making it essential for him to deviate from his route and hide out. The only trace of him that Smith could find was an abandoned white man's camp trampled over by Indian moccasins. Obviously, Clyman had been surprised and killed by the natives. By the time Clyman had eluded the Indians, Smith had gone back upstream bearing the sad news that Old Jim was no longer a trapper.

The failure to find his party left Clyman uncertain about his best course of action. He was alone in mighty big country. A man could roam around forever out here and probably still not find Captain Smith or Old Fitz. Clyman set off walking downstream again, sometimes confused about where he really was, and wondering all the while if he might still locate his group.

Near the mouth of the Sweetwater, where it empties into the North Platte, Clyman stopped to set up a small camp in a clump of thick-growing willows. He was about to strike a fire when he thought he heard voices. As he explained in his journal, he watched through the screen of willows as twenty-two Indians and thirty horses arrived on the other side of the narrow stream. Said Clyman in a masterful understatement, "I did not feel myself perfectly safe . . ."

Night came on. There was bright moonlight. Clyman figured that a guard could spot him quickly if he tried to move back across the half mile of open sandy country behind him. He worked himself into a good observation point and settled down to watch. About midnight the Indians departed.

Clyman then made his way downstream, to another location where he believed his party might be, but found only wildlife and another small group of Indians. He waited for eleven days, and the longer he waited, the more edgy he became. This was his first prolonged stay alone in the wilderness. He considered spending one more week trying to find his party. But he took careful stock of his supplies and knew the extra week would increase his risk. His lead pouch now held only eleven bullets, and unless he found the other trappers soon, he might never get back.

He decided that his only sound choice was to strike out downstream for Fort Atkinson. He did not fully understand that he had seven hundred miles of wilderness travel ahead of him to reach his destination. Clyman traveled all that summer. One day he decided to try to capture one of the wild horses he so often saw across the plains. He remembered stories of capturing horses by creasing them in the neck with a bullet and temporarily stunning the animal until it could be captured. He made a halter from strips of buffalo hide. He hid by a water hole and waited. A fine black stallion came to drink. Clyman, using one of his few remaining bullets, aimed carefully, squeezed off the shot, hit the animal in the neck, then ran up and slipped the halter over its head. But the stallion never moved again. Clyman's bullet had broken its neck.

Another day, Clyman crossed the trail of an Indian party and soon found himself in a Pawnee village. Men and boys descended on him, threatening death. One of them snatched Clyman's butcher knife and made slashing motions across the trapper's breast. This was no time to show fear or timidity and Clyman lifted his shirt to bare his chest. Instead of killing him at once, the Indians, impressed with his fearlessness, began taking his property and soon, although allowed to keep his rifle, he was without his flint and steel, powder, blankets, and the few remaining bullets he carried.

That night he was kept under guard, but early the next morning an elderly Indian and his son came with three horses and escorted Clyman some miles out from the village in the direction from which he had come. There, he was given a small supply of parched corn and released, and he once more set off on foot, headed for the distant fort.

Before leaving him, the friendly Indian asked one favor. Clyman's long brown hair had not been cut since he left St. Louis. The Indian who had saved his life admired it, and Clyman, thinking this a relatively painless way for a trapper to lose his hair, later explained that the Indian, "barbered me with a dull butcher knife."

Clyman faced periods of hunger when game was scarce. He once encountered two badgers fighting, shot at and missed them. He then found a bleached horse bone, ran the badgers down and clubbed them. Using his flintlock, he struck a fire and roasted the badger meat. There followed uncounted days of walking, and nights of half-sleeping and half-listening. He swam streams, fought mosquitoes, studied the landscape, and tried to figure out where he was until he came, at last, to a trail that seemed to lead in the right direction.

Confused, hungry, numb with fatigue, Clyman was stumbling

along, head down, one September day when he lifted his eyes and beheld a beautiful sight. There was Fort Atkinson and, above it in the breeze, the stars and stripes. Said Clyman, "I swooned immediately." After he recovered, and rested enough to move forward, Clyman made his way down to the fort.

His adventures as a trapper took him to wild and scenic parts of the West, often in company with Jed Smith, Jim Bridger, Tom Fitzpatrick, and other famous mountain men. He was with Smith on an early exploring trip into what became Yellowstone National Park, and the party was able to report that the unbelievably strange sights recorded earlier by Colter had been true after all. "That was some, that was."

In the late summer of 1827, Clyman came back to St. Louis, leading a party of mountain men coming in to sell their furs. He made enough profit on his furs this year to buy a farm near Danville, Illinois. But he was not yet ready to quit the mountains. He installed his brothers on the farm.

He later led wagon trains of settlers over the mountains into California. On one of these trips, in 1848, he met the McCombs of Indiana, including their daughter Hannah. James Clyman and Hannah McCombs were married, and they settled on a ranch near Napa, California. The time had finally come for Clyman to settle down. Perhaps he had conquered the wanderlust. Perhaps not.

When he was eighty years old, Clyman, bent and weathered, was still working his orchards, pruning trees, shearing his sheep, making hay, and hauling wood.

Even in his later years, he often took his gun and wandered, with the careful slow steps of an old man, into the nearby mountains seeking a deer, a bear—or perhaps a memory.

Jim Clyman had accomplished what many of his long-ago trapper companions had not; he had lived to be an old man. He died on his ranch in 1881, in his ninetieth year, a fortunate man, knowing that he had the courage in his youth to go where the action was. He had been a free trapper. He had been his own man.

Bibliography

Alter, J. Cecil. *Jim Bridger*. The University of Oklahoma Press. 1962.

Athearn, Robert G. *Forts of the Upper Missouri*. University of Nebraska Press. 1967.

Berry, Don. *A Majority of Scoundrels*. Comstock Editions, Inc. 1961.

Blevins, Winfred. *Give Your Heart to the Hawks*. Avon Books. 1973.

Bonner, Thomas D. *Life and Adventures of James P. Beckwourth, Mountaineer, Scout, Pioneer and Chief of the Crow Nation*. 1856.

Bradbury, John. *Travels in the Interior of America*. 1819.

Camp, Charles L. *James Clyman, American Frontiersman*. 1928.

Cleland, Robert Glass. *This Reckless Breed of Men*. Alfred A. Knopf, Inc., 1950. University of New Mexico Press. 1976.

Coues, Elliott (ed.). *The History of the Lewis and Clark Expedition*. Four vols. F. P. Harper. 1893.

Chittenden, Hiram M. *The American Fur Trade of the Far West*. Three vols. F. P. Harper. 1902.

DeVoto, Bernard. *Across the Wide Missouri*. Houghton Mifflin Company. 1947.

Drips, Andrew. Papers of. (Unpublished.) Missouri Historical Society. St. Louis.

Ferris, Warren. *Life in the Rocky Mountains*. Old West Publishing Company. 1842–1844.

Garavagila, Louis A., and Charles G. Worman. *Firearms of the American West* 1803–1865. University of New Mexico Press. 1984.

Gibson, W. Hamilton. *Camp Life and the Tricks of Trapping*. 1881.

Gilbert, Bil. *The Trail Blazers*. Time-Life Books. 1973.

———. *Westering Man, The Life of Joseph Walker*. Atheneum. 1983.

Gowans, Fred R. *Rocky Mountain Rendezvous: A History of the Fur Trade Rendezvous* 1825–1840. Peregrine Smith Books. 1985.

Hafen, LeRoy R. *Broken Hand*. The Old West Publishing Company. 1931.

———. *Mountain Men and Fur Traders of the Far West* (ed.). Ten vols. Arthur H. Clark Company. 1965–1972.

Hanson, Charles E., Jr., *The Hawken Rifle: Its Place in History*. The Fur Press. 1979.

Hamilton, W. T. *My Sixty Years on the Plains*. Forest and Stream Publishing Co. 1905.

Irving, Washington. *The Adventures of Captain Bonneville*. G.P. Putnam's Sons. 1898.

Jacob, J.G. *The Life and Times of Patrick Glass*. Jacob and Smith. 1859.

James, Thomas. *Three Years Among the Indians and Mexicans*. 1846.

Larpenteur, Charles. *Forty Years a Fur Trader on the Upper Missouri*. 1898.

Leonard, Zenas. *Adventures of a Mountain Man: The Narrative of Zenas Leonard*. R.R. Donnelly & Sons. 1934.

Myers, John M. *The Saga of Hugh Glass*. Little Brown. 1963.

Morgan, Dale I. *Jedediah Smith and the Opening of the West*. Bobbs-Merrill Company. 1953.

Oglesby, Richard Edward. *Manuel Lisa and the Opening of the Missouri Fur Trade*. University of Oklahoma Press. 1963.

Pattie, James Ohio. *The Personal Narrative of James Ohio Pattie*. J. H. Wood. 1831.

Ross, Alexander. *Fur Hunters of the Far West*. 1855.

Russell, Carl P. *Firearms, Traps & Tools of the Mountain Men*. Alfred A. Knopf, Inc. 1967.

———. *Guns of the Early Frontiers*. University of California Press. 1957.

Russell, Osborne. *Journal of a Trapper*. Oregon Historical Society. 1955.

Ruxton, George Frederick. *Ruxton of the Rockies*. Collected and edited by Mae Reed Porter and LeRoy R. Hafen. University of Oklahoma Press. 1950.

Sage, Rufus B. *Scenes in the Rocky Mountains.* 1846.

Schraf, J. Thomas. *History of St. Louis City and County.* 1883.

Shepard, E. H. *The Early History of St. Louis and Missouri.* 1870.

Smith, Jedediah S. *Journals.* (unpublished). Missouri Historical Society. St. Louis.

Steward, William Drummond. *Edward Warren.* G. Walker. 1854.

Sublette Papers. (Unpublished.) Missouri Historical Society. St. Louis.

Sunder, John E. *Bill Sublette, Mountain Man.* University of Oklahoma Press. 1959.

Thwaites, Reuben Gold (ed.). *The Original Journals of the Lewis and Clark Expedition.* Eight vols. 1904–1907.

Townsend, John Kirk. *Narrative of a Journey Across the Rocky Mountains to the Columbia River.* Philadelphia, 1839.

Victor, Frances Fuller. *The River of the West: The Adventures of Joe Meek.* R. W. Bliss. 1870.

Wilson, Elinor. *James Beckwourth.* University of Oklahoma Press. 1972.

Index

Across the Wide Missouri (DeVoto),
153, 226
Adventures of a Mountain Man
(Leonard), 37
Adventures of Captain Bonneville, The
(Irving), 86, 141
American Fur Company, 6–9, 78, 142, 192
Ashley, Gen. William, 7, 76–82, 84, 85,
93, 120–121, 210, 211, 236
Astor, John Jacob, 6–9

bait, for beaver traps, 24–26
beaver, 5–6, 9–12, 14–22, 58, 63, 93,
115, 125, 140, 148, 196
Beaver World (Mills), 20
Beckwourth, James P., 71, 190–196, 208
Benton, Sen. Thomas Hart, 112, 177
bighorn sheep, 43–44, 159
bison. *See* buffalo
Bissonette, Antoine, 59, 60
blackpowder gun tools, 110, 110*illus.*
boats, 233–235 and *illus.*
Bonner, T.D., 190, 191
Bonneville, Capt. Benjamin, 178
Brewerton, George, 147, 154
Bridger, Old Jim, 7, 83–92, 95, 136,
205, 209, 240
buffalo, 27–34, 91, 121, 203
buffalo hunters, 31–32
"buffer," 28, 34
bullboats, 233, 234*illus.*

caches, 223–224*illus.*, 225
canoes, 235, 235*illus.*
Carson, Kit, 113, 147–154, 156
Castor canadensis. See beaver
Charbonneau, Toussaint, 49–50
Clark, Capt. William, 25, 29–30, 40,
47–48, 55, 64, 223, 225
Clyman, James, 122, 132, 214, 236–240
Cody, Buffalo Bill, 31
Colter, John, 59–60, 68–75
Colt six-shooters, 229
Columbia River Fishing and Trading
Company, 202
Continental Divide, 5, 53, 55, 84, 93–94
cougars, 40–41
coyotes, 39

deer, 42, 49, 91, 182
DeVoto, Bernard, 153, 201, 226
dime novels, 147–148
Dixon, Joe, 68, 69
Drewyer, George. *See* Drouillard, George
Drips, Andrew, 8, 152
Drouillard, George, 37, 48–49, 52,
59–60, 62–63
duels, 81–82, 152–153

elk, 41–42, 91, 121, 182
Evans, Robert, 126–127

Ferris, Warren Angus, 14, 209
fire, 185–188 and *illus.*
*Firearms of the American West
1803–1865* (Garavaglia and
Worman), 103
fishing, 206–207
Fitzpatrick, Tom, 7, 39–40, 93–101,
113, 136, 137, 149, 237, 240
Flint, Timothy, 221
flintlock rifles, 104, 229
Fort Bent, 113, 114
Fort Bridger, 89–90, 230
Fraeb, Henry, 7, 95
Frémont, John C., 100, 112–114,
118–119, 147, 154
fur companies, 2–3, 5–9, 59, 63, 95, 130
fur industry, winding down of, 117, 162

gambling, 81–82
Gervais, Jean Baptiste, 7, 95
Glass, Hugh, 132–138
Gore, Sir George, 90–91
"Great Pathfinder, the." *See* Frémont,
John C.
Great Salt Lake, 85, 92, 123–124,
126–127, 178–179
Green River, 80, 94, 152, 177, 178, 210
grizzly bears, 35–39, 50, 51, 91, 96,
106, 121–123, 129, 134–135,
153–154, 157–158, 159–160,
203–205, 217–218, 220
guns, 32–33, 102–106, 229, 230

Hamilton, Billy, 175, 226–232
hands (gambling game), 81

"hand talking," 228
Harpers Ferry rifle, 103*illus.*
Harris, Moses "Black," 208–214
hats, fur trade and, 12
Hawken brothers (Jacob and Samuel), 104–105
Hawken rifle, 103–104, 106*illus.*
Hawken Rifle: Its Place in History, The (Hanson), 104
Henry, Andrew, 7, 76, 77, 121, 132
horn utensils, 131, 131*illus.*, 196, 196*illus.*
horse thieves, 149–153, 219
horse trading, 117–118
Hudson's Bay Company, 6, 7, 12, 130, 228
Hunting of the Buffalo, The (Branch), 31

Indians, 8, 9, 57–58, 60, 64
  beaver and, 17–18
  buffalo and, 28–30
  conflict with trappers, 63, 68, 71–75, 78–79, 84, 86–89, 94–95, 97–100, 102, 116, 121, 128–131, 133–134, 137–138, 143–146, 149–152, 155–157, 179–180, 197–201, 216–217, 219–220, 228–231, 236, 239
  cooperation with trappers, 64, 70, 81, 99, 100, 114–115, 127–128, 191–195, 212–213, 220, 231, 239
  leatherwork of, 164, 165*illus.*, 166
  Lewis and Clark expedition encounters with, 48, 49, 52–54
  as wives of mountain men, 43, 49–50, 81, 87, 90, 115, 141, 153, 162, 164, 171, 174, 191–196, 213

Jackson, David E., 7, 82, 123, 210
James, Thomas, 36, 61, 62, 71, 233
James Clyman, American Frontiersman (Camp, ed.), 236
Jedediah Smith and the Opening of the West (Morgan), 126
Jefferson, President Thomas, 46, 47, 50, 55
Journal of a Trapper (Russell), 28, 160, 197, 202
Journals of Lewis and Clark, 29

Kentucky rifle, 102–103, 104*illus.*
Kit Carson's Own Life Story, 149
knives, 110, 110*illus.*

Lafitte, Jean, 133, 138
leatherwork, 164, 165*illus.*, 166–176
leggings, 170, 170*illus.*
leg hold traps, 10, 11
Leonard, Zenas, 37, 38, 97, 105, 106, 178, 184, 235
Lewis, Capt. Meriwether, 14, 40, 46–48, 54, 55–56, 67, 106
Lewis and Clark expedition, 5, 6, 25, 29, 37, 40, 46–56, 51–52, 57, 68–69
Life and Adventures of James P. Beckwourth (Bonner), 191
Life in the Far West (Ruxton), 116
Life in the Rocky Mountains (Ferris), 209
Lisa, Manuel, 57–64, 69, 78
Louisiana Territory/Purchase, 46, 49, 55, 58

Mammals of Wisconsin (Jackson), 18
Manifest Destiny, 112
marksmanship, 102, 116, 129, 150, 229–231
medical emergencies, 122
"medicine," 24–26, 117
Meek, Joe, 71, 87–89, 141, 155–163
merchants, 57, 76–82
Mexicans, relations with trappers, 125, 128–129, 139–140, 183, 220–221
Mills, Enos, 14, 20
Mississippi River, 57, 65
Missouri Fur Company, 63, 69, 77
Missouri Historical Society, 99, 130
Missouri River, 49, 57, 61, 77–78, 84, 114, 154, 215
mittens, 169, 169*illus.*
moccasins, 168*illus.*, 168–169
mountaineers. *See* mountain men
Mountain Lamb (Milton Sublette's wife), 141, 162
mountain lions, 40–41
mountain men. *See also* trappers
  beaver and, 22–26
  boats of, 233–235 and *illus.*
  buffalo and, 28, 30–34
  caches of, 223–224*illus.*, 225
  exploration by, 65–66, 92, 123–130
  as fishermen, 206–207
  as guides, 112–113
  guns and, 102–106
  language of, 116–117
  nature of, 2–5
  as storytellers, 157–161, 190–191, 208–210

summer rendezvous gatherings of, 81–82, 94, 95, 117, 127, 141–145, 152, 177
  wildlife and, 35–45
Mountain Men and Fur Traders of the Far West, The (Walker), 183
Museum of the Fur Trade (Chadron, Nebraska), 25, 104, 206, 226, 233
muskets, 105–106
My Sixty Years on the Plains (Hamilton), 227
Mystic Warriors of the Plains, The (Mails), 33

Newhouse, Sewell, 10–11
Northwest Fur Trapping and Fur Trading Company, 202
nutria, 12

Ohio River, 57, 67
outfitters, 82
overhunting, 18, 43, 91

Pacific Fur Company, 7
Pattie, James Ohio, 40–41, 215–222
Personal Narrative of James O. Pattie, 216, 221
Pierre's Hole, Battle of, 143–146
pirates, 133
pistols, 105
Plains rifle, 103–104, 105*illus.*
Powell, John Wesley, 80–81
prairie dogs, 45, 121
pronghorn antelope, 42–43, 121

rattlesnakes, 136
ravens, 45, 212, 218
rawhide hobbles for horses, 176, 176*illus.*
religion, 114–115, 120
Remington rifles, 32
rendezvous, 81–82, 94, 95, 117, 127, 141–145, 152, 177
revolvers, 105
River of the West, The (Victor), 156
Rocky Mountain Fur Company, 7, 8, 86, 95, 100, 141, 146, 202
Rocky Mountains, 2, 12, 46, 67, 178, 215
Russell, Osborne, 28, 31, 35, 41, 160, 197–205
Ruxton, George Frederick, 3, 28, 29, 43, 81, 116–117, 208
Ruxton of the Rockies (Ruxton), 43

Sacajawea, 49–50, 53
Saga of Hugh Glass, Pirate, Pawnee, and Mountain Man, The (Myers), 133
Sage, Rufus B., 4, 8, 44, 168
St. Louis, 1–2, 55, 57, 63, 68, 80, 89, 104, 120, 130, 139, 234
scouts, 91, 100, 113, 121, 231
Sharps buffalo guns, 32–33
shelter, 189, 189*illus.*
shooting bags, 106–107, 107*illus.*
shotguns, 105, 229–230
sign language, 228–229, 231
Smith, Jedediah, 7, 45, 79, 80, 82, 93, 120–131, 210, 237, 240
Smith, Thomas L., 140
snowshoes, 211
steel traps, 10–11
storytelling, 40, 157–161, 190–191, 208–210
Sublette, Milton, 95, 139–146, 158, 162
Sublette, William, 7, 82, 95, 99, 123, 210

Thirty Years of Army Life on the Border (Marcy), 90
Three Years Among the Indians and Mexicans (James), 36
trappers, 2–5, 23–26, 58–66, 139–140, 143–146, 182. *See also* mountain men
trapper's awls, 166*illus.*, 166–167
Trappers of the Far West (ed. Hafen), 141
traps, 9–13, 23–26, 29

Vasquez, Louis, 89
Victor, Frances Fuller, 87, 156

Walker, Joe, 177–184
War of 1812, 12, 64, 76, 236
weather conditions, 187, 211–212, 236
Wilburn, Karl, 110, 111, 173, 174
wild turkeys, 44–45, 212
Williams, Old Bill, 112–119, 226
wolves, 39–40, 136

yarners. *See* storytelling
Yellowstone River, 70, 78
York (slave), 48
Young, Ewing, 139, 140, 148, 150